MW01076402

Made in Quebec

MADE IN QUEBEC

A CULINARY JOURNEY

JULIAN ARMSTRONG

HarperCollins*Publishers*Ltd

HarperCollins Publishers Ltd
2 Bloor Street East, 20th Floor
Toronto, Ontario, Canada
M4W 1A8

www.harpercollins.ca

Library and Archives Canada Cataloguing in Publication
information is available upon request

ISBN 978-1-44342-531-5

Printed and bound in the People's Republic of China

PP 9 8 7 6 5 4 3 2 1

Photography: RYAN SZULC (pages 2, 13, 21, 35, 47, 54, 61, 62, 65, 66, 77, 78, 85, 87, 95, 113, 121,
126, 131, 134, 145, 150, 161, 163, 168, 174, 186, 188, 217, 218, 222, 232, 234, 239, 246, 258, 261, 264,
278, 287, 312, 315, 318, 324, 334, 338, 342, 347, 361, 362, 375, 378, 394, 396)
All other photography by GORDON BECK
Recipe testing: MICHELLE GÉLINAS

To the chefs and cooks of Quebec
whose generosity with their recipes made this book possible

Contents

The story of Quebec food is a love story...

Quebecers love to eat. They talk enthusiastically about the best foods and where to find them, they recommend recipes, and they turn misty-eyed remembering their food traditions. In North America, Quebec is distinct in language and culture, distinguished by its obsession with good food and drink, lively restaurant scenes, bustling food shops and markets, and interest in the latest food trends and loyalty to heritage dishes. So it's not surprising that one of Montreal's top restaurants is called Toqué!, which means infatuated, cracked—a little crazy.

Travellers to the province can experience the French culinary tradition, adapted long ago to native foods. They soon notice the preoccupation of Quebecers with what's for dinner, and their belief that cuisine is a vital part of life. Quebecers eagerly share tips on the best or newest restaurants, yet home cooking is also alive and well. So is fast food. Quebecers don't mind some teasing over their celebrated poutine, and they are always happy to argue about where to get the best bagel or smoked meat sandwich.

I have called Quebec home for most of my life and have been lucky enough to work as a food reporter for my entire career. I've had the opportunity to take regular tasting trips around the province, venturing far off the beaten track to country restaurants and to cheesemakers, wild-food foragers, specialty livestock breeders, and fishermen maintaining centuries-old practices and organic gardeners using the latest agricultural techniques. It's a newspaper beat to beat all others, and one of my great satisfactions is the encouragement I've always been given by native Quebecers, who have never stopped providing me with tips, recipes, background, and referrals to specialists I should consult on my travels. Quebec, to me, is a region of generosity, at table and in every other way.

My findings have sometimes surprised my Quebec-born friends because, not having grown up in the province, I have spotted the distinctive and unusual in the food of one region after another. These differences have been right under their noses—or forks—from birth, but I made stories out of them, and native Quebecers seem to have enjoyed the tales.

Everywhere I travel in the province, I find that French cuisine is alive and well. Sure we like Italian and Asian, Middle Eastern and American, but, as chefs will state, the mother cuisine is French.

The 17th-century settlers came to New France with their cast-iron pots and pans and their simple country recipes for tourtières and ragouts, pâtés and terrines, tarts and galettes. Those dishes continue to be part of today's cuisine, particularly at holidays and family gatherings. Year-round, the tourtière is the most-sold ready-made dish in Quebec food stores. Pâtés and terrines are part of any cocktail reception; pies and cakes, regulars in pastry counters. And, on Christmas Eve, the finer pâtisseries are jammed with shoppers picking up their *bûche de Noël*, the Christmas sponge cake rolled up with chocolate buttercream and iced to look like a yule log.

Quebec has not forgotten the medieval cooking of its original settlers, country folk from northwestern France who were still cooking in the style of the 1400s. Those long-ago cooking practices still in use in Quebec family cooking include seasoning meat dishes with spices such as cinnamon and cloves; using salted herbs; boiling bones to make stock; using bread and crumbs as frugal ingredients in recipes; making stale bread into bread pudding or French toast; using browned flour as both a seasoning and a thickener; making boiled dinners and chowders; using dried legumes to make pea soup and baked beans; combining dried fruit with fresh in such desserts as apple-raisin pie and spiced date cake; and flavouring desserts with honey and nuts.

Preserving the Cuisine

Quebec's cooking maintains its past in part because a small group of Montreal chefs realized in the 1970s that traditional dishes were in danger of disappearing. Ready-made products were proliferating, and pasta appeared to be becoming Quebec's number one ingredient. The chefs launched a province-wide study with the Institut de tourisme et d'hôtellerie du Québec, Montreal's government-run professional cooking school. Student researchers conducted interviews with home cooks throughout Quebec about traditional family cooking. They talked to senior citizens, farming groups, regional cooks, and tourist associations. The students and chefs collected vintage recipes from every region, some 30,000 in all. The institute's research centre tested thousands of recipes and selected 630 of them for a cookbook, *Cuisine traditionelle des régions du Québec*. It's a remarkable record of simple, homey, regional dishes that reveals how the original French cuisine was adapted to foods and ingredients found in the New World.

More encouragement was given to making Quebec cuisine distinctive in 1990 when top chefs all over the province started a movement called La Cuisine régionale au Québec. The chefs went to

work encouraging producers in their areas to turn out more of their region's best fruit and vegetables, meats and cheeses, and the chefs, in turn, committed to replacing as many imported ingredients as they could in their cooking with these products. They began to name their suppliers on their menus, a practice you still find in restaurants as prestigious as Toqué!, in Montreal, and Laurie Raphaël, in both Quebec City and Montreal.

Chefs regularly say that the best Quebec cooking starts with the best foods, and they have long encouraged improvements in livestock-farming techniques, crossbreeding of fruits to extend their season, automated harvesting systems

Montreal bagels are trimmed with either poppy seeds or sesame seeds.

to a recipe. Many are so popular that they are sold across Canada and in the United States.

A Quebec cookbook cannot neglect maple, the favourite sweetener. After all, Quebec makes 72 per cent of the world's supply (with 7 per cent coming from the rest of Canada and 21 per cent from the United States). Honey and molasses are other traditional Quebec sweeteners, but the syrup French explorers learned to make from the First Nations peoples leads the pack. Maple recipes abound in this book; a few call for maple sugar, which is now being marketed in greater quantity and sold in specialty stores.

Travelling around Quebec, I have found that the visitor's passport to a friendly welcome is the effort they make to speak French, however haltingly. As a journalist whose French reveals my Ontario roots from my first *bonjour*, I've found that, everywhere in my adopted homeland, Quebecers are people of goodwill.

When asked how to manage travelling the province without being totally bilingual, particularly when off the beaten track, I am always reminded of one night near Sorel-Tracy, southeast of Montreal. I'd spent the day scouting goose farms for a story and couldn't find the highway back to Montreal. It was just past dusk when I rolled into a gas station in a small village. The attendant came toward me and, in a bit of a panic, I could only manage, "Je suis perdue." (I am lost.)

He grinned, and I'll never forget his friendly response: "Tu n'es pas perdue . . . tu es ici avec moi." (You're not lost . . . you're here with me.)

for vegetables, and even streamlining of wild-food foraging for such delicacies as fiddleheads and mushrooms. Even some wines, ciders, and liqueurs come with a Quebec flavour, like the wonderful ice cider from winter-chilled apple orchards, and the liqueur known as chicoutai, made from the wild northern cloudberry.

The perpetual newsmaker among Quebec foods is cheese. Winning prizes throughout North America has become an annual event for Quebec cheesemakers. Again, the French influence reigns. Cheesemakers have developed an array of soft and semi-soft cheeses in every corner of Quebec, some succulent on a cheese tray, others adding zest

Cook's Notes

Quebec's founding recipes, still popular with families, appear in this book with less fat and fresher ingredients. The chefs' recipes have been simplified from the versions they make in their restaurants but still offer distinctive flavours.

The theme throughout the book is the pleasure to be derived from using fresh foods in season. It's a custom long popular in Quebec but strengthening in the province as the number of farmers' markets grows, improvements in foods—livestock feeding methods, new varieties of vegetables and fruits—appear, and wild foraging becomes ever more popular. A leading Quebec chef, whose winter cuisine includes the root vegetables of her ancestors, rebels against the general acceptance of year-round produce, much of it lacking flavour, imported from far away. "We don't need broccoli," is how she puts it. Another scorns out-of-season asparagus, preferring to wait for the superb spears of local asparagus each May and June. And there's a groundswell of complaint about strawberries that come to Canada with hard, white centres and little flavour. Better, say Quebec fruit scientists, to crossbreed our own strawberries to extend their season. In short, we are finding new pleasure in eating our own food at its best.

Eggs and Dairy

Recipes in this book use large eggs, whole or partially skimmed milk, and unsalted butter. If you use salted butter, reduce the amount of added salt to your taste. There is no margarine or shortening in this book; if you desire, you can emulate early Quebec cooks by making pastry with lard rather than butter. Most recipes call for table salt, but other salts are suggested in some recipes to give the best flavour and texture.

Quebec, a major dairy-product producer, now makes heat-treated creams of various fat contents. These products are labelled "for cooking" or "old-fashioned," and they are supposedly more resistant to curdling when heated and, in the case of 35% cream, able to keep their shape longer when whipped. The rest of Canada has yet to be offered these products. Regular whipping cream continues to be the best option for a sauce that is heated, but overheating it may cause curdling. Heating lower-fat creams requires even more caution. In recipes, whipping cream means 35% butterfat; cream refers to 15% butterfat.

Convenience Foods

Maple sugar and maple butter (a spread made by whipping maple syrup to a spreading consistency) are sold in many specialty stores. They can be obtained from Marché des Saveurs du Québec, 280 Place du Marché-du-Nord, Montreal, Quebec, H2S 1A1; tel: 514-271-3811; email: marchedessaveurs@gmail.com.

Frozen baby green peas and canned artichokes are used in a few recipes. It's worth it to spend more on top-grade canned tomatoes such as San Marzano. Quebec is fortunate in having packaged, pre-sliced fresh leeks, able to stay fresh for up to two weeks in their porous plastic bags. Technology is allowing us more fresh foods in convenient containers, pre-cut vegetables in particular.

Stock

When using ready-made stocks, it's worth it to find varieties that have good flavour without too much salt. Fresh fish stock is easy to make with scraps from the fishmonger and a few seasonings, but you can substitute bottled clam juice.

Measuring

Both imperial and metric measures are given. Meats and common package sizes for products are given in their metric weight. Take your pick as to which volume or weight system you use. With baking, precision is required. With everything else, remember we're only a few generations removed from the era when our grandmothers would measure butter by "the size of an egg." We should relax about exact amounts of most ingredients.

Spring

Trailing a fiddlehead forager in the Quebec woods is a good way to experience the excitement of the first spring foods. Stepping cautiously on moist earth beside a rushing stream, I could barely see the shoots of the ostrich fern that cause such a flurry each spring in stores, markets, and restaurants—a pale green blur of growth concealed the fiddleheads and their curled heads. All around us, mosquitoes buzzed us for their early-May feed. The forager lent an air of mystery to the occasion, leading my photographer and me back and forth along side roads to his picking woods to make sure, we decided, that we could never find his secret spot again.

We had just come from a cultivated display of spring growth—a large asparagus farm where rows of pale green stalks had begun poking up a few inches from the sandy soil. A family farm formerly devoted to tobacco production, it was an example of new and renewed Quebec agriculture: the varieties of asparagus had been carefully researched, soil and windbreaks of trees adapted, and a state-of-the-art packing plant built across the road from the family farmhouse. The latest project of the grower, Mario Rondeau, is to encourage asparagus plants to produce a second crop in mid-summer. That is almost as innovative as Quebec's autumn strawberry and raspberry crops.

Down the road in the Lanaudière, a pastoral region of heritage farms northeast of Montreal, kids were fishing for trout along the rivers and a goat farm was offering its first spring cheese, the chèvre—extra fresh, full of flavour, and perfect on a baguette made of stone-ground flour from a nearby mill.

Perhaps because Quebec's winters are so severe—long, cold, and banked up with snow and ice for what feels like six months—a near-hysteria erupts when the first foods of spring appear.

Take lobster, for instance. As soon as the East Coast lobster season opens and planes fly the first Îles de la Madeleine and Gaspé catches to market, we go wild for this delicately sweet seafood. Off the shore of Percé, a special lobster catch gets underway next to the celebrated rock. An adventurous restaurateur who is also a deep-sea diver starts filling his underwater cages with lobsters. He'll feed them in their watery prisons all summer, bringing up just the quantity his chefs need, day by day, until Thanksgiving.

Other foods prove equally compelling come spring. Snow crab from the Gulf of St. Lawrence appears in April through mid-May and is particularly prized for crab cakes. Lamb and ham are favourite spring meats. It's still greenhouse time, with the plentiful big three of hydroponically grown crops—cherry tomatoes, seedless cucumbers, and Boston lettuce—and the first herbs—mint, chives, and sorrel—to enjoy in salads and on hot and buttery new potatoes.

A great spring meal winds up with a perfect soft cheese or strong, aged cheddar, followed by a maple dessert—or, as the season advances, a rhubarb pie or bowl of the first strawberries topped with whipped cream and a dusting of maple sugar.

First Courses

Smoked Salmon Tartare

Lobster in Cointreau Cream Sauce

Smoked Trout Croquettes

Seared Scallops on a Bed of Spicy Avocado with Truffle Oil

Greek Spring Salad

Russian Radish Salad

Fiddlehead Omelette

Main Courses

Crêpes with Asparagus and Cheese

Snow Crab with Celery Root

Poached Salmon on Sorrel Mashed Potatoes

Scallops with Miso, the Nobu Way

Cedar Planked Trout Fillets

Beef Steaks with Red Onions

Concentrated Veal Stock

Tartare of Horsemeat or Beef with Butter and Radishes

Leg of Lamb Roasted in Parchment Paper

Leg of Lamb Flavoured with Juniper Berries

Ham Braised in Maple Beer

Chicken with Dumplings

Side Dishes

Risotto with Asparagus or Fiddleheads

Spring Salad with Green Peas and Artichokes

Field Dandelion and Strawberry Salad

Old Country Nubbins

Desserts

Maple Syrup Pie

Maple Syrup Crème Brûlée

The Simplest Maple Dessert

Rhubarb Strawberry Compote

Aunt Ida's Rhubarb Cake

Strawberry Crisp

Lemon Pudding

Scones

Date Squares

Maple Ice Cream

Maple Sorbet

Tartare de saumon fumé

SMOKED SALMON TARTARE

Down the road from the little restaurant called La Broue dans l'Toupet, in the old fishing village of Mont-Louis, on the Gaspé's north coast, you'll find one of Quebec's finest fish-smoking enterprises, Atkins & Frères. Chef Daniel Gasse likes using its products in his cooking, in particular the Atlantic salmon, and the mackerel and shrimp from the Gulf of St. Lawrence. You can reduce the smoked salmon flavour in this appetizer by replacing half of it with fresh sushi-grade salmon.

SERVES 4

12 slices (250 g) cold-smoked salmon

2 sprigs fresh dill, chopped

2 peeled mandarin oranges or clementines, pith removed, in segments and chopped

Juice of 1 lemon

2 tablespoons (30 mL) capers, rinsed and patted dry

2 tablespoons (30 mL) olive oil

Salt and freshly ground pepper

Lemon quarters

Capers

Baguette, to serve

✤ Using a sharp knife, chop salmon finely. In a bowl, place salmon, dill, mandarins, lemon juice, capers, and oil. Mix well and season with salt and pepper. Cover and refrigerate 2 to 3 hours.

✤ Tartare may be spooned onto 4 serving plates or packed into 4 moulds or ramekins (½ cup/125 mL each), then unmoulded onto the plates.

✤ Trim plates with lemons and capers. Serve with baguette slices, toasted or grilled until crisp.

Smoked Seafood Headquarters

Driving east to the Gaspé along the St. Lawrence River, I was amazed to find a perfect little restaurant on that remote and spectacular northern coast. Tucked in along the shore among fishermen's houses in the tiny fishing port of Mont-Louis is La Broue dans l'Toupet. There, the Gasse family of cooks, led by Chef Daniel Gasse, cooks the fish and seafood of the lower St. Lawrence region—as well as a steak or two. I'd stopped on my way into town at Atkins & Frères, the Gaspé fish-smoking company whose sleek black packages of smoked fish sell briskly in the best Montreal fish stores. And there, on Daniel's menu, were unique combinations of fresh fish and Atkins & Frères' smoked seafoods.

The Atkins brothers, James Henry, Charles, and Bernard, are Quebecers who were, for a time, West Coast hippies, but they happened into town and stayed. They opened a modest-looking smokehouse that now produces a host of delicacies for much of eastern Canada and the U.S. northeast.

Their bestseller is salmon smoked the old-fashioned way using the hot-smoke method. James Henry explains that they invented their system using an old camp stove in their backyard. Their salmon has a slightly cooked, almost ham-like texture that differs from the usual silky East Coast smoked salmon.

James Henry Atkins sells his smoked salmon at Jean-Talon Market.

Homard en sauce au Cointreau

LOBSTER IN COINTREAU CREAM SAUCE

This luxurious dish, perfect for a special occasion, comes from chef-owner Georges Mamelonet of the Percé restaurant La Maison du Pêcheur. Although lobster may be fished only at certain times during the season, it's on his menu daily from May to October, for he has devised a system of imprisoning and feeding lobsters in deep-water cages just off Percé Rock, the ancient landmark that dominates Percé's harbour. Every day, Georges dons a wetsuit to descend about 60 feet (18 m) to feed his catch and bring up just the quantities he needs.

SERVES 2

Grated peel of 1 orange
1/3 cup (75 mL) fresh orange juice
Salt and freshly ground pepper
2 tablespoons (30 mL) Cointreau
1/3 cup (75 mL) whipping cream
1 cup (250 mL) thinly sliced, cooked lobster meat
Chopped fresh flat-leaf parsley
Lime slices

+ In a heavy frying pan, cook orange peel and juice over medium heat, stirring often, until almost dried out. Add salt, pepper, and Cointreau and cook for 1 minute. Add cream and continue cooking, stirring often, for 1 to 2 minutes.
+ Add lobster and heat, turning the meat in the cream sauce and stirring gently to coat. Serve on warmed serving plates, topped with parsley and a lime slice.

Note
+ You will need a 1-pound (500 g) lobster, cooked and shelled, or 1 can (11.3 ounces/320 g) frozen lobster meat, thawed.

LOBSTER

H ow long to boil lobster is an ongoing debate. In the Gaspé, where lobster season means party time, the tradition is to boil lobsters for 12 to 15 minutes. However, chefs compare that custom to the sacrilege of cooking a tender steak to well done. They like to boil a lobster weighing 1 to 1 1/4 pounds (500 to 625 g) for only 8 to 10 minutes, counting from when the water comes back to a boil. And take those elastics off the claws because they can flavour the lobster with rubber. Let the lobster cool at room temperature.

Montreal chef and fish specialist Jean-Paul Grappe suggests that you have a big pot of boiling water ready, but only boil your lobsters one at a time. Drop the lobster into the pot and boil it for 1 minute, which kills it, he says. (If you put four in the pot at once, you are giving them a slow death while the water returns to a boil.) After 1 minute, remove the lobster and set it aside while you boil the others, one by one, the same way. Then, when all have been given this quick finale, return them to the pot and boil for about another 10 minutes, depending on size. Finally, says the chef, let them rest at room temperature as you would roast beef, to tenderize the meat. Only then should you start your lobster feed.

Croquettes de truite fumée

SMOKED TROUT CROQUETTES

Trout farms are dotted throughout Quebec, but spring means fishing for the wild stuff in the province's cold, fast-flowing rivers and in ponds. Geneviève Longère, a chef who, with her husband, Yves, ran a table champêtre (country restaurant) at their farm near St-Alexis-de-Montcalm, northeast of Montreal, likes to use smoked trout in these light and flavourful croquettes. Serve with a salad of spring lettuce, radishes, and green onions, with an oil and balsamic vinegar dressing.

MAKES 12

7 ounces (200 g) smoked trout, skinned
2 cups (500 mL) cubed dried bread
1/2 cup (125 mL) light cream
2 tablespoons (30 mL) chopped green onions
1/2 teaspoon (2 mL) Espelette pepper or cayenne pepper
Sea salt
1 to 2 egg whites
4 cups (1 L) sunflower oil, for frying

+ Using a sharp knife, chop fish finely and set aside.
+ Place bread cubes in a food processor, add cream, let stand 5 minutes, then pulse just until smooth. Add fish, green onions, pepper, and salt and pulse to thoroughly combine. Add 1 egg white and whirl to mix in; texture should be firm but not dry. Whirl in another egg white if necessary to make a firm paste.
+ Divide fish mixture into 12 equal portions and form into small, fat sausage shapes. Arrange on a pan lined with plastic wrap, cover, and refrigerate for 1 hour.
+ Pour oil into a deep fryer, a large, heavy, stovetop-safe casserole dish, or an electric frying pan, to a depth of about 1½ inches (4 cm) and heat to 350°F (180°C). Deep-fry croquettes until golden brown, about 3 to 5 minutes.
+ Transfer to a tray lined with paper towels to drain. Serve warm. Croquettes can be kept warm for up to 30 minutes in an oven heated to 150 to 170°F (65 to 77°C).

Note

Instead of deep-frying, you can fry croquettes in 2 tablespoons (30 mL) sunflower oil over medium-high heat for 3 minutes per side or until golden brown.

Pétoncles sur un lit d'avocat et huile de truffe

SEARED SCALLOPS ON A BED OF SPICY AVOCADO WITH TRUFFLE OIL

When Jacques Hendlisz, an experienced amateur chef, offers this appetizer at Alex H, the Montreal restaurant where he works as sous-chef on Tuesday nights, it usually sells out early. Regulars love the combination of crisp, sweet seafood and nippy avocado. A wine connoisseur and retired hospital director, Jacques downplays his culinary skills. "Food is the underpinning of a great conversation . . . it touches all your senses," he says. This appetizer will help any conversation along.

SERVES 6

6 large scallops

Salt and freshly ground white pepper

4 ripe medium avocados

Juice of 1/2 lemon

Dashes hot pepper sauce or 1/4 teaspoon (1 mL) sambal oelek

1 ripe large tomato

1 tablespoon (15 mL) fruity olive oil, preferably from Provence

2 tablespoons (30 mL) butter

1 tablespoon (15 mL) olive oil, for searing

Truffle oil or olive oil, for drizzling

1 tablespoon (15 mL) balsamic vinegar

+ Rinse scallops in cold water and pat dry with paper towels. Sprinkle both sides with salt and white pepper. Place scallops on a plate lined with a paper towel and refrigerate until ready to cook.

+ Dice avocados into ½-inch (1 cm) pieces. Place in a resealable plastic bag with lemon juice, salt, and hot pepper sauce to taste. Seal the bag and refrigerate.

+ Dice tomatos, discard seeds, and place in a bowl with salt, white pepper, and fruity olive oil.

+ Heat butter with olive oil in a large, heavy frying pan over high heat for about 1 minute. When the butter is past foaming, add the scallops and sear for 1 to 2 minutes a side or until lightly browned. Set aside on a plate.

+ When ready to serve, fill 6 ramekins (2 inches/5 cm in diameter) with avocado mixture. Unmould onto 6 serving plates. Top each avocado mound with a seared scallop. Decorate the plates with tomatoes. Drizzle truffle oil on scallops, and balsamic vinegar around the rim of the plates.

Notes

Sambal oelek is a hot chili sauce commonly used in Malaysian and Thai cooking. It is sold at specialty food stores, Asian markets, and most supermarkets.

If desired, reduce the vinegar to a glaze by simmering it until it has reduced by half.

ROMAINE LETTUCE

Lettuce grower Thérèse Riendeau, the matriarch of the family that runs the 1,730-acre (700 hectare) Potager Riendeau romaine farm at St-Rémi, south of Montreal, rates her crop as superior to romaine from California because Quebec has more moisture in its lettuce fields and therefore more flavour in its romaine. She likes to rinse and dry her lettuce, tear it into bite-size pieces, then toss it with freshly made croutons and a simple vinaigrette flavoured with chopped fresh basil.

Salata Pashkalini

GREEK SPRING SALAD

Menus at Montreal's celebrated Greek restaurant Milos have been setting a standard for the city's Greek chefs ever since Costas Spiliadis opened his cheerful blue-and-white taverna in 1979. Even when he is away supervising his other Milos restaurants (in New York, Athens, Las Vegas, and Miami's South Beach), his mother's cooking lives on at his original Montreal establishment.

SERVES 8

1 large head romaine lettuce (or 2 small heads), leaves separated
4 green onions, finely chopped
1/2 bunch fresh dill, finely chopped
1/3 cup (75 mL) olive oil
1/4 cup (60 mL) red wine vinegar or 2 tablespoons (30 mL) balsamic vinegar
Salt and freshly ground pepper
1/2 cup (125 mL) Kalamata olives, pitted
4 ounces (125 g) feta cheese, preferably Greek, rinsed and thinly sliced

- ✦ Trim romaine leaves, stack them up, and slice into thin strips. Place in a salad bowl with green onions and dill, tossing to mix.
- ✦ In a cup, whisk together oil and vinegar. Season with salt and pepper. Pour dressing over salad, tossing again to mix. Arrange olives and cheese over top.

Radishes

Radishes go well with a little salt, but the French fashion is to accent them with butter. Spread a slice from a fresh baguette with a little unsalted butter or mayonnaise, then top with sliced, lightly salted radishes. Or slice a ripe avocado, lay it on bread, then arrange sliced radishes on the avocado. Special salt—smoked, sea, or coarse—adds punch. And, if you're all set to serve radishes but they seem just a little soft, you may be able to refresh them by immersing them in ice water for 30 minutes.

At the radish farm Leclair & Frères, at Sherrington, south of Montreal, Solange Leclair slices her radishes thinly and tosses them with a vinaigrette that has plenty of freshly ground black pepper to accent the radish's natural peppery flavour. The dish is prettier if you use mixed bunches of red, white, and purple radishes. Quebec's favourite radish is round and red, but a long, red-and-white variety called French or breakfast has become popular too, particularly with people of European background. Clément Guérin, a Sherrington radish grower, produces both types. Lined up next to carrot and celery sticks, this radish looks pretty when served with a dip.

Left: Pascal Guérin checks radishes at his Sherrington farm.

Salade de radis à la Russe

Russian radish salad

Quebec has long, cold winters, and the settlers became expert at storing vegetables in root cellars. Russians, used to a similar climate, take the credit for storing the radish, one of spring's first crops, all winter, and varying its use far beyond the crudité platter. This radish salad, accompanied by two other spring arrivals—green onions and tender spring lettuce—was served at a buffet of Russian-Quebec cuisine prepared by a group of Russian-born Montreal women. Nina Gann of Pointe-Claire, who made this salad, warned against oversalting: "Radishes don't like much salt," she says.

Serves 4

1 large bunch radishes, sliced (2 cups/500 mL)
2/3 cup (150 mL) sliced green onions
1/3 cup (75 mL) sour cream (or half mayonnaise, half sour cream)
Salt and freshly ground pepper
1 hard-boiled egg, chopped

+ In a bowl, mix together radishes and green onions. Cover and refrigerate for 30 minutes.
+ In another bowl, combine sour cream, salt, and pepper. Cover and refrigerate up to 5 hours.
+ Just before serving, stir sour cream into vegetables, mixing well. Transfer to a serving bowl and sprinkle with chopped egg.

Omelette aux têtes de violon

FIDDLEHEAD OMELETTE

Caroline Dumas considers fiddleheads "the star of the plate" because, as she puts it, they are rare, delicate, and unique-looking. Running her chain of Montreal soup restaurants, Soupesoup, she never attempts fiddlehead soup because her soups usually are ready and waiting for her customers' orders, and fiddleheads lose their bright green colour if kept waiting.

SERVES 2

Fiddleheads
2 cups (500 mL) fresh fiddleheads
3 tablespoons (45 mL) olive oil
3 cloves garlic, minced
1 shallot, finely chopped
3 tablespoons (45 mL) verjus, cider vinegar,
   or white balsamic vinegar
Sea salt and freshly ground pepper

Omelette
1 tablespoon (15 mL) butter
4 eggs
3 tablespoons (45 mL) whipping cream
   or whole milk
Salt and freshly ground pepper
1 cup (250 mL) shredded Le Maréchal,
   Comté, or aged cheddar cheese

✦ Put fiddleheads in a large, resealable plastic bag, add cold water to cover, close and shake to clean off the brown husks and any dirt from the fiddleheads. With your hands, pick out the fiddleheads and place in a bowl. Discard water in the bag. Repeat the washing process with clean water at least once more, until water in the bag is clear. Drain and dry fiddleheads with towels. Cut tail ends off fiddleheads.

✦ Bring a large pot of water to a boil, add fiddleheads and boil for 4 minutes. Drain and rinse in cold water. Set aside.

✦ In a large, heavy frying pan, heat oil over medium heat and sauté garlic and shallot until softened and lightly coloured, 3 to 4 minutes. Add fiddleheads and stir constantly for 3 minutes. Drizzle with verjus and sprinkle with salt and pepper. Set aside.

✦ In an 8-inch (20 cm) heavy omelette pan or nonstick frying pan, melt butter over low heat. In a bowl, whisk eggs with cream. Add pinches of salt and pepper. Pour egg mixture into the heated pan and cook for 2 to 3 minutes, shaking the pan to distribute the egg mixture. While the omelette is still fairly moist, spread cheese and fiddleheads in the centre of the egg mixture. Continue cooking for another minute. When cheese starts to melt, fold half the omelette over itself and tip out onto a warmed serving plate. Cut in half if sharing. Serve with a crisp tossed green salad.

Note
Verjus is a mild-tasting, sweet-and-sour vinegar made from unripe grapes. It dates back to medieval times. It is available in specialty stores.

FIDDLEHEADS

Cooking fiddleheads is as easy as cooking asparagus. Simply remove the fiddleheads' papery brown husks, trim off stalks, rinse in several changes of cold water, then boil for 6 to 10 minutes, depending on size, until crisp-tender, or steam for 8 to 10 minutes. Their flavour is distinctive; all you need is butter.

Fiddleheads make a modest dish special because of their beautiful curled shape and punchy, slightly bitter flavour. Once cooked and cooled, fiddleheads can be quickly sizzled with finely chopped garlic and used as filling for an omelette; folded into hot, creamy pasta along with chopped mushrooms and ham; or added last minute to potato soup made with chicken stock and flavoured with thyme and lemon juice.

The arrival of the celebrated spring delicacy on vegetable stands prompts the annual Quebec government safety warnings to handle these furled fronds carefully or you might suffer food poisoning. The concern, explains veteran Montreal chef-professor Jean-Paul Grappe, is that your fiddleheads may not all be fronds from the ostrich fern (*Matteuccia struthiopteris*), which are safe to eat. Experienced foragers know the variety to harvest, but amateurs may make mistakes. Grappe considers us to be completely safe if we buy fiddleheads at a reputable store.

Fiddlehead forager François Lamontagne
harvests near St-Jacques-de-Montcalm.

Gerry van Winden

When summer weather turns steaming hot, we think with pleasure of a cooling salad. But Gerry van Winden starts watching the sky and yearning for a cold snap.

"Heat and salad don't go together," contends the salad grower, known throughout eastern North America for his baby greens, grown on his 7,500 acres (3,035 hectares) near Sherrington. Produced in Quebec from May to November, and in Florida in wintertime, the tiny spinach, baby romaine, arugula, oak leaf lettuce, and another half-dozen varieties of leaves have made him Canada's largest producer of ready-made salad, sold under the name Fresh Attitude.

On six or seven days each summer, Quebec temperatures rise to 85°F (30°C) or higher. Gerry grits his teeth at his wilting fields and braces for the thunderstorm that will end the heat wave —"but also break my leaves," he says, throwing up his hands.

To mitigate the damage, Gerry, an agriculture graduate and descendant of a Dutch gardening family, has improved the drainage on his land and invested in tents of netting, to be cast over the crops at the first sign of a storm. When the rain or hail ends, he removes the nets quickly. "We want our leaves to dry fast before mould can develop."

His business, VegPro International, had its beginnings in 1952 when his father, Peter, and uncle, John, emigrated from Holland. At that time, the Quebec government was digging in

the L'Acadie River, southeast of Montreal, and draining what's still called "the muckland." The soil is black and extra fertile, perfect for growing tender vegetables—it's estimated to have four times the capacity of Quebec's ordinary soil to absorb water.

Acquiring more land and increasing the varieties of vegetables they grew, the van Windens—there are seven of them in the company now—saw a trend to baby greens in Italy and California, and gradually moved their business in that direction.

A field of his tiny leaves is a spectacle: delicate greens and reds low to the ground and stretching off to the horizon. Another sight to be seen is when one of his specially designed harvesting machines starts chomping its way through a sea of baby spinach. Within a few hours, those little leaves will have been washed, dried, sorted, and packed for sale.

Fresh and local is the future, says Gerry. Although Quebec, with its long winters, is a major region for importing foreign produce, Gerry forecasts continued strength for the local growing industry. "Local is going to have more and more value," he says.

Gerry van Winden supervises the baby lettuce harvest at St-Rémi.

Fishermen unload mackerel at Douglastown on the Gaspé coast.

Crêpes aux asperges gratinées

CRÊPES WITH ASPARAGUS AND CHEESE

Asparagus season has now been extended to 12 months of the year, thanks to growers in Mexico and Peru. But Quebec asparagus plays a unique role in heralding spring. Debbi Eaman of Knowlton, a talented family cook, likes to use the slimmest spears in this classic lunch or dinner dish. She uses a couple of cheeses here: cheddar or Parmesan to flavour the sauce, and Le Migneron or Gruyère to tuck into the asparagus rolls along with slices of ham.

SERVES 4 AS A MAIN COURSE OR 8 AS A FIRST COURSE

Crêpes

2 cups (500 mL) milk

2 eggs

1 cup (250 mL) all-purpose flour

4 tablespoons (60 mL) melted butter

1 teaspoon (5 mL) salt

Butter, for cooking crêpes

Sauce

2 tablespoons (30 mL) butter

2 tablespoons (30 mL) all-purpose flour

1 1/2 cups (375 mL) heated milk

Salt and freshly ground pepper

1/2 cup (125 mL) shredded medium cheddar cheese, such as the mild cheddar from Fromagerie
Île-aux-Grues

Filling

1 1/2 pounds (750 g) slim asparagus spears

8 thin slices Gruyère cheese

8 thin slices Black Forest ham

For crêpes:

+ Whirl milk and eggs together in a blender, adding flour a little at a time, followed by butter and salt, until all ingredients are combined.
+ Coat a crêpe pan or 8- or 9-inch (20 or 23 cm) nonstick frying pan with a little butter and set over medium-high heat. When the pan is hot, add ½ cup (125 mL) of the batter, tilting pan to spread batter widely. Cook just until crêpe begins to turn golden brown. Use a spatula to loosen it from the pan and flip it to cook the other side just until golden brown.
+ Place crêpe on a large plate lined with waxed paper. Top with another piece of waxed paper. Continue in this way until all batter is cooked, placing each crêpe in turn on waxed paper to keep them separate.

For sauce:

+ In a medium, heavy saucepan, melt butter over medium-low heat and stir in flour. Stir constantly for 2 minutes. Stir in the hot milk, stirring briskly to blend, until sauce thickens. Season with salt and pepper, then add cheese, stirring until melted. Remove mixture from heat and cover to keep warm.

For assembly and baking:

+ Butter a shallow baking pan (13 × 9 inches/33 × 23 cm) or gratin dish large enough to hold 8 rolled-up crêpes.
+ Drop the asparagus into a pot of boiling salted water. Cook for 2 minutes, then drain and run under cold water to stop the cooking.
+ Place a crêpe on a flat surface. Place a slice of cheese on crêpe, followed by a slice of ham. Top with 4 or 5 spears of asparagus. Roll up crêpe and place in the pan, seam side down. Repeat, lining up rolled crêpes neatly side by side. Pour sauce over the crêpes, leaving the ends unsauced.
+ Preheat the oven to 375°F (190°C).
+ Place the pan of crêpes uncovered in the oven and bake for 30 minutes. Turn on the broiler and broil until lightly browned.

Notes

Unfilled crêpes can be wrapped in waxed paper and refrigerated for up to 1 week, or frozen for up to 6 months.

Filled, unsauced crêpes can be prepared up to 3 hours in advance, covered, and refrigerated. Refrigerate sauce separately.

Organic foods blooming

The organic movement in Quebec has long roots that date back to the all-natural farming methods of pioneer times. Each year, more converts turn to "biologique" foods produced without the use of chemicals. A separate counter offering fruit and vegetables grown without chemical fertilizers or pesticides is standard in supermarket produce sections. Farmers' markets usually include organic growers, and major produce companies import and distribute these foods year-round. A vital part of Quebec's burgeoning organic-food business is played by a group of organic farmers who are members of Équiterre, based in Montreal. These farmers bring orders weekly to urban customers, who pay for their orders six months in advance, thereby helping finance smaller growers. Équiterre has been expanding its customer base ever since 1995, when one organic farm supplied 15 families. Today, this family farmers network (formerly called community supported agriculture, or CSA) is made up of more than 100 farms that feed an estimated 12,000 families. Baskets of organic fruit and vegetables are delivered summer and winter to about 450 urban drop-off points all over Quebec, with each basket containing a selection of 6 to 12 foods. Some farms also offer eggs, meat and herbs. Customers sign up for the season via the website www.paniersbio.org. The site also offers free recipes. A sign of the general acceptance of this type of food program is the recent addition of drop-off points in supermarket parking lots and at commuter train stations.

Brandade de crabe des neiges au celeri-rave

SNOW CRAB WITH CELERY ROOT

Spring means snow crab season in the Lower St. Lawrence. Snow crab, shaped like a giant spider, is also called spider crab, tanner crab, and queen crab. The meat is in their many legs and can be boiled, fried, or baked. Chef Colombe St-Pierre, who runs a restaurant in Le Bic on the lower south coast, likes to combine this shellfish with creamy puréed potatoes flavoured with celery root and shallots.

SERVES 4

2 cups (500 mL) finely chopped cooked crabmeat, fresh or frozen and thawed
4 medium yellow-fleshed potatoes, peeled and quartered
1 small celery root, peeled and cubed
1 tablespoon (15 mL) vegetable oil
2 shallots, minced
1/2 cup (125 mL) dry white wine
1/2 cup (125 mL) whipping cream
Salt and freshly ground pepper
Sprigs fresh parsley or chives

+ Put crabmeat in a bowl and heat gently by placing the bowl in a larger bowl of hot water. Cook potatoes and celery root together in a pot of boiling salted water just until tender, then drain and purée in a blender or food processor. Return to the pot and set over very low heat to dry out mixture slightly, stirring constantly. Set aside.
+ In a small, heavy frying pan, heat oil over medium heat and cook shallots, stirring often, just until golden. Add wine and cook until mixture is reduced to about ⅓ cup (75 mL). Stir into potato purée.
+ In a small saucepan, boil cream gently over medium heat, just until it is reduced to about ⅓ cup (75 mL). Stir into potato purée. Set purée over low heat and stir constantly until heated.
+ At the last moment, stir in crabmeat and season with salt and pepper. Avoid overheating mixture. Serve hot, sprinkled with parsley.

Saumon poché, purée de pommes de terre à l'oseille et beurre blanc

POACHED SALMON ON SORREL MASHED POTATOES

The pink of the fish, the pale green of the potatoes, and the cream of the sauce make this dish a tempting sight at Bistro Beaux Lieux, in Sutton, in the Eastern Townships. Chef-owner Christian Beaulieu regards it as one of his signature dishes. Smaller Quebec communities tend to be a little conservative in their tastes, favouring meat over fish, says Beaulieu, who was self-taught while working in Montreal restaurants. So he talks up his fish cuisine as customers are reading their menus. "They order it, and they like it," he says.

SERVES 4

1 pound (500 g) Yukon Gold potatoes, peeled and quartered
1/2 cup (125 mL) whipping cream, plus more as needed
1/2 cup (125 mL) dry white wine
Juice of 1 lemon
4 1-inch (2.5 cm) thick salmon fillets (4 ounces/125 g each)
1/2 cup (125 mL) cold unsalted butter, cubed
1 bunch fresh sorrel, finely chopped
Salt and freshly ground pepper
2 tablespoons (30 mL) olive oil

+ Place potatoes in a large pot of cold salted water. Bring to a boil and cook just until tender, then drain and return to the pot with the heat off so the potatoes dry out.
+ Meanwhile, in a large, heavy frying pan, combine cream, wine, and lemon juice. Add salmon and cook over medium-high heat until sauce comes to a boil. Reduce heat to low, cover, and cook gently for 10 minutes, or just until fish flakes with a fork. Transfer fish to a hot platter, cover, and keep warm.
+ Gently boil sauce until reduced to the consistency of thick cream. Remove from heat and stir in half the butter, piece by piece. Cover and keep warm.
+ Mash potatoes with a potato masher, then blend in remaining butter, sorrel, salt, pepper, and oil. If necessary, blend in a few extra spoonfuls of cream to give the desired consistency.
+ To serve, scoop potatoes into the centre of 4 warmed serving plates. Set a piece of salmon on top and pour sauce over fish. Accompany with hot steamed asparagus or fiddleheads.

Boreal Flavours

Wild-food foragers return from the Quebec wilderness with uncommon plants, leaves, tree sap, mushrooms, and other finds to use in vinaigrettes, essences, syrups, and seasonings. They have found the boreal forests of northern Quebec and the Gaspé Peninsula to be rich sources of these products, often selling them to Quebec chefs on the lookout for ways to make their cooking unique. "Chefs want to have the exotic, they learn fast, and they integrate these products into their cooking," says Ste-Adèle chef Anne Desjardins. Dried wild mushrooms are one example; they can be ground into a powder and used instead of flour as a coating for fish fillets. Syrup from the yellow birch tree is another. This Gaspé product can be used in place of maple syrup to make a glaze, sauce, or vinaigrette for meat, fish, or vegetables. The essence from the fir tree is combined with wild fruits such as blueberries and cranberries, and maple syrup is paired with pine essence to make vinaigrettes and jellies. Roots of burdock, when dried, give the flavour of hazelnuts or almonds to foods, and lovage root, which smells like celery, makes a salt substitute. Another source for wild foods is the Quebec coastline. One company that does coastal foraging, Les Jardins de la Mer, is in St-André-de-Kamouraska, on the south shore of the lower St. Lawrence River. The company produces fresh and dried marine plants such as salicorne (sea asparagus) and sea parsley, as well as dried algae and mint tisane. Two stores in Montreal's Jean-Talon Market are sources for wild products: Marché des Saveurs du Québec and Les Jardins Sauvages. My best advice when experimenting with these delicacies in cooking is to use a tiny amount to start.

Claudie Gagné forages for sweetgrass at Les Jardins de la Mer.

Pétoncles au miso

SCALLOPS WITH MISO, THE NOBU WAY

Johanne Vigneau, chef-owner of La Table des Roy restaurant, in Îles de la Madeleine, knows that customers like scallops for their delicate sweetness and meaty texture. She was inspired by the cuisine of the Nobu restaurants, of the worldwide Japanese chain, to create this recipe. The marinade can also be used with white fish, such as cod or halibut, or with salmon. The shallot vinaigrette can be made a few hours in advance.

SERVES 4

Marinade

1/2 cup (125 mL) sake

3 tablespoons (45 mL) mirin

1/2 cup (125 mL) light miso

3 tablespoons (45 mL) granulated sugar

Vinaigrette

2 tablespoons (30 mL) granulated sugar

1 cup (250 mL) mirin

2 tablespoons (30 mL) miso

1 tablespoon (15 mL) rice vinegar

1 tablespoon (15 mL) wasabi powder

2 shallots, finely chopped

Pinch freshly ground black pepper

Dash sambal oelek, or to taste

Scallops

12 large scallops

1 package (8 ounces/250 g) soba noodles

2 to 3 green onions, finely chopped

For marinade:

+ In a small saucepan, heat sake and mirin over medium heat. Boil for 15 seconds to evaporate the alcohol. Remove from heat and add miso, mixing it in with a wooden spoon. When miso is well dissolved, put the pan back on the heat and stir in sugar. As soon as sugar has dissolved, remove from heat. Refrigerate to cool.

For vinaigrette:

+ In a large cup, dissolve sugar in the mirin. Stir in miso, rice vinegar, wasabi powder, shallots, pepper, and sambal oelek.

For scallops:

+ Rinse scallops and pat dry with paper towels. Reserving ¼ cup (60 mL) of the marinade, pour remainder into a resealable plastic bag. Place scallops in the bag, seal, and refrigerate for 1 to 3 hours.
+ When ready to cook, prepare noodles according to package directions. Then remove scallops from marinade and pat dry with paper towels, taking care not to blot off all the marinade.
+ Preheat the broiler. Place scallops in a baking pan. Grill about 3 inches (7.5 cm) from the broiler until golden, about 3 minutes. Turn and grill the other side for another 2 minutes. Or spray a large, heavy frying pan with olive oil and fry scallops for 3 minutes. Turn scallops, remove the pan from the heat, and let scallops finish cooking in the hot pan for 2 minutes.
+ Toss cooked noodles with enough shallot vinaigrette to lightly coat. Taste and add more if you like. Toss with green onions. Arrange grilled scallops on top and drizzle with the reserved marinade. Serve at once.

SCALLOPS: A SPECIALTY

It doesn't matter how far you venture off the beaten track, Quebec offers unexpected treasures. In the windy and wave-swept Îles de la Madeleine, in the Gulf of St. Lawrence, is a celebrated Quebec restaurant where local seafood, veal, and cheese dominate the menu. Called La Table des Roy, it's run by the dedicated, self-taught chef Johanne Vigneau, in the community of Étang-du-Nord. Not content with making it into the best restaurant guides, she has opened a cooking school and kitchen shop called Gourmande de Nature. Among the classes she gives is one on cooking local seafood with international flavours. (You'll find her scallop recipe on page 50.)

Filets de truite sur une planche de cèdre

Cedar planked trout fillets

Delicately flavoured fish acquires a slightly smoky taste if you bake it on a cedar plank, says chef Geneviève Longère of St-Alexis-de-Montcalm. The planks are sold at building-supply and kitchen stores.

Serves 4

1 untreated 1-inch (2.5 cm) thick cedar plank
   (8 x 12 inches/20 x 30 cm)
1/4 cup (60 mL) olive oil
1 cup (250 mL) finely chopped celery
2 cups (500 mL) finely chopped unpeeled Cortland or Granny Smith apples
1 1/3 cups (325 mL) peeled, chopped potatoes
Salt and freshly ground pepper

2 cups (500 mL) celery juice
2 tablespoons (30 mL) butter
1 cup (250 mL) finely chopped onions
1 1/3 cups (325 mL) fresh or frozen fiddleheads
4 skin-on trout fillets (3 ounces/85 g each)
2 tablespoons (30 mL) chopped chives
2 tablespoons (30 mL) chopped chervil

+ Soak the plank in water for at least 3 hours, then dry the surface and rub generously with oil. Place on a baking sheet in an oven preheated to 425°F (220°C) for 20 minutes.
+ Meanwhile, place celery and half the apples in a medium saucepan, cover with cold water and bring to a boil. Reduce heat to low and simmer for 7 minutes, or until almost tender. Drain.
+ Meanwhile, in another saucepan, simmer potatoes in enough salted water to cover. When tender, drain and add to apple mixture. Using a potato masher or ricer (not a food processor), mash until almost smooth. Season with salt and pepper and keep warm in the bowl of a double boiler.
+ In a saucepan, bring celery juice and remaining apples to a boil over medium heat. Reduce heat to low and simmer for 15 minutes. Strain through a sieve. Season with salt and pepper, and stir in 1 tablespoon (15 mL) of the butter. Keep sauce warm.
+ In a large, heavy frying pan, heat remaining 1 tablespoon (15 mL) butter over medium heat and cook onions until browned and caramelized.
+ Meanwhile, in a large saucepan of boiling salted water over medium heat, cook fiddleheads for 2 minutes. Drain and season with salt and pepper.
+ Bake trout skin side down on the heated plank for about 7 minutes, or just until fish flakes with a fork.
+ Divide hot purée among 4 warmed plates and top with a trout fillet, skin side up. Arrange fiddleheads and onions around fish and pour sauce over top. Finish with chives and chervil.

Note
Celery juice is available in natural food stores. To make fresh, use a juice extractor; 1 bunch celery produces about 2 cups (500 mL) juice.

Filet de boeuf aux oignons rouges

BEEF STEAKS WITH RED ONIONS

Jean Soulard, the French-born chef who was executive chef for 20 years at the Fairmont Le Château Frontenac, in Quebec City, has been a pioneer among Quebec chefs, seeking out local products and making them shine in the cuisine at his landmark hotel. Author of eight cookbooks, he has collected all his favourite dishes in one big book, Le Grand Soulard de la Cuisine, *including this lively treatment for steak. Fond de veau is available at butcher shops, but it is also easy to make.*

SERVES 4

2 tablespoons (30 mL) olive oil
2 tablespoons (30 mL) butter
3 red onions, thinly sliced
3 tablespoons (45 mL) red wine vinegar
2 cups (500 mL) fond de veau (page 56)
2 tablespoons (30 mL) honey
Salt and freshly ground pepper
4 beef sirloin, rib eye, or tenderloin steaks (5 ounces/150 g each)

✦ In a large, heavy frying pan, heat half the oil and half the butter over medium heat and cook onions, turning often, until softened and golden but not browned. Add vinegar and simmer, stirring often, for 2 to 3 minutes. Add fond de veau and cook until reduced by half. Stir in honey, salt, and pepper and keep warm over low heat.

✦ In another heavy frying pan, heat remaining butter and oil over medium-high heat and sear steaks for 4 minutes per side for rare, a little longer for medium-done. Sprinkle with salt and pepper.

✦ To serve, divide onions among 4 warmed serving plates. Top with steaks and pour extra sauce over.

Fond de veau

CONCENTRATED VEAL STOCK

MAKES 4 CUPS (1 L)

2 pounds (1 kg) veal bones, cracked, with trimmings
1/2 small carrot, chopped
1/2 onion, chopped
1/2 stalk celery, chopped
1 Roma or plum tomato, chopped
1 tablespoon (15 mL) tomato paste
1 clove garlic, crushed
1 small bouquet garni (1 bay leaf, and sprigs of fresh thyme and flat-leaf parsley tied together, or tied
   in a cheesecloth bag)
1 teaspoon (5 mL) salt
Freshly ground pepper

✦ Preheat the oven to 400°F (200°C).
✦ Spread bones and trimmings in a baking pan and roast until browned, 30 to 45 minutes, turning occasionally. Add carrot, onion, celery, and tomato and roast for another 4 to 5 minutes. Transfer ingredients to a
   large, heavy pot. Add tomato paste, garlic, and bouquet garni. Add water to cover, and salt and pepper.
   Simmer over medium heat, uncovered, for 2 hours, skimming off surface froth occasionally.
✦ Strain through a sieve into a bowl; you should have about 4 cups (1 L). Cool, then refrigerate until
   chilled. Skim off fat. Mixture can be frozen, ideally in 1-cup (250 mL) portions, which are the most convenient to use.

Tartare de cheval ou boeuf au beurre et radis

TARTARE OF HORSEMEAT OR BEEF WITH BUTTER AND RADISHES

The Montreal restaurant Joe Beef regularly makes waves in the city's culinary scene. Chef-owners David McMillan and Frédéric Morin adapted a more traditional beef tartare to horsemeat, a delicacy with Québécois diners. Tartare means piquancy, and onion flavour is traditional. This recipe has both. The chefs like to serve tartare with frites. Essential to its preparation is well-chilled meat of the highest quality and equally cold, scrupulously clean equipment.

SERVES 4 AS A MAIN COURSE OR 6 AS AN APPETIZER

1 1/2 pound (750 g) horse or beef fillet, chilled
1/2 cup (125 mL) unsalted butter, chilled
3 tablespoons (45 mL) Dijon mustard
4 tablespoons (60 mL) minced shallots
4 tablespoons (60 mL) chopped chives

1 tablespoon (15 mL) chopped fresh chervil
1 tablespoon (15 mL) grated fresh horseradish
Salt and freshly ground pepper
Sliced radishes

+ Have meat thoroughly chilled. Place a cutting board, sharp knife, and bowl in the refrigerator several hours in advance.
+ Place meat on the cutting board and cut in 1-inch (2.5 cm) slices. Return all but 1 slice to the refrigerator. Cut slice of meat in tiny cubes the size of small capers. (Do not grind or cut in a food processor.) Repeat with remaining slices, placing cut meat in a plastic bag and refrigerating it as you work so it stays cold.
+ In a large frying pan, melt butter over medium heat until it starts to brown lightly. Remove the pan from the heat and let it cool down for 2 minutes.
+ Meanwhile, in a small bowl, combine Dijon, shallots, chives, chervil, horseradish, salt, and pepper. Taste and adjust seasoning.
+ In the chilled bowl, combine meat with cooled butter and mustard mixture. Refrigerate until serving time.
+ To serve, make a mound of tartare on each plate and arrange radishes on top. Serve at once.

Note

The chefs like to use a mix of French radishes (long, with a white tip), red radishes, and black radishes, shaved into paper-thin slices with a mandoline.

Potatoes on a Roll

Small, new potatoes are called "grelots" in Quebec and are enjoyed from spring through autumn, even though, as St-Rémi potato grower Daniel Oligny explains, they cost twice the price of regular potatoes. That's because they are so much more work to harvest than those of regular size. Daniel estimates he needs at least five little potatoes to make a pound (500 g). Shoppers pay the price, partly because these potatoes are sweet and tender, and partly because they are a convenience food, requiring no peeling and only a quick boil or steam until tender, then a roll in a hot frying pan of butter or oil to crisp the skin. Sales of grelots have almost doubled in the past five years.

Another boost in potato sales has come as a result of increased variety. First, growers watched red-skinned potatoes steal part of the white potato market. Then, they started trying to grow different varieties. I saw that development still in the fields at Réal Pinsonneault's property at St-Michel. It looked more like a flower garden than a farm, swaths of greenery accented with contrasting colours of blossoms, from white to rosy mauve. The colour indicated white, red, or blue potatoes.

Réal is helping turn the humble spud into a variable feast by marketing eight different varieties as they ripen through summer and fall. He uses small three-pound bags to encourage testing, and labels each variety with its best uses. Early Jemsegs are good for potato salad; early Belmonts and red Norlands are both excellent for boiling; and there are mid- and late-season types such as Vivaldi, a creamy baker, and Chieftain, for boiling or frying. Freshly dug potatoes are as perishable as strawberries, I learned, watching workers shake earth from the potatoes, fill buckets, and spread potato leaves on top. The leaves protect the potatoes from sunburn until they can be trucked to the packing plant, washed, and cooled. I now know that delicate new potatoes should always be refrigerated.

Arnaki kleftiko

LEG OF LAMB ROASTED IN PARCHMENT PAPER

Spring means lamb to Greek Montrealers—even though the era when lamb was really plentiful only in the spring has long gone and lamb producers in Quebec and elsewhere keep the market supplied year-round. At Restaurant Mythos Ouzeri Estiatorio, cooks prepare traditional foods each Easter, including this festive dish called kleftiko. Go easy on the salt, owner Dimitri Galanis warns, because the Greek cheese kefalotiri is salty. The meat is extra tender and the cheese accents the rich lamb flavour.

SERVES 6

1 leg of lamb (4 pounds/2 kg), trimmed of fat
12 cloves garlic, slivered
4 ounces (125 g) kefalotiri or Pecorino Romano cheese, slivered
Olive oil, for rubbing
1 tablespoon (15 mL) freshly ground black pepper
1 teaspoon (5 mL) freshly ground white pepper
1 teaspoon (5 mL) sea salt
15 bay leaves

+ Preheat the oven to 325°F (160°C).
+ Using a sharp, pointed knife, make slits at intervals all over the meat surface and insert slivers of garlic and cheese. Rub meat with oil and then sprinkle with black and white pepper and salt.
+ Have ready a large square of parchment paper and a large square of aluminum foil. Place about half the bay leaves on the paper, set meat on top, and place remaining bay leaves on the meat. Wrap meat in the paper and fold ends tightly closed, then wrap the package in the foil.
+ Place wrapped meat in a roasting pan and roast for 90 minutes or until a meat thermometer inserted in the thickest part of the leg registers 120°F (49°C) for rare, 130°F (54°C) for medium. Let stand, in its wrapping, for 15 minutes before carving.

Notes

Both kefalotiri and Pecorino Romano cheese are salty, so be sure not to oversalt the meat.
The meat can be prepared in advance, refrigerated, then brought to room temperature before roasting.

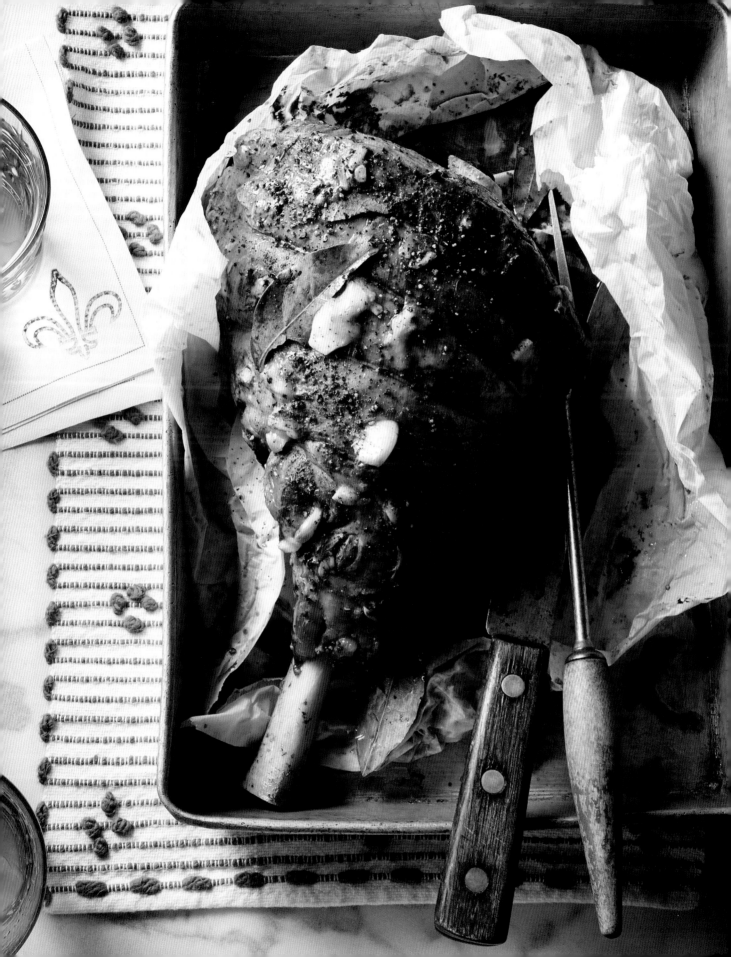

Quebec's first television chef was ahead of her time, from her first food projects in the 1930s when she ran a Montreal cooking school and then a vegetarian restaurant, The Salad Bar, to her final years demonstrating how to use the microwave and cook in metric measures. The lesson of Jehane Benoit (1904–87) that lives on today is the importance of seeking out the best fresh food, preferably in season, and letting it shine in simple ways. It's been called "cuisine du marché," "terroir," and "local," but long before these terms became fashionable, Madame Benoit knew they meant the best.

Whenever I cook a leg of lamb, I recall sitting at the kitchen table at her lamb farm near Sutton and listening to her talk about her favourite easy meals. Jehane, whose many cookbooks are now collector's items, pushed us all to seek out the best family cooks, including those who cooked in an ethnic tradition new to us, and to write down the recipes they made from memory. A few good pieces of cooking equipment can make cooking easier, she would say, and the simpler the better. Sturdy pots and pans, sharp knives, a wire whisk, wooden spoons, a good vegetable peeler, kitchen scissors, and a meat thermometer—these were her essentials. I keep her old wooden ladle in my kitchen as a reminder of her teachings.

Gigot d'agneau aux baies de genièvre

LEG OF LAMB FLAVOURED WITH JUNIPER BERRIES

Charlevoix, the hilly region of the lower St. Lawrence valley, is home to many lamb farms. Chef Marthe Lemire of the town of La Malbaie livens up roast lamb with juniper berries and cognac. My family has been enjoying this recipe for years, ever since Marthe, at the time chef-owner of an inn specializing in lamb cuisine, gave it to me. Juniper berries are sold at well-stocked spice shops. Marthe, now chef-owner of the Crêperie Le Passe-Temps, likes to serve the lamb with green beans with bacon, and steamed baby potatoes.

SERVES 6 TO 8

1 leg of lamb (4 pounds/2 kg)

2 tablespoons (30 mL) dried juniper berries, crushed

2 tablespoons (30 mL) butter, softened

1/4 teaspoon (1 mL) each salt and freshly ground pepper

3 tablespoons (45 mL) cognac or brandy

1 small onion, chopped

1 clove garlic, finely chopped

2 tablespoons (30 mL) butter

1 cup (250 mL) lamb or chicken stock

✦ Cut a shallow slit along the length of the lamb leg and fill with 1 tablespoon (15 mL) of the juniper berries. In a cup, stir butter with remaining juniper berries, salt, and pepper. Spread over lamb. Insert a meat thermometer in lamb and place in a shallow roasting pan. Roast in a 375°F (190°C) oven for 1 to 1¼ hours, until a meat thermometer inserted in the thickest part of the leg registers 120°F (49°C) for rare, 130°F (54°C) for medium.

✦ Transfer meat to a warm platter. Pour off fat from the pan and reserve. Return meat to the pan and pour cognac over top. Carefully bring a lighted match close to the lamb to flambé it. Return meat to the hot platter and keep warm.

✦ In a small frying pan over medium heat, sauté onion and garlic in butter until softened. Add reserved lamb drippings and stock and simmer over low heat 3 to 4 minutes until sauce is reduced and slightly thickened. Strain sauce and serve hot over sliced lamb.

Jambon braisé à la bière et à l'érable

HAM BRAISED IN MAPLE BEER

Belgian-born brewer Patrice Schoune, who runs Ferme Brassicole Schoune in St-Polycarpe, southwest of Montreal, recommends the delicate effect his maple-flavoured beer gives to meat dishes. He makes this beer, sold at beer specialty shops, by adding maple syrup as the beer ferments.

SERVES 6

3 tablespoons (45 mL) butter

1 medium onion, finely chopped

1 leek, white part only, finely chopped

1 carrot, diced

2 tablespoons (30 mL) granulated maple sugar

2 pounds (1 kg) smoked ham with bone, pierced with 8 or more cloves

1 tomato, peeled, seeded, and coarsely chopped

1 bouquet garni (1 bay leaf and sprigs of fresh thyme and flat-leaf parsley tied together, or tied in a cheesecloth bag)

2 bottles (12 ounces/341 mL each) Schoune L'Érabière maple-flavoured beer

✢ Preheat the oven to 375°F (190°C).

✢ In a deep, heavy, stovetop-safe casserole dish, melt butter over medium heat and cook onion, leek, and carrot just until tender, about 5 minutes. Add maple sugar and continue cooking, stirring often, until mixture is lightly caramelized. Set ham on vegetables and then add tomato, bouquet garni, and beer to the casserole dish.

✢ Roast, uncovered, for 20 minutes. Reduce the oven temperature to 325°F (160°C) and roast for another 45 minutes, basting occasionally.

✢ Remove casserole dish from the oven, place ham on a warmed serving platter, cover loosely with foil and let stand for 10 minutes. Carve ham and serve on warmed serving plates, accompanied by vegetables and beer sauce.

Note

You can use light beer mixed with 2 tablespoons (30 mL) maple syrup instead of Schoune L'Érabière.

Poulet aux grands-pères

CHICKEN WITH DUMPLINGS

In early times, this homey dish would be simmered on a cast-iron stove, using a chicken from the flock on the farm. That's Chef Serge Caplette's memory of how his grandmother, who raised her own poultry, cooked this dish at her home in St-Robert, east of Montreal near Sorel-Tracy. "The grands-pères *(dumplings) could replace potatoes or bread at the meal," recalls the chef, who teaches at the École hôtelière de Laval, north of Montreal. Be sure the chicken simmers very slowly.*

SERVES 6

1 whole chicken (4 pounds/2 kg)
1 bay leaf
1 sprig fresh thyme
1/2 teaspoon (2 mL) salt
1 cup (250 mL) cubed fresh carrots
1/2 cup (125 mL) chopped onion
1/2 cup (125 mL) coarsely chopped celery
1/2 cup (125 mL) cubed rutabaga

Dumplings
1 cup (250 mL) all-purpose flour
1 teaspoon (5 mL) baking powder
1/4 teaspoon (1 mL) salt
Generous pinch freshly ground pepper
1/2 cup (125 mL) packed, finely chopped celery leaves
2 eggs

✦ Place chicken in a large pot with bay leaf, thyme, and salt. Add water (about 4 cups/1 L) to about halfway up chicken. Cover and bring to a boil over medium-high heat, then reduce heat so water is at just a simmer. Simmer very slowly, covered, for 1 hour and 10 minutes, then stir in carrots, onion, celery, and rutabaga. Cover and simmer slowly for another 1 hour and 10 minutes.

✦ Remove chicken from pot, reserving stock and vegetables. When chicken is cool enough to handle, remove meat. Discard skin and bones or save to make stock for another dish. Cut or break up chicken into about 8 pieces and place in a bowl. Add vegetables to chicken.

✦ Strain reserved stock through a sieve into another bowl, then return to the pot and keep warm, covered, over low heat.

For dumplings:

✤ In a mixing bowl, stir flour with baking powder, salt, and pepper. Stir in celery leaves. Make a well in the centre of flour mixture and break the eggs into it. Using a fork, whisk eggs and then gradually incorporate them into flour mixture until it is a soft, sticky batter.

✤ Coat hands with flour and form batter into small balls, about 2 teaspoons (10 mL) each. Set on a plate lined with plastic wrap.

✤ Bring stock to a boil and gradually add all the dumplings. Cover and adjust heat so stock simmers. Simmer for 15 minutes without lifting the lid.

✤ Remove the pot from heat. Using a slotted spoon, transfer dumplings to a plate. Immediately return the pot to medium heat and add chicken and vegetables. Cover and, when stock starts to boil, add dumplings. Heat for 2 to 3 minutes, then serve in warmed bowls.

If you travel the back roads of Quebec, you will find countless temptations to enjoy local food and drink, either on the spot or to buy and take home. It's called agri-tourism, and refers to establishments welcoming visitors to taste, tour, and shop: farms and cheesemakers, wineries and orchards, bakeries and specialty meat shops. When setting out to drive about the province, I never leave home without a cooler and ice packs for storing food finds. Staying in small inns, I can usually arrange to stash my treats in the inn's refrigerator overnight, and have my ice packs refrozen too.

One of the most popular tours, particularly when the autumn wine harvest gets underway, is the wine route around Dunham, in the Eastern Townships. You can sip vintages for free, often with a snack included; buy wines you don't find anywhere else; have a picnic; and take a tour of vineyards and orchards. The spring apple-blossom time each May is a fine time to travel in apple country. Orchards in Rougemont, Mont-Saint-Hilaire, and St-Joseph-du-Lac welcome visitors then and during the autumn apple harvest.

Summer offers Le Circuit du Paysan (The Rural Tour), which goes all over the far-flung "garden" region to the south and west of Montreal. The Lanaudière, a fertile territory about an hour's drive northeast of the city, offers a visual feast of tranquil rivers and heritage stone farmhouses, along with superb cheese and wine, and good restaurants.

In eastern Quebec, Charlevoix has one of the longest established gastronomic tours, the Route des Saveurs. On the southeast coast of the St. Lawrence River, the brochure *Saveurs du Bas-Saint-Laurent* is published annually, as is the excellent magazine *Gaspésie Gourmande*. The website for the guidebook *Terroir et saveurs du Québec* lists gastronomic stops all over the province. French predominates, but most sites offer English information.

Festivals are another way Quebec celebrates gastronomy. Knowlton, home of Brome Lake Ducks, has an annual September duck festival. The blueberry harvest is celebrated each August with a festival in Lac St-Jean blueberry country, in Dolbeau-Mistassini. Magog winds up the summer with a wine festival, while the South Shore town of Chambly holds a beer festival. Montreal has a February dining-out festival, and the city celebrates the food markets of yesteryear each August at an 18th-century-style festival beside the Pointe-à-Callière architectural museum. For information visit www.bonjourquebec.com or watch for Tourisme Québec offices in the various regions, marked with a large question mark, where you can obtain free regional guides in English or French.

Lucie Cadieux cuddles a friend at her lamb farm, La Ferme Éboulmontaise, in Charlevoix.

Risotto aux asperges ou têtes de violon

RISOTTO WITH ASPARAGUS OR FIDDLEHEADS

Charlevoix, a hilly region in the Lower St. Lawrence where livestock graze on the hillsides, produces fine cheeses, used by many chefs, including La Malbaie's Dominique Truchon, to enhance their cuisine. He livens up a traditional risotto with Charlevoix cheese such as Tomme d'Elles, a semi-firm washed-rind cheese made by Baie-St-Paul cheesemaker Maurice Dufour from half cow's milk, half sheep's milk. At Chez Truchon, located in a century-old mansion, the chef adds crunch and colour to his risotto with either fiddleheads or asparagus.

SERVES 4 TO 6 AS A MAIN COURSE, OR 8 AS AN APPETIZER

1 cup (250 mL) fresh fiddleheads or 12 spears asparagus
1 tablespoon (15 mL) olive oil
2 shallots, chopped
1 1/3 cups (325 mL) unrinsed arborio rice
1 cup (250 mL) dry white wine
2 cups (500 mL) hot chicken stock
1/3 cup (75 mL) whipping cream
1/3 cup (75 mL) shredded Tomme d'Elles or cheddar cheese

✦ Clean fiddleheads (see page 34). (If using asparagus, cut into 1-inch/2.5 cm pieces.) Blanch for 2 minutes in boiling salted water, then drain, rinse in cold water to stop the cooking, and set aside.

✦ In a heavy, stovetop-safe casserole dish, heat oil over medium heat and cook shallots just until softened, 2 to 3 minutes. Add rice, turning to coat the grains. Add wine and cook, stirring constantly, just until it is all absorbed by the rice.

✦ Add half the stock a little at a time and cook, stirring constantly, just until it is all absorbed by the rice. Add remaining stock a little at a time and cook, stirring constantly, until all of it is absorbed. The rice should be lightly al dente. Stir in fiddleheads, then cream and cheese. Serve at once.

Asparagus

Shop for this perishable vegetable where turnover is fast, and store it in wet paper towels in a plastic bag in the refrigerator, says grower Mario Rondeau. Enjoy it as soon as possible, he advises. On his Primera-brand packaging, he suggests boiling or stir-frying medium-thick spears for 3 to 5 minutes, steaming for 5 minutes, microwaving for 3 to 6 minutes, or roasting for 8 to 10 minutes. He also brushes spears with olive oil, sprinkles on freshly ground black pepper and chopped fresh thyme and either basil or tarragon, and then barbecues them over medium heat for 2 to 5 minutes a side.

An asparagus salad calls for a lemon Dijon vinaigrette, says Michelle Rajotte, who helps husband Louis-Marie Jutras run their big asparagus farm, Cultures de Chez Nous, in Ste-Brigitte-des-Saults, on the south shore of the St. Lawrence River. Boil or steam spears just until crisp-tender, immerse in cold water to stop the cooking, then add a dressing of vegetable oil, lemon juice or white wine vinegar, Dijon mustard, salt, pepper, and chopped fresh herbs. Let stand for 10 minutes to give asparagus time to absorb the dressing.

Michelle makes hot, freshly cooked asparagus into a more substantial dish by adding warmed olive oil, freshly grated Parmesan, chopped flat-leaf parsley, finely chopped hard-boiled eggs, and capers.

Salade pascale aux pois verts et aux artichauts

SPRING SALAD WITH GREEN PEAS AND ARTICHOKES

This salad can be served with a meat or fish dish, or as a fine lunch on its own. It's a specialty on the spring menu at Restaurant Mythos Ouzeri Estiatorio in Montreal. Owner Dimitri Galanis likes to use fresh peas but settles out of season for the best small frozen peas. Canned artichokes are another concession to convenience here.

SERVES 6

4 medium yellow-fleshed potatoes, peeled and cubed

1 bunch green onions

3 tablespoons (45 mL) olive oil

1 clove garlic, finely chopped

1 can (14 ounces/398 mL) artichokes, drained, patted dry, and quartered

2 tablespoons (30 mL) fresh lemon juice

1 pound (500 g) frozen green peas, thawed

2 tablespoons (30 mL) chopped fresh dill

+ Cook potatoes in boiling water until tender, then drain. Meanwhile, cut green onions into white and green parts. Chop both parts, keeping them separate.
+ In a large, heavy frying pan, heat oil over medium heat and cook white part of onions just until softened but not coloured, about 5 minutes. Add garlic and continue cooking just until the garlic releases its scent. Add potatoes and cook, stirring occasionally, for 10 minutes.
+ Add quartered artichokes and cook, stirring occasionally, for 5 minutes. Add lemon juice and peas and cook for 3 minutes, shaking the pan. Transfer vegetables to a serving plate and scatter with remaining chopped onions and dill. Serve at room temperature.

Salade de pissenlits aux fraises

FIELD DANDELION AND STRAWBERRY SALAD

Laval chef Franca Mazza reveals her Italian heritage in her love of fresh fruit and vegetables, as well as of Parmigiano Reggiano cheese. After running successful Montreal restaurant kitchens, Franca has turned to a combination of catering and teaching at the Marché 440 public market in Laval, north of Montreal. Her buffets are a visual and edible feast of colourful ingredients, such as this spring salad. Fresh dandelion greens can be found at most vegetable markets.

SERVES 4

30 fresh-picked baby dandelion leaves
10 ripe large strawberries, sliced
4 green onions, thinly sliced
12 fresh mint leaves, chopped
Balsamic maple dressing (below)
Shavings of Parmigiano Reggiano cheese, for topping

✦ Soak dandelion in cold water for 30 minutes. Drain, pat dry with paper towels, then cut out the thick rib in the centre of each leaf and discard. Chop leaves coarsely.
✦ In a salad bowl, mix together dandelion leaves, strawberries, green onions, and mint; toss with dressing. Serve topped with cheese shavings.

Balsamic maple dressing

MAKES ABOUT 1/3 CUP (75 mL)

4 tablespoons (60 mL) extra-virgin olive oil
2 tablespoons (30 mL) white balsamic vinegar
1 teaspoon (5 mL) to 1 tablespoon (15 mL) maple syrup, or more to taste
Sea salt

✦ In a cup, whisk together oil and vinegar. Season with maple syrup and salt.

EARLY LETTUCE

Treat early spring lettuce gently, say Quebec growers. At the giant Sherrington lettuce farm Les Fermes V. Forino, huge machines descend on fields to cut five kinds of lettuce with a system partly controlled by computers. The harvesters travel between the rows, cutting, washing, and packing the lettuce. Carmen Forino calls it "gentle harvesting."

A descendant of one of a group of families of Italian background who started farms half a century ago on the lush black soil of "the muckland," south of Montreal, Carmen likes her salad dressing mild enough so it doesn't mask the delicate flavours of these early greens. Try using lemon juice or a mild vinegar such as cider, white wine, or rice vinegar. Don't overload the dressing with a strong-flavoured oil either, and toss the salad with the dressing only at the last minute. Additions to the leaves should be mild-flavoured too: chopped green onions, fresh herbs such as mint or sorrel, or greenhouse cucumbers that can be sliced thinly, salted, then drained dry and mixed with the spring lettuce. Chopped celery leaves, fresh flat-leaf parsley, and cherry tomatoes are other possible additions. Don't drown a leaf lettuce salad with dressing or the leaves collapse: estimate 1/3 cup (75 mL) dressing for 6 to 8 cups (1.5 to 2 L) greens.

Grelots grillés au four

OLD COUNTRY NUBBINS

Tiny potatoes are known as "nubbins" in Montreal's Irish and Scottish communities. Peggy Regan, a baker in Montreal, considers this recipe a blend of her Irish-Scottish family traditions. She likes to serve the smallest potatoes as an hors d'oeuvre. She cooks them, then roasts them or swirls them briefly in a hot pan coated with butter. Roll in chopped parsley, sprinkle with salt and pepper, and serve on sticks with drinks, she says. Michelle Gélinas of Montreal tested the recipe using duck fat and liked the added flavour.

SERVES 4

12 to 16 baby potatoes (grelots), unpeeled
1/3 cup (75 mL) butter or duck fat
Salt and coarsely ground pepper
Chopped fresh flat-leaf parsley

✦ Place potatoes in a medium saucepan of cold salted water. Bring to a boil over medium-high heat. Lower heat and simmer, covered, just until potatoes can easily be pierced with a fork. Do not overcook. Drain potatoes, return to the pan, and place the pan back on the burner over medium-high heat to dry potatoes. Shake the pan constantly for about 1 minute.

✦ Add butter, increase heat to high, and, as butter melts, shake the potatoes in the pan to coat each one with butter. When butter starts to turn brown, remove the pan from heat.

✦ Add salt, pepper, and parsley. Gently toss potatoes to mix and serve at once.

Anne Desjardins

Tucked away in the Laurentian Mountains, north of Montreal, is a petite chef with a wide-ranging influence. Anne Desjardins has been setting an example for Quebec chefs for three decades, ever since she returned from a trip to France and started persuading farmers to grow what she wanted to cook.

"It was my odyssey," says the woman who for 34 years was chef and co-owner of L'Eau à la Bouche ("mouthwatering" in English), the Ste-Adèle restaurant that pioneered what Anne calls northern gastronomy.

Never mind that she opened her restaurant in a mountain valley with skimpy soil and fences made of rocks—and more than an hour's drive to the food markets of Montreal. Anne, whose friendly face conceals a determined will, remembered how the French chefs who were her teachers tracked down their ingredients and developed relationships with suppliers, whom they treated as treasured associates.

From the beginning, she sought out growers who would provide her with vegetables beyond Quebec's staple potatoes, carrots, rutabaga, and cabbage. Early on, she had to work tirelessly to obtain the foods that are now regulars on the menus of 21st-century chefs: tiny green beans, once only available imported from Kenya; different-coloured beets and carrots; heirloom tomatoes; saskatoon berries and elderberries; and—from the wild-food foragers she encouraged—wild mushrooms, salicorne (sea asparagus), and purslane.

Meats were originally limited to beef, pork, and some veal and lamb. Anne had to encourage farmers to produce quail, guinea hen, squab, and rabbit. She also sought out fish farms for trout and Arctic char.

Always, what she calls her credo has been "Go local," meaning find and cook quality products from nearby. "Terroir is the thing," she says. "There was no problem with the land," she continues, recalling earlier days. "The plain between the mountains and Montreal is fertile, and we have sunshine and cheap energy. The problem was in our heads."

To Anne's rescue came a woman called Henriette. "She had a small truck and would drive up to the restaurant with vegetables from her garden—green beans, kale, special carrots, Jerusalem artichokes, arugula," the chef recalls. In return, with her French contacts, Anne obtained seeds for specialty foods, which Henriette then grew for her. Farmers began producing specialty meats, fish farms were started, and wild-food foragers learned that Anne would welcome their discoveries in the wilderness.

Anne's menus began attracting attention: dishes such as duck foie gras with spiced honey, wild chanterelle mushrooms with miniature squash, guinea hen with cranberries, caribou steaks with wild garlic, and Abitibi farmed trout with fresh herbs (see page 321). Her same philosophy—along with that of careful cooking— continues to hold today: "You have to have the best suppliers . . . sending gatherers into the woods for the first wild garlic . . . the first crop of fiddleheads."

Chefs are using foods they have never seen before, foods not yet in home kitchens, Anne says, holding out a handful of peppery green alder berries harvested north of Lac St-Jean. "We are discovering boreal cuisine. This is right, because we live in the north," says the chef. "We are Nordic."

Anne was named Quebec's woman chef of the year in 1996, the same year she cooked a "hunter's" lunch at Quebec House in Paris—goose confit with cranberries, beaver consommé, and Arctic caribou. Two years later, she won a Grand Prix award from Tourisme Québec, for

developing fine restaurant dining in the Laurentians. Then, in 2001, she was honoured with the Quebec agriculture department's award for food innovation, called the Renaud-Cyr, and, in 2002, was named *chevalière* (knight) of the Ordre nationale du Québec, the highest honour for a chef.

"I am so happy to see that now the new generation of chefs believes in 'Go local,'" says Anne. They understand the link their cooking provides with the land. That harmony—"earth and climate, products and producers, cooks and eaters"—is one of her pleasures.

Chef Anne Desjardins obtains wild mushrooms from foragers. She likes to include Swiss chard and kale in her cuisine.

Tarte au sirop d'érable

Maple syrup pie

Residents of the Eastern Townships regard this dessert highly and debate which bakery makes the better pie. Both Les Sucreries de l'Érable in Frelighsburg, where the pie originated, and Désirables Gâteries in Bromont, where Andrée Gadoury, who developed the original recipe, makes and sells it, keep the recipe confidential. How the filling, a combination of maple syrup, butter, eggs, and brown sugar, but no thickener, takes on a luscious maple jelly texture when baked is their secret. I spent years testing versions of the pie, listening to tips from former bakery employees, and then retesting. I made many a delicious, if runny, pie. Finally, my gifted recipe developer, Michelle Gélinas, came up with a method that works in the home oven: bake the pie on a hot pizza stone or upside-down cast-iron pan. The darker your syrup, the better the flavour. Do not freeze this pie, and be sure to serve it at room temperature.

MAKES 2 PIES, 6 SERVINGS EACH

2/3 cup (150 mL) butter, softened
1 1/2 cups (375 mL) firmly packed light brown sugar
5 eggs, at room temperature
2 cups (500 mL) maple syrup, preferably amber or dark
1/2 teaspoon (2 mL) vanilla extract
2 9-inch (23 cm) unbaked pie shells (or ready-made thawed frozen pie shells), not pricked

+ Place a large pizza stone, 2 cast-iron rings from a wood stove, or 2 large cast-iron frying pans on the centre rack of the oven (the frying pans upside down, if using), and preheat the oven to 400°F (200°C) for 20 minutes to make sure the pizza stone or frying pans are very hot. The heat from the stone or the cast-iron, along with the oven heat, is essential for the pies to gel properly.
+ In a mixing bowl, beat the butter until creamy, then gradually beat in the brown sugar until mixture is creamy. Add eggs one at a time, beating well after each addition. Beat in maple syrup and then vanilla.
+ Divide mixture between the pie shells. For best results, place the filled pie pans in larger ovenproof glass pie plates for baking. Place pies on the pizza stone and bake for 45 minutes. Filling will swell in the pie shells.
+ Remove pies from the oven. Test for doneness by inserting a knife in the centre of a pie; it should come out clean but moist. Cool pies on a rack; filling will thicken as it cools. Transfer cooled pies to plates and refrigerate overnight.
+ Bring to room temperature before serving.

Crème brûlée à l'érable

Maple syrup crème brûlée

A double dose of maple—syrup as well as sugar—plus rosemary lift this version of the popular dessert out of the ordinary. French chef Denis Mareuge likes to cook with maple at Boulangerie Owl's Bread, his bakery-delicatessen-restaurant in Mansonville, in the Eastern Townships. It's named in honour of the nearby Owl's Head ski and golf resort. This dessert is his latest maple invention.

Serves 6

1 1/3 cups (325 mL) whipping cream
2/3 cup (150 mL) 2% milk
1 sprig fresh rosemary
5 eggs
7 tablespoons (105 mL) maple syrup
1/3 cup (75 mL) granulated maple sugar or light brown sugar

+ In a heavy saucepan, combine cream and milk and bring to a boil over medium heat. Remove from heat, add rosemary, and let stand, covered, for 2 hours.
+ Preheat the oven to 350°F (180°C). Place 6 ramekins (½ cup/125 mL each) in a baking pan with sides at least 1 inch (2.5 cm) deep.
+ Discard rosemary and reheat cream mixture to the boiling point. Meanwhile, beat eggs and maple syrup in a bowl using a hand-held electric mixer until foaming and pale.
+ Pour hot liquid in a thin stream into the egg mixture, beating continuously with the electric mixer. Pour mixture into the ramekins. Pour very hot water into the pan around the ramekins. Bake for 30 to 35 minutes, until a knife inserted in the centre of a crème comes out clean.
+ Remove the baking pan from the oven and let stand, the ramekins still in the water, until water is lukewarm. Remove the ramekins and place in the refrigerator, covered with plastic wrap, for several hours until cold.
+ Shortly before serving time, place the oven rack close to the broiler and preheat the broiler. Sprinkle each ramekin with maple sugar. Broil just until sugar caramelizes, then remove from heat and serve. Alternatively, use a propane torch to caramelize the sugar.

Note

The crème brûlée can be refrigerated for up to 24 hours once it comes out of the oven and has cooled. Bring to room temperature before broiling.

John Rhicard checks maple
syrup boiling at Owl Hoot
Maple Farm, Stanbridge East.

Maple syrup is taken for granted as an indigenous Quebec ingredient, since the province produces 72 per cent of the world's supply, but for both connoisseurs and maple producers it has an almost mystical quality. "I associate maple with beautiful moments, singular and special times," says Danny St-Pierre, chef-owner of the Sherbrooke restaurants Auguste and Chez Augustine. The maple industry is so much a part of Quebec's history and image that a giant *cabane à sucre* (sugar shack) called Sucrerie de la Montagne operates year-round on Mont Rigaud, west of Montreal. Hundreds of tourists (its three dining halls can seat more than 500) come to see the buckets on the sugar maples and the horses tramping through the forest to collect the sap, their wagons on skis in winter.

When the maple sap is running, the "sugaring off" meal is traditional, and huge: maple-glazed ham, maple-sweetened pork and beans, sausages, omelettes, tourtière, crisp-fried pork rinds called *oreilles de crisse* (Christ's ears), ketchup, and pickles. Then maple syrup pie and pancakes for dessert. The finale, if you have any room at all, is *tire* (maple taffy—boiling syrup poured on snow, where it hardens to candy instantly), served from a snow-filled wooden trough. It takes a little detective work to find them, but the most popular and best sugar shacks are still those run by families using their barns as their restaurants, many with a fiddler playing traditional French-Canadian songs. The industrial-tinged *sucreries* are giant dining halls built with a rustic look and usually equipped with electric guitars or canned music. The menu is similar.

The Fine Points of Maple Harvesting

John Rhicard, who runs a family farm near Stanbridge East and installs 3,600 taps on his sugar maple trees each spring, has been "boiling," as he calls maple syrup making, for more than 65 years. "The sap gets in your blood," he said as we walked the woods of Owl Hoot Maple Farm on a brisk March day. Many Quebec maple farms have switched to plastic tubing and a vacuum process to draw out the sap, but John sticks with natural gravity. He uses tubing and traditional buckets in equal measure, and has his own horses transporting cans of sap through the wood on sleds or—when the snow has melted—on drays. While warm sunny days and freezing cold nights are essential for the sap to run, John also keeps an eye on the barometric pressure to determine how long he'll have to boil the sap before it thickens into syrup. "On a sunny day, we have to boil longer than on a grey day," says his wife, Dianne. "But the work must be done because the trees don't wait for a sunny day. It's the same reason you don't make fudge on a dark, cloudy day."

The ability to walk on snowshoes carrying cans of sap comes in handy on this farm. Rhicard family members, including six grandchildren, pitch in each spring, working as long as the trees require, from a short season of 10 days to a long one of six weeks. "That's why maple syrup costs as much as it does," Dianne says.

The Simplest Maple Dessert

I first enjoyed this at a 17th-century stone farmhouse on Île d'Orléans, near Quebec City, and it's probably the best confection I've ever eaten. It's called Tartine d'Antan. Take a thick slice of fresh country bread, sprinkle it generously with maple sugar, and pour over it the best thick cream you can get.

Horses draw a dray through the woods to collect maple syrup at Owl Hoot Maple Farm.

Compote de rhubarbe et de fraises

RHUBARB STRAWBERRY COMPOTE

Suzanne Bigras, who runs Quebec's largest rhubarb farm, Les Fermes Serbi, in St-Eustache, northwest of Montreal, attaches family recipes for rhubarb to each bunch of rhubarb she sends to market. This easy recipe can be made with rhubarb on its own—her first choice—or with added strawberries, which brighten the colour to a deep red. If using only rhubarb, use 1 cup (250 mL) sugar. If using strawberries too, add only ½ cup (125 mL) sugar because the strawberries bring their own sweetness.

MAKES 4 CUPS (1 L)

4 cups (1 L) cubed fresh rhubarb
2 cups (500 mL) strawberries, cut in half if large
1/2 to 1 cup (125 to 250 mL) granulated sugar
5 tablespoons (75 mL) cold water
1/2 teaspoon (2 mL) cornstarch

✢ In a large saucepan, stir together rhubarb, strawberries, ½ cup (125 mL) of the sugar, and 4 tablespoons (60 mL) of the water. Bring to a boil over medium heat, stirring until sugar is dissolved. Reduce heat to low and simmer, stirring occasionally, for 5 minutes.

✢ In a cup, stir cornstarch with remaining 1 tablespoon (15 mL) water until dissolved. Stir into rhubarb mixture and continue cooking over low heat, stirring constantly, for 3 minutes. Refrigerate until cold. Serve with vanilla ice cream or plain yogurt, fresh or frozen.

Gâteau à la rhubarbe de tante Ida

AUNT IDA'S RHUBARB CAKE

This recipe dates back almost a century, as Leah Curley, a talented Knowlton cook, remembers it. Her aunt taught her how to make the cake when Leah was about 10 years old, and it's still her favourite way to enjoy the plentiful pink shoots of the rhubarb plant. Baked in a wide pan, this cake can be cut in squares to serve with ice cream, frozen yogurt, or whipped cream.

SERVES 8 TO 10

1 cup (250 mL) granulated sugar

1/2 cup (125 mL) butter, softened

1 teaspoon (5 mL) vanilla extract

1 teaspoon (5 mL) salt

1 3/4 cups (425 mL) all-purpose flour

3/4 cup (175 mL) buttermilk

1 egg

1 teaspoon (5 mL) baking soda

2 cups (500 mL) cubed fresh rhubarb

1/2 cup (125 mL) brown sugar, packed, or granulated maple sugar

1/2 cup (125 mL) coarsely chopped pecans or walnuts

Fresh orange juice, for moistening

✦ Preheat the oven to 350°F (180°C). Grease a 13 × 9 inch (33 × 23 cm) baking pan.

✦ In a large bowl, beat together granulated sugar and butter, then blend in vanilla and salt. Gradually beat in the flour. In a large measuring cup, whisk buttermilk with the egg and baking soda, then beat into the sugar mixture. Stir in rhubarb, mixing well. Pour batter into the prepared pan.

✦ In a small bowl, mix together brown sugar, nuts, and just enough orange juice to bind together. Sprinkle mixture over batter. Bake for 35 minutes or until a cake tester inserted in the centre comes out clean. Cut cake in squares in the pan and serve warm or cooled to room temperature.

Drinks with a History

Six unique Quebec liqueurs have been attracting attention ever since their launch in the mid-1990s. Each is inspired by a drink made long ago, some dating back to the 17th century, others products of imaginative winemakers who have concocted drinks reminiscent of Quebec's earliest traditions of home-brewing. The bestseller is Sortilège, a combination of Canadian rye whisky and maple syrup that sells throughout Canada. Next in popularity are two with names derived from the First Nations: Chicoutai, made from the tart-flavoured Nordic cloudberry, and Minaki, a blueberry aperitif named with the Algonquin word meaning "land of blueberries." Amour en Cage is made with ground cherries, comparable to gooseberries. L'Orléane is crème de cassis, the black currant liqueur. It is modelled on a prize-winning liqueur made on Île d'Orléans by French-born Bernard Monna. Fine Sève is an aged maple syrup eau-de-vie with 40 per cent alcohol content. The other drinks have alcohol contents ranging from 18 to 25 per cent.

"The history of distilling in Quebec dates back to the end of the 1700s," says Philip Tieman, marketing director of bottling company Maison des Futailles. "Quebecers have a tradition of making their own drinks and serving them at the réveillon and other special occasions. They buy alcool, which is unflavoured alcohol, and use it as a base. These liqueurs are made with authentic Quebec recipes, created in yesteryear and brought back to life."

Croustillant de fraises

STRAWBERRY CRISP

When the Quebec strawberry season opens and we can buy or pick the early varieties—small, shiny, dark red berries—all the fruit needs is hulling, washing, and eating. Trimmings could be a sprinkle of sugar, or a dollop of whipped cream or yogurt sprinkled with maple sugar. As the strawberry season advances, we want to do a little more to this favourite summer fruit, perhaps by making a pie such as the popular strawberry-rhubarb, or a strawberry shortcake. This simple dessert comes from Janice Paulino, a professional Montreal cake baker and decorator. She finds it a warm, homey change from the elaborate party cakes she makes at Gâteaux Janice. If desired, you can prepare the dessert an hour or so before baking.

SERVES 6

1 1/2 pounds (750 g) fresh strawberries, halved if large (6 cups/1.5 L)
3 tablespoons (45 mL) quick-cooking tapioca (instant or minute)
Ground cinnamon, for sprinkling
1 cup (250 mL) firmly packed brown sugar
1/3 cup (75 mL) all-purpose flour
1/3 cup (75 mL) rolled oats (quick-cooking or old-fashioned)
1/4 cup (60 mL) melted butter or vegetable oil
1/4 cup (60 mL) finely chopped pecans (optional)

✛ Preheat the oven to 350°F (180°C).
✛ In a large bowl, toss the strawberries with the tapioca. Place in a deep, 8- or 9-inch (20 or 23 cm) baking pan or 6 individual baking dishes or ramekins, piling fruit high, as it will reduce during cooking. Set on a baking sheet with a rim to catch any drips. Sprinkle with cinnamon.
✛ In the same bowl, stir brown sugar with flour and oats. Mix in melted butter until ingredients are evenly moistened; mixture will be lumpy. Mix in pecans (if using). Spread mixture over top of berries.
✛ Bake for 30 to 40 minutes, until topping is crisp and lightly browned. Serve warm with ice cream or sweetened whipped cream.

STRAWBERRIES, THE EASY WAY

When Quebec berries are in season, serve them plain, with cream or yogurt. Once the season is underway, Montreal cakemaker Janice Paulino slices open vanilla cupcakes and layers them with fresh, sliced strawberries and sweetened whipped cream, topping each serving with shaved white chocolate.

To make an easy dessert for entertaining, cut berries in quarters or halves, combine with ruby port and a little brown sugar, and sprinkle with ground cinnamon. Let stand for 1 hour at room temperature, then add chopped fresh mint and serve with vanilla ice cream.

Another easy way to enjoy strawberries is to drizzle them with a little balsamic vinegar or a generous grind of black pepper and serve topped with plain Greek yogurt and a sprinkling of maple sugar.

Pouding au citron

Lemon pudding

British recipes are part of Quebec cuisine, and have been ever since the British conquest of New France in 1759. The Scottish-Irish culinary tradition is particularly strong in Montreal. Pudding is a good example; it's called "pouding" in French. This one is from my Toronto background, but I have found it in Montreal anglophone families too. No one in my family can remember how many generations back it dates. My mother considered it a reliable basic dessert. I acquired it when I was newly married, when Mum typed it out on her old Smith-Corona and included it in a three-ring binder of family recipes, which I still use regularly. I like the pudding for its serious lemon flavour. It suits any season because it can be served plain or with seasonal fresh fruit, warm, at room temperature, or even cold from the refrigerator.

SERVES 6

1 cup (250 mL) milk
2 tablespoons (30 mL) all-purpose flour
1 cup (250 mL) granulated sugar
1 tablespoon (15 mL) melted butter
Grated peel and juice of 1 lemon
2 eggs, at room temperature, separated

+ Preheat the oven to 350°F (180°C). Butter an 8-inch (20 cm) baking pan and fill a larger baking pan half full of water. Place the pan of water in the oven.
+ In a bowl, combine milk and flour, then stir in sugar, butter, lemon peel, and lemon juice, mixing well. In a cup, beat egg yolks and stir into milk mixture.
+ In a small, deep bowl, beat egg whites until they stand in stiff peaks. Fold milk mixture into beaten egg whites.
+ Pour batter into the prepared baking pan. Place in the pan of hot water and oven-poach for 40 minutes or until pudding is firm to the touch.

Scones

Peggy Regan, a Montreal baker of Irish-Scottish background, specializes in comforting basics such as these scones. Customers at Gryphon d'Or, her shop and restaurant in the Notre-Dame-de-Grâce district, enjoy a warm scone with coffee or tea. Seville orange marmalade, made every winter by Montrealers of British background, goes well with a scone. So do fruit jams, strawberry or raspberry in particular. Since the ingredients are on hand in most kitchens, the recipe is handy because it's quick to make and can be used as the base for a last-minute dessert. Split the scones in half and top with fresh or stewed fruit and whipped cream, or toast and serve with cheese.

MAKES 8

2 cups (500 mL) all-purpose flour
4 teaspoons (20 mL) baking powder
1 to 2 tablespoons (15 to 30 mL) granulated sugar
Generous pinch salt
1/4 cup (60 mL) cold butter or shortening, cubed
3/4 cup (175 mL) milk
1 egg

✦ Preheat the oven to 425°F (220°C). Line a baking sheet with parchment paper or dust it lightly with flour; do not grease.

✦ In a large bowl, stir flour, baking powder, sugar, and salt until well blended. Add butter and cut it in with a pastry blender or 2 knives until butter chunks are the size of peas.

✦ Using a fork, whisk milk with egg in a small bowl. Add mixture all at once to dry ingredients. Using a rubber spatula, mix with a folding action. Do not stir, and do not try to blend completely—just until all the dry streaks of flour are gone.

✦ Turn dough onto a floured surface. Knead it gently two or three times. Pat into a flat round, about 1½ inches (4 cm) thick. Cut into quarters, and then cut each quarter in half, to make 8 triangular scones. Or cut dough with a 2-inch (5 cm) cookie cutter.

✦ Lightly shake off excess flour and set scones on the prepared baking sheet. Bake for 14 to 15 minutes, until golden brown. Transfer to a rack to cool.

Carrés aux dattes

DATE SQUARES

If you want to test the quality of a Quebec bakery, try its carrés aux dattes. *One of the best I have found is sold at La Rumeur Affamée, a delicatessen–bakery–cheese shop in Sutton, in the Eastern Townships. The squares are so big, you can eat just a quarter of one and still be satisfied. Serge Boivin of Les Sucreries de l'Érable, who supplies baked specialties to the Sutton store and others in the Eastern Townships and Montreal, credits his mother, Gisèle Campeau of Mont-Laurier, in the Laurentians, with the recipe. He remembers that his grandfather would have a square with liquid* sucre à la crème *(maple fudge) poured on top. "It's really piggy," says Serge, "but it's a treat."*

MAKES 16 LARGE SQUARES

1 package (500 g) pitted dates

1 teaspoon (5 mL) cornstarch, as needed

2 tablespoons (30 mL) granulated maple sugar (optional)

3 cups (750 mL) quick-cooking rolled oats (not instant)

1 cup (250 mL) all-purpose flour

2 cups (500 mL) loosely packed brown sugar

1/2 teaspoon (2 mL) baking soda

1/2 teaspoon (2 mL) salt

1 cup (250 mL) melted butter

+ Preheat the oven to 350°F (180°C). Butter an 8-inch (20 cm) square baking pan.

+ In a medium saucepan, cover dates with water (about 3 cups/750 mL) and bring to a boil over medium heat, stirring occasionally. Boil, stirring every few minutes, for 10 minutes.

+ Remove from heat and, if mixture is runny, stir in cornstarch to thicken it. Stir in maple sugar (if using). Set aside to cool.

+ In a mixing bowl, stir oats with flour, brown sugar, baking soda, and salt, breaking up any lumps in brown sugar. Add melted butter to dry ingredients and blend in with a fork.

+ Spread half of oat mixture in the prepared pan and press into an even layer. Spread dates evenly over top, then top with remaining oat mixture, spreading it out in an even layer.

+ Bake for 20 to 30 minutes or until lightly browned. Set the pan on a rack to cool, then cut slab into squares.

Notes

Brown sugar may be substituted for maple sugar.

Squares will keep well at room temperature stored in an airtight container for 2 days or in the freezer for at least 2 months.

Crème glacée au sirop d'érable

MAPLE ICE CREAM

If you like your ice cream maple-flavoured, Robert Lachapelle, proprietor with his brother Richard of the Havre-aux-Glaces (Ice Cream Haven in English) ice cream stands in Montreal's two large public markets, Jean-Talon and Atwater, has been hailed for offering the best version in town. The brothers use maple sugar, once the product everyone made from their sugar maples, but now outrun by maple syrup. Maple sugar, sold in textures ranging from powdered to coarse, is expensive and in limited distribution. It lends a delicate tang to food. Brown sugar may be used but it won't give the same flavour. Maple-coated pecans enhance the flavour of Robert's recipe for maple ice cream.

MAKES 4 CUPS (1 L)

2 cups (500 mL) whipping cream
1/2 cup + 1/3 cup (200 mL) whole milk
2 tablespoons (30 mL) powdered maple sugar
4 egg yolks
2/3 cup (150 mL) light or amber maple syrup
2 teaspoons (10 mL) corn syrup
Pecans coated with maple syrup (see below) or coarse maple sugar for topping

✤ In a medium saucepan, combine cream, milk, and maple sugar over medium heat, and heat until a candy thermometer reaches 68°F (20°C). Do not overheat or you could overcook the egg yolks once they are added.

✤ Meanwhile, place egg yolks in another medium saucepan over medium heat. Beat continuously with a hand-held electric mixer. Add cream mixture, a ladleful at a time, continuing to beat vigorously.

✤ Whisk the maple syrup and corn syrup together in a cup and add, little by little, to the egg mixture, continuing to beat vigorously.

✤ Continue to cook, beating, until the mixture reaches the temperature of 176°F (80°C). Remove from heat, cool, and then refrigerate, covered, for 12 hours or overnight.

✤ Using a wire whisk, beat the cold mixture just until it is smooth.

✤ Pour into an ice cream maker and freeze according to manufacturer's directions.

✤ Serve topped with the maple pecans or maple sugar.

Note

To make maple-coated pecans, spread whole pecans on a baking sheet, drizzle with maple syrup, and bake for 5 minutes at 350°F (180°C). Cool before using.

Neige d'érable

MAPLE SORBET

Making sorbet with maple syrup requires inside knowledge of the syrup's composition, says Robert Lachapelle, who runs Montreal's Havre-aux-Glaces (Ice Cream Haven) stands with his brother, Richard. Maple syrup is 66 percent sugar, which is too high a percentage for making sorbet without adding water, Robert explains. So he reduces the sugar to a concentration of 29 per cent by adding either the new maple sap product called maple water, or ordinary water. The result is this delicately flavoured sorbet.

MAKES 2 CUPS (500 mL)

2/3 cup (150 mL) maple syrup
1 tablespoon (15 mL) corn syrup
1 1/3 cups (325 mL) maple water or water

+ In a medium saucepan, heat together the maple syrup, corn syrup, and maple water over medium heat, until a candy thermometer reads 145°F (63 °C). Remove from heat and refrigerate, covered, for 4 to 6 hours.
+ Transfer mixture to the freezer and chill until it is reduced in temperature to 32°F (0°C) or ice crystals have formed.
+ Use a hand-held electric mixer or blender to incorporate air into mixture, beating for about 1 minute. Transfer it to an ice cream maker and freeze according to the manufacturer's directions.
+ If not serving right away, cover and store in the freezer for up to 2 days.

Note

Maple water is sterilized maple sap, launched in Quebec in 2012. A clear beverage with a delicate maple flavour, it is promoted as a natural energy drink and for use in cooking.

A Thing for Sweet and Creamy

Driving east along the south coast of the St. Lawrence River, experienced travellers approaching Rivière-du-Loup know to stop for ice cream at Les Glaces Ali-Baba. The place looks more like a gas station than a centre of gastronomy, but inside, the long counter is usually crowded with a swarm of people trying to decide among 20 flavours of ice cream, a dozen sorbets, and a few frozen yogurts, as well as how many scoops to order.

That little stand, with none of the glitz and marketing of big-name ice cream companies, is a fixture in the Bas-St-Laurent (Lower St. Lawrence). The products, ice cream in particular, are just plain good, all produced by owner and ice cream maker Jean-Marc Dubé with the best and freshest cream and eggs he can obtain. He's been at it for some 30 years, ever since he took a crash course in ice cream making in Italy. Why "Ali-Baba"? Dubé says he wanted a magical name that reminded him of a treasure cave from a childhood story.

Independent ice cream makers are dotted about Quebec. A large company in the Eastern Townships is called Coaticook, which is also the name of the town where it has flourished since 1940. "There are people today who recognize Coaticook only as ice cream," says Jean

Provencher, co-owner with his sister Johanne. "They have no idea it's also a place," he says, even though the town is a major dairy-farming centre, and tourists flock to see its spectacular gorge with a suspension bridge that is, according to Guinness World Records, the world's longest—almost 555 feet (170 metres). Provencher welcomes tourists with an ice cream stand in the gorge. The ice cream is excellent, made with pure, local ingredients.

Contrasting in size with the major Quebec ice cream player Coaticook is the small specialty company Havre-aux-Glaces (Ice Cream Haven) which has stores in Montreal's big public markets, Jean-Talon and Atwater. Ice cream makers Robert and Richard Lachapelle are so hands-on with their products, they make their own maple syrup at their sugar bush north of Shawinigan at Lac Mékinac. Their brother, Normand, helps produce enough maple syrup to make the 8 maple flavours on their list of 24 different ice creams. Robert says the maple ice cream made with both maple syrup and maple sugar is tops (see recipe, page 101).

Facing page: Jeimy Oviedo enjoys the best-selling maple ice cream at Havre aux Glaces in Jean-Talon Market

Summer

When summer sun starts to warm the air, a festive spirit takes hold in Quebec. It's partly because, all year long, we are haunted by the big winter chill Gilles Vigneault sang about: "Mon pays ce n'est pas un pays, c'est l'hiver" (my country is not a country, it's winter). Quebec's first summer holiday, St-Jean-Baptiste Day on June 24, launches a season of intense pleasure in the outdoors. We watch for the first lettuce and radishes to push up in our gardens, plan barbecues and picnics, and dine on restaurant terraces. It's not unusual to see a cyclist wheel by with a baguette and bottle of wine or families clogging highways with campers as they head to Quebec's big parks on rivers, lakes, or the ocean.

The first food to cause a summer celebration is the early strawberry—small, red, juicy, and as sweet as candy. In fact, the sweetest foods of summer are our most anticipated. After the first strawberries comes the first corn on the cob, sweet and dripping with butter. At mid-summer, field-grown tomatoes arrive, heavy with sun-warmed juice. Early varieties of apples provide sharp contrast to all this natural sugar.

By mid-summer, Italian-Quebecers have produced lush gardens of seemingly every vegetable, both fence and trellis of their front gardens or backyards draped with tomato and grape vines, even though many will buy American grapes to make their wines.

It's an efficient business, growing Quebec's food. I remember a day on a huge lettuce farm at St-Rémi south of Montreal, when workers were harvesting romaine. Men were trimming big heads down into the pale-green cones that have become a new lettuce fashion. Gentler in flavour than the deep green outer leaves, these skinny cores are sold washed and packaged. As the truck moved along the rows of tall, bushy heads of romaine, the workers slashed away at each head, tossing aside enough big, dark leaves to make countless salads. Remonstrating about waste to Clermont Riendeau, the farm owner, I was soothed with his explanation that the trimmings would be ploughed under the rich, black soil to make green fertilizer for the next crop.

The blueberry farms ("bleuetières") around Lac St-Jean or in the Abitibi region keep their crop well hidden. The dusky blue berries, called "wild" to distinguish them from the larger, cultivated variety, are produced by a system of wild blueberry management to make the wild plants produce plentiful amounts of fruit. By late August, when all the fruit has been harvested, machines chop the plants down to about 3 inches (7.5 cm) in height and the field is left alone for two years, the better to encourage big crops.

Each summer's fruit is sorted, washed, and frozen in a highly automated plant at Dolbeau-Mistassini, later to be trucked to distribution points for transfer to about 30 countries around the world. Quebec, second only to Maine in "wild" blueberry production, freezes 90 per cent of its crop for food manufacturers.

In early August, there is so much fruit, Dolbeau-Mistassini stages an annual blueberry festival that includes baking an enormous blueberry pie. Blueberry pies are summer favourites and they never look or taste better than when the berries are combined with peaches from neighbouring Ontario.

First Courses

Îles de la Madeleine Scallops with Lovage Sauce

Cheese-Baked Snails

Bruschetta with Goat Cheese

Curried Lobster Apple Soup with Thyme

Green Tomato Gazpacho

Cream of Corn Soup

Scallop and Smoked Duck Mousse

Gourgane Bean Soup

Main Courses

Bouillabaisse de Mont-Louis

Fish Stock

Ginger Trout

Salmon Gaspé Style

Halibut Steaks with Fresh Tomato, Avocado, and Shrimp Salsa

Dr. Joe's Vegetarian Goulash

Skirt Steak with Gorgonzola Sauce

Warm Salad with Braised Veal Cheeks, Wild Mushrooms, and New Potatoes

Charlevoix Lamb Burgers

Fennel, Ham, and Cheese Casserole

Side Dishes

Deep Green Salad

Chunky Lemon Potatoes

Summer Tomatoes with Cider-Chive Dressing

Roasted Tomatoes with Fresh Herbs

Warm Bean Salad

Eggplant Tomato Tart

Raspberry Salad

Creamed Corn with Coriander and Feta

Pickled Spiced Corn

Desserts

Economy Pudding

Glazed Raspberry Pie

Raspberry Jelly with Fresh Blueberries and Raspberries

Blackberry Pie

Rhubarb Orange Pie

Strawberry-Season Cake

Blueberry–Sour Cream Torte

Pétoncles des Îles de la Madeleine au jus de livèche

ÎLES DE LA MADELEINE SCALLOPS WITH LOVAGE SAUCE

As the St. Lawrence River widens east of Rivière-du-Loup, the waters turn salty, there's a whiff of salt water in the air, and the local people refer to the river as the sea. Chefs along both the north and south shores consider the river's mouth and the Gulf of St. Lawrence a principal source for food. Scallops are only one of the seafoods they like to cook. Colombe St-Pierre, daughter of a lighthouse keeper at Le Bic and chef-owner of Chez Saint-Pierre in the village, prides herself on serving foods native to the gulf region, such as big scallops from Îles de la Madeleine. She uses lime juice to "cook" the scallops, ceviche style, accenting the flavours with lovage, the celery-flavoured herb.

SERVES 4

8 large scallops
1 cup (250 mL) fresh lovage or celery leaves
1 cucumber, peeled, seeded, and cut in chunks
2 egg yolks
1/2 cup (125 mL) whole milk
1/3 cup (75 mL) olive oil
1 teaspoon (5 mL) Dijon mustard
1 small clove garlic, finely chopped
Grated peel and juice of 2 limes
Pinches salt and freshly ground pepper

+ Rinse scallops and pat dry with paper towels. Place in a bowl, cover, and refrigerate for up to 4 hours.
+ Plunge lovage into a saucepan of boiling water. Boil for 1 minute, then rinse under cold water, squeeze dry with your hands, and pat dry with paper towels.
+ In a blender, blend lovage, cucumber, egg yolks, milk, oil, Dijon, garlic, lime peel, salt, and pepper until mixture liquefies. If desired, strain sauce through a sieve. Set aside.
+ About 30 minutes before serving time, sprinkle scallops with lime juice and pinches of salt and pepper, and refrigerate.
+ Pour cucumber liquid into 4 soup bowls and add 2 scallops to each.

Cassolettes d'escargots

CHEESE-BAKED SNAILS

The Charlevoix cheese called Le 1608, launched in 2008 by Laiterie Charlevoix to mark the 400th anniversary of the founding of Quebec, is made with the milk of Quebec's first cows, the Vache canadienne. The cheese has been welcomed by chefs, who like to cook with it. Marthe Lemire, chef-owner of Crêperie Le Passe-Temps in La Malbaie, uses it for her sauce for snails and mushrooms in this rich and delectable appetizer.

SERVES 4

2 tablespoons (30 mL) butter

8 ounces (250 g) mushrooms, minced

1 clove garlic, chopped

1 small shallot, chopped

Pinch ground nutmeg

Pinches salt and freshly ground pepper

1 can (4 ounces/125 g) snails (about 24), rinsed and patted dry

1/2 cup (125 mL) dry white wine

1 tablespoon (15 mL) chopped fresh flat-leaf parsley

4 tablespoons (60 mL) grated Le 1608, Emmenthal, or Gruyère cheese

+ Have ready 4 ramekins or individual baking dishes that hold ½ cup (125 mL) each. In a medium saucepan, melt butter over medium heat and cook mushrooms, garlic, and shallot, stirring constantly, until mushrooms release their liquid, about 2 to 3 minutes.

+ Season with nutmeg, salt, and pepper. Add snails and wine. Reduce heat to low and simmer mixture until liquid has almost evaporated, about 10 minutes. Stir often near the end of cooking.

+ Stir in parsley and divide mixture among the ramekins. Sprinkle each ramekin with cheese. Arrange the ramekins on a baking sheet. Preheat the broiler and broil snails just until cheese melts, 1 to 2 minutes. Do not let cheese burn.

Note

Ramekins can be filled and topped with cheese up to 6 hours in advance, then covered and refrigerated. Bring to room temperature before broiling.

Bruschetta au Barbu

BRUSCHETTA WITH GOAT CHEESE

Serve these easy hors d'oeuvres made with fresh chopped tomatoes and goat cheese with a well-chilled rosé wine, suggests Fabienne Guitel. She runs La Fromagerie La Suisse Normande with husband Frédéric near St-Roch-de-l'Achigan, in the Lanaudière region, northeast of Montreal. Le Barbu, a soft goat cheese with a bloomy rind, has more flavour than Le Crottin, a fresh goat cheese. Fabienne likes to marinate Le Crottin in olive oil to give it a Mediterranean touch. Both their goat cheeses and others made of cow's milk reflect her French heritage and his Norman background.

SERVES 8

8 slices baguette
2 tomatoes, seeded and finely chopped
2 green onions, finely minced
1/2 yellow or orange bell pepper, finely chopped
1/4 teaspoon (1 mL) salt
2 rounds Le Barbu or Le Crottin cheese (3 ounces/85 g each), or 1 round aged goat cheese

✦ Toast baguette slices.
✦ In a strainer, mix together tomatoes, green onions, and bell pepper and set in the sink. Sprinkle with salt, let drain for 30 minutes, then pat dry with paper towels.
✦ Spread mixture on baguette toasts. Cut cheese into 8 slices. Place a slice on each bruschetta and arrange on a baking sheet.
✦ Preheat the broiler and grill bruschetta for 1 to 2 minutes, just to crisp and melt the cheese. Serve at room temperature.

Note
The bruschetta can be assembled in advance and broiled just before serving.

Quebec has cheesemakers in every region, and each has its own flavour for the visitor. The most gratifying cheese places to visit, in my opinion, are goat farms, because the goats seem so intelligent and friendly, pressing forward to greet visitors, even nuzzling your hand. Sheep, particularly with a full coat of wool, are probably the most appealing in looks, but so timid that they keep their distance. Cows add to the sylvan scene, whatever their breed.

Thinking of my most satisfying visits to cheesemakers, I am reminded of Fromagerie Lehmann in the Saguenay–Lac St-Jean region of northern Quebec. The Lehmanns are Swiss-born, and have a herd—appropriately—of Brown Swiss cattle, beautiful gold-coloured animals. The cows were lazing about their pasture when I came to call one sunny August day. Cheesemaker Jacob Lehmann, a lean and bearded veteran, was on the job, but his wife, Marie, running the farm boutique, appeared and sold me their three washed-rind, semi-soft cheeses and took the time to explain how they changed from making their Kéno-gami, Pikauba, and Valbert cheeses with raw milk to using a method of part-pasteurization of the milk called thermizing, combined with a 60-day aging to destroy all harmful bacteria.

Left: Cheesemaker Dominique Labbé brushes Le 1608 cheese at Laiterie Charlevoix in Baie-St-Paul.

Only 18 of Quebec's cheeses are made with unpasteurized milk, and about half that number with completely raw milk. Makers of these cheeses, mostly soft or semi-soft products, have over the years attracted the attention of federal and provincial health authorities. They regulate and watch over such food-safety factors as the bacteria in milk, be it from cows, goats, or sheep, and the production and sanitation standards that are maintained in cheese plants, large and small.

Connoisseurs believe that if these specialty cheeses are made with raw milk, they likely have the best flavour. Government regulations are strict. To make sure any unwanted bacteria are killed, these cheeses must be stored in the controlled conditions of maturing rooms for at least 30 days. Another group of these cheeses is made by thermizing, a method of milk pasteurization wherein, instead of heating the milk to the pasteurization temperature of 159.8°F (71°C) for 15 seconds, the cheesemaker heats it for the same amount of time to between 143.6 and 154.4°F (62 and 68°C). The lower temperature allows more flavour than if the milk were pasteurized, goes the theory. If a cheesemaker thermizes the milk, the cheese must be stored for 60 days in order to kill unwanted bacteria before it may be sold.

Since 2008, Quebec's agriculture department has allowed raw milk cheeses to be sold only if the milk used is no more than 24 hours old and strict regulations are adhered to concerning microbiological content. Tests must be conducted regularly and records kept for government inspectors. If a cheesemaker uses milk from his or her own animals rather than buying it, the animals' health must be monitored by a veterinarian.

Health Canada warns that raw milk cheeses may present a risk of food-borne illness. Its recommendation is that these products not be consumed by children, pregnant women, the elderly, or people with weakened immune systems. To help consumers, Quebec requires that these cheeses be labelled as unpasteurized. Quebec cheeses sold outside the province must have a federal permit indicating they are in compliance with all standards and inspection requirements.

Dominique Labbé mixes milk from La Canadienne cows to make cheese at Laiterie Charlevoix.

Soupe de homard et aux pommes perfumée au thym

CURRIED LOBSTER APPLE SOUP WITH THYME

Quebec's lobster season runs from May through June, but chefs find lobster sources in various regions of the Gulf of St. Lawrence until early August. Alain Labrie, chef-owner of La Table du Chef in Sherbrooke, likes to use local products such as trout from nearby trout farms. But lobster remains a favourite from the time he trained at the Gaspé's Fort-Prével chef school. His soup stretches one lobster into a soup for six, using Quebec's exceptional cooking apple, the Cortland, and livening up the flavour with thyme and curry.

SERVES 6

2 lemons

12 firm cooking apples, such as Cortland or
   Golden Delicious

1 tablespoon (15 mL) butter

1 large onion, coarsely chopped

2 tablespoons (30 mL) fresh thyme leaves

1 tablespoon (15 mL) curry powder

8 cups (2 L) chicken stock

2 large potatoes, peeled and coarsely chopped

1 cup (250 mL) light cream

Salt and freshly ground pepper

Meat from 2 cooked lobsters (1 to 1 1/4
   pounds/500 to 625 g each), in bite-size
   pieces, at room temperature

6 sprigs fresh thyme

✦ Using a vegetable peeler, remove strips of peel from lemons. Squeeze juice from 1 lemon and set aside. Place lemon peel in a small saucepan of cold water. Bring to a boil over medium-high heat, drain peel, fill saucepan with more cold water, and bring peel to a boil a second time. Drain again, immerse in cold water, and when cool, drain again.

✦ Peel, core, and chop 10 of the apples coarsely, reserving remaining 2 whole. In a large, heavy saucepan, melt butter over medium heat and cook onion and chopped apples with lemon peel, thyme leaves, and curry powder, just until apples and onion are tender, about 15 minutes. Reduce heat to low, add stock and potatoes, and simmer gently for 30 minutes or until potatoes are tender.

✦ Use a blender to purée soup until smooth; you will need to do this in batches. Transfer mixture to a large, heavy saucepan. Stir in cream.

✦ When ready to serve, reheat soup. Chop remaining 2 unpeeled apples finely and add to soup with the reserved lemon juice to taste, and salt and pepper.

✦ Warm 6 wide, shallow bowls. Divide lobster between the bowls and pour hot soup over top. Decorate each with a sprig of thyme.

Note
The soup can be refrigerated, covered, for up to 1 day once the cream has been added.

Gaspacho de tomates vertes

GREEN TOMATO GAZPACHO

Quebec's tomato season is a time for celebrating over a feed of sweet, juicy tomatoes from the fields, unadorned and preferably still warm from the sun. But there are those summers when the sun won't shine hot or long enough to turn green tomatoes red. Sutton chef Christian Beaulieu combines green tomatoes—either unripened red or his favourite green- and yellow-striped zebra variety—with bell peppers and cucumbers in this easy soup. His customers at Bistro Beaux Lieux like the combination.

SERVES 8

8 medium green zebra tomatoes or unripened red tomatoes
1 green bell pepper, cut into small pieces
1 red bell pepper, cut into small pieces
1 English cucumber, peeled, seeded, and cut into small pieces
1 clove garlic, peeled
1 shallot, quartered
1/2 cup (125 mL) mix of fresh mint and basil leaves
3 tablespoons (45 mL) olive oil
Dash hot pepper sauce or sambal oelek
Salt and freshly ground pepper
1 ball buffalo mozzarella cheese (3 1/2 to 4 ounces/100 to 125 g), cut into 8 slices
Extra-virgin olive oil, for drizzling

+ In a large food processor, pulse all the ingredients except cheese to a purée consistency. (If your food processor is small, purée mixture in batches, placing some of each ingredient, except cheese, in the food processor and pulsing until smooth.)
+ Pour soup into a bowl or pitcher and refrigerate, covered, until ready to serve. Serve in chilled bowls, each topped with a slice of cheese and a drizzle of olive oil.

Velouté de maïs

CREAM OF CORN SOUP

Chefs are skilled at preserving food at its best. Chefs Marc de Canck and his son-in-law Olivier de Montigny of the Montreal restaurant La Chronique offer this soup as a signature dish in and out of corn season. Marc, Belgian-born, flash-freezes kernels of summer cobs to use throughout the year. The two chefs like to pour the soup over a single scallop that's then covered with truffle shavings and surrounded by sautéed leeks. This recipe is their adaptation of this dish for the home cook.

SERVES 6 TO 8

4 tablespoons (60 mL) butter
1 large onion, finely chopped
2 pounds (1 kg) fresh or frozen corn kernels
4 cups (1 L) chicken stock
2 cups (500 mL) whole milk
2 cups (500 mL) whipping cream
Salt and freshly ground pepper
Large grilled scallops, cooked shrimp, or cubed cooked crab or lobster meat (optional)
Thinly sliced fresh chives

✤ Melt butter in a large, heavy saucepan over medium heat. Add onion and sauté until softened. Add corn and stock, bring to a boil, and boil gently until reduced by half.

✤ Add milk and cream, and reduce heat to low. Cover and barely simmer, stirring occasionally, for about 15 minutes. Do not let mixture boil or milk will curdle.

✤ Purée half the mixture in a blender or food processor. Return to remaining soup and stir to combine. Season with salt and pepper.

✤ Serve hot in warmed bowls, each topped with your choice of cooked shellfish (if using) and chives.

CORN ON THE COB

Two-colour corn, sometimes called peaches and cream (the name of one popular variety) because its kernels alternate between yellow and cream, is the big seller in Quebec. Only a minority of corn lovers continue to buy the all-yellow cobs of yesteryear, believing they offer more flavour. Bicolore corn, as growers term the two-colour type, is sweet, tender, and bred to stay fresh longer. Organic grower Ken Taylor explains: "The bicolore has a super-sweet gene, which protects the conversion of sugar to starch." Yellow corn goes stale faster, becoming starchy in a matter of hours. But, if you can obtain it fresh and enjoy it right away, it offers considerably more flavour, say connoisseurs.

Only a few growers still produce yellow corn, and those with stands at Montreal's two big public markets have their faithful customers who know to wait out the first corn pickings for a few weeks until the slower-ripening yellow cobs come into season. At Atwater Market, Gaétan Prairie from the South Shore community of L'Acadie grows both kinds. His wife, Céline, who remembers when two-colour corn came into fashion in the late 1980s, sells more of the two-colour variety but welcomes the yellow-corn faithful when that variety ripens. At Jean-Talon Market, dubbing himself "Le roi du maïs sucré" (The king of sweet corn), is Georges Deneault, another grower offering both two-colour and yellow corn. He usually has a pot of boiling water on the go and will cook you a free cob as an enticement to load up.

Mousse de pétoncles et canard fumé

SCALLOP AND SMOKED DUCK MOUSSE

Denis Mareuge always has a specialty mousse in the takeout counter of Boulangerie Owl's Bread, an Eastern Townships headquarters for fine food. The French-born chef feeds Quebec's love of pâtés and rillettes, smoked salmon, and foie gras. A baker at heart, he offers a daily assortment of traditional French loaves at his store and restaurant in Mansonville, and at the summer Saturday farmers' market in Knowlton. His logo is an owl—inspired by nearby Owl's Head Mountain—holding a loaf of country bread on a baker's traditional wooden paddle.

SERVES 6

7 ounces (200 g) fresh scallops
1 egg
1 ounce (30 g) smoked duck breast, trimmed
   of fat, finely chopped
Salt and freshly ground pepper
Unsalted butter, for greasing
1 cup (250 mL) whipping cream

Balsamic vinaigrette
2 tablespoons (30 mL) extra-virgin olive oil
1 tablespoon (15 mL) fine balsamic vinegar
Sea salt and freshly ground pepper

✦ Rinse scallops and pat dry with paper towels. Place in a food processor with egg, smoked duck, salt, and pepper. Pulse until smooth, using a spatula to scrape down the sides of the food processor as necessary. Cover mousse with plastic wrap and refrigerate for about 30 minutes.

✦ Meanwhile, butter 8 ramekins (1/3 cup/75 mL) each. Cut parchment paper to fit the bottoms of the ramekins and butter the paper. About 15 minutes before serving time, preheat the oven to 350°F (180°C).

✦ Blend cream into scallop mixture, then scoop into the ramekins. Set ramekins in 1 or 2 baking pans and pour boiling water around the ramekins to three-quarters of the way up the sides. Bake for 8 to 10 minutes, until a knife inserted in the centre of a mousse comes out clean.

✦ Meanwhile, prepare balsamic vinaigrette: In a cup, combine oil with balsamic vinegar. Beat in sea salt and pepper to taste.

✦ Remove pan from the oven and remove ramekins from the pan. Loosen mousse from ramekins by sliding a knife around the edges, then unmould onto 8 serving plates. Serve with vinaigrette.

Note

The mousse can be cooked several hours in advance, then covered and refrigerated. Shortly before serving time, warm mousse by placing ramekins in a large, stovetop-safe pan, adding cold water to a depth of about 1 inch (2.5 cm), and setting over high heat until water boils. Remove from heat and unmould.

Soupe aux gourganes

GOURGANE BEAN SOUP

This version of the traditional soup of Saguenay–Lac-St-Jean is a third-generation favourite with food writer Monique Girard-Solomita. She comes from Roberval, on the shores of Lac St-Jean, and was for many years my counterpart in covering food news at Le Journal de Montréal, *Montreal's French tabloid newspaper. Her mother, one of the northern region's large Gagnon clan, always made the soup, having learned the recipe from her mother. When the big, fat, green gourgane beans come into season each August, Monique gets out her soup pot. "We even enjoy it in hot weather," she says.*

SERVES 8 TO 10

2 tablespoons (30 mL) vegetable oil
2 onions, finely chopped
12 cups (3 L) water
2 chicken stock cubes
2 to 3 cups (500 to 750 mL) shelled fresh gourgane or broad beans
7 ounces (200 g) salt pork, cut in large pieces
1 tablespoon (15 mL) dried savory
Freshly ground pepper
1/3 cup (75 mL) pearl barley, carefully rinsed
1/2 cup (125 mL) coarsely chopped celery
1/2 cup (125 mL) coarsely chopped carrots
1/2 cup (125 mL) yellow string beans cut in 1/2 inch (1 cm) pieces
Finely chopped fresh flat-leaf parsley
Finely chopped green onion

+ In a large saucepan, heat oil over medium heat and cook onions just until tender but not browned, 2 to 3 minutes. Add water and stock cubes and bring to a boil. Add gourgane beans, salt pork, savory, and pepper. Reduce heat to low and simmer, uncovered, for 1 hour.
+ Add barley and simmer for another 30 minutes. Add celery and carrots and continue simmering for 25 minutes. Add string beans and cook for 5 minutes.
+ Check seasoning, adding salt and pepper to taste. Serve sprinkled with parsley and green onions.

Gourgane beans are harvested
by Philippe Legault at Le Potager
Grandmont in St-Gédéon.

GOURGANE BEANS

I had an inkling of what to expect when I visited my first gourgane bean farm near Lac St-Jean, in northern Quebec. That bean, a cousin of the fava and broad bean that dates back to medieval times, makes a traditional thick soup that's a basic August treat in both the Saguenay and Charlevoix regions. Remembering the soup from years back when I took a French immersion course in Jonquière, and aware that the fat, green pods appear in Montreal markets each August, I once bought a packet of gourgane seeds and planted them in my garden. It was a Jack-and-the-beanstalk experience. Allowing the seeds a space about the size of a card table, I soon had to provide trellises to support what ended up

as waist-high plants. My harvest? Once shelled, I had only about two big handfuls, enough for a single batch of soup.

Walking the tall, leafy rows of gourgane plants on the big Grandmont bean farm in St-Gédéon, near Lac St-Jean, I plucked handfuls of pods from tree-like stalks that were thick with dark green leaves. My little harvest survived two days' travel back to Montreal in a cooler. I then tried to replicate the beans I'd enjoyed at Auberge-Bistro Rose & Basilic in Alma, a town in the centre of gourgane country. Chef Mathieu Gagnon had served them alongside a crumb-crusted fillet of lamb, the bright green beans resembling large, firm, fresh peas. He shelled them, steamed them, and flavoured them with lamb stock, then added crumbled crisp bacon. They were delicious. Shelling gourganes is easy if you first blanch them for 30 seconds, he told me, and then slip off the skins. He was right. Fresh gourgane beans are imported from Mexico a good part of the winter and spring. Chez Nino in Montreal's Jean-Talon Market is one specialty store that carries them.

Costas Spiliadis

To Costas Spiliadis, Greek cuisine has a certain style and, ever since 1980, when he opened Milos in Montreal, the goal of this Greek-born restaurateur has been to bring that style to the Western world. His dedication to fresh food in its season has made him Quebec's most influential promoter of quality fresh ingredients, known for tracking down the finest foods from as far away as the mountains above Thessaloniki (for wild greens) to as close as a goat farm in Ontario (for goat yogurt). Called "a crazy man" for his food principles, Costas has been helping set Quebec standards for the best fresh foods for more than three decades.

Offering the finest products takes detective work, determination, and money, says the restaurateur, who has cloned his Montreal restaurant in New York, Athens, Las Vegas, and Miami's South Beach and has plans for London. His chefs strive to obtain Greece's wild greens, or get enough of My Sister's Olive Oil as he calls his own brand, or find a certain fish for his lavishly stocked fresh fish counters, or enough wildflower honey to drizzle on thick Greek yogurt. Costas never stops fighting distance and time to find the foods he remembers from his childhood. "Sometimes," he explained to me once, "I am talking on the phone to a fisherman who has just found octopus in the Mediterranean off Tunisia. He hasn't caught the fish yet but we both know those waters are the cleanest in the Mediterranean. I buy in that phone call and the next day those octopus are grilling in my restaurants."

His cooking style is simple. His zucchini and eggplant slices, called Milos Special, are cut paper-thin, battered and deep-fried until crisp, and served with salty fried saganaki cheese and tzatziki. His potatoes are simply quartered, brushed with olive oil and lemon juice, sprinkled with dried oregano, salt, and pepper and baked until tender. Costas decided to go upscale when he opened New York's Estiatorio Milos in 1997 and left those potatoes off his menu. "But Montrealers would come to New York and ask for them, we'd do a special order and the New Yorkers would see them. I ended up putting them on the menu," he said, grinning. They are also offered in his Miami restaurant.

Those potatoes were on his mother's menu when he was growing up on the Aegean island of Patras. "Food at home was, for us, the single element that brought the family together," he says, remembering happy hours at table with parents he describes as "fanatic" about good food. To hear him reminisce is to wonder if his mother, Evridi Theodoridou, ever sat down between food shopping, growing vegetables, and cooking. "Her moussaka took her seven hours," said her son.

The Greek salad, established on Quebec salad bars, must never contain lettuce, he maintains. When tomatoes ripen in Greece, it's too hot for good lettuce to grow, he explained. "So only people who have no idea of anything will add lettuce to a Greek tomato salad."

Ideally, he wrote, that salad has tomatoes still warm from the sun, the wild greens called purslane, Greek fleur de sel, extra-virgin olive oil, red wine vinegar, small Santorini capers, Greek feta cheese, cucumbers, green peppers, sweet red onions, and dried oregano. The only allowable extras: a coating of the vinegar on the cucumber slices, some sun-dried Greek olives, and some flat-leaf parsley.

Olive oil, quality and quantity, is more than an oil. It's a seasoning and one to go big on, in his view. "Just close your eyes and pour," he says, quoting his mother.

Costas, who immigrated to the United States at 18, and then studied for a degree in sociology at Montreal's Concordia University, was first a broadcaster; he helped to found Radio Centre Ville and ran its Greek programming. But he was dis-turbed that, to Montrealers, Greek food appeared to be souvlaki and no more. Nostalgic for his mother's cooking, he opened Milos. One of the actions fellow Greeks called "crazy" was to use his car, an old taxi, to drive twice a week to the Fulton Fish Market in New York to buy fresh fish.

Costas preaches patience when waiting for foods such as tomatoes to come into season. "A tomato is worth waiting for. When you get it, you treat it with respect, like the marble on the Parthenon."

His perfect meal? Fresh grilled fish and, for dessert, a fruit platter with watermelon. Just as his mother would have served it.

Costas Spiliadis prides himself on his fresh fish counter at Milos restaurant, Montreal.

Bouillabaisse de Mont-Louis

It's not surprising that Chef Daniel Gasse specializes in fish and seafood at his little restaurant, La Broue dans l'Toupet, on the north coast of the Gaspé in Mont-Louis. A fishing and lumbering village dating back to the 17th century, the place had a reputation as an ideal spot from which to fish for cod. When that species ran out, Daniel adapted his cuisine to others, in particular the plentiful scallops and shrimp. He uses the freshest catches in this meal-in-one soup.

SERVES 4

2 tablespoons (30 mL) butter	1 1/2 pounds (750 g) fresh salmon or halibut, cubed
2 shallots, minced	
1 small leek, white part only, finely chopped	4 large scallops
1 teaspoon (5 mL) finely chopped garlic	4 tiger shrimp, peeled and deveined
1 teaspoon (5 mL) grated fresh gingerroot	12 mussels
Pinch cayenne pepper	1 or 2 ripe tomatoes, seeded, peeled and chopped
2 to 3 medium potatoes, peeled and cubed	1 or 2 green onions, chopped
4 cups (1 L) fish stock (page 136)	Chopped fresh flat-leaf parsley, for garnish

+ In a large, heavy pot, melt butter over medium heat and sauté shallots, leek, garlic, gingerroot, and cayenne for about 3 minutes.
+ Add potatoes and stock and bring to a boil. Reduce heat to low, cover, and simmer until potatoes are almost cooked.
+ Add salmon and continue cooking for 5 minutes. Add scallops, shrimp, and mussels and cook just until shrimp turn pink, scallops are becoming tender, and mussels have opened. Discard any mussels that do not open.
+ Serve in large, warmed bowls, topped with tomatoes, green onions, and parsley.

Court-Bouillon

Fish stock

2 tablespoons (30 mL) butter

1 medium onion, cut in large chunks

2 carrots, cut in large chunks

2 stalks celery, coarsely sliced

5 to 6 mushrooms, cut in chunks

1 pound (500 g) fish bones and heads

12 cups (3 L) cold water

1 bouquet garni (2 bay leaves and sprigs
of fresh thyme and flat-leaf parsley tied
together, or tied in a cheesecloth bag)

Grated peel and juice of 1 lemon

Pinch salt

4 whole peppercorns

+ In a large, heavy saucepan, melt butter over medium heat and sauté onion, carrots, celery, and mushrooms just until softened, about 5 minutes.

+ Add fish bones and heads, water, bouquet garni, lemon peel and juice, salt, and peppercorns. Bring to a boil and simmer for 25 minutes, partially covered. Strain. Set aside or refrigerate, covered, for up to 1 day.

GREEN ONIONS

This long, thin, mild-flavoured member of the onion family is a staple in Quebec kitchens. Produced in huge quantities on several farms, it has a different look when compared with imported versions. A Quebec green onion has a little bulb on the end, rather than a skinny base. Grower Olivier Barbeau, who runs a green onion farm in St-Michel, south of Montreal, thinks his onions have more flavour than imports from California or Mexico. Their bulbous end is an advantage because the onions can be pickled.

Essential to the salad bowl, green onions can add flavour to many cooked dishes, say Quebec growers. Olivier likes to cut them into lengths of a few inches (10 cm or so), fry them in butter until lightly browned, and add them to a grilled cheese sandwich. Steven Lemelin, of Les Fermes du Soleil, in Ste-Clotilde, lays green onions on a hot grill, then adds his steak. He finds the onions prevent the meat from burning. He adds olive oil, salt, and pepper and enjoys the onions with the meat.

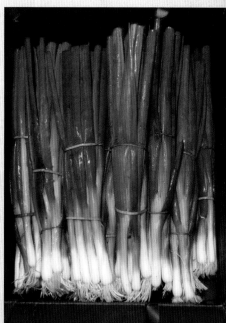

Truite au gingembre

GINGER TROUT

The wildest of flavour combinations came to Stanstead, a sleepy southern Quebec town a stone's throw from the Vermont border, when film producer Bashar Shbib opened Millie's Diner. The cuisine of his Syrian father and German mother received a boost when Bashar immersed himself in Middle and Far Eastern spicing. Farmed trout, zapped up with fresh gingerroot and coriander, licorice liqueur, and cardamom, was a favourite on his eclectic menu. He's moved on to other ventures but still gingers up his trout.

SERVES 4

1 whole trout or Arctic char (2 pounds/1 kg)
4 or 5 sprigs fresh coriander
1 cup (250 mL) coarsely grated fresh gingerroot
1/2 cup (125 mL) finely chopped garlic
2 tablespoons (30 mL) finely chopped onion
2 tablespoons (30 mL) honey
1 tablespoon (15 mL) sesame oil
1 1/2 teaspoons (7 mL) coarse salt
1/2 cup (125 mL) ouzo, arak, Ricard, or Pernod
1/2 teaspoon (2 mL) freshly ground cardamom

✤ Line a baking sheet with aluminum foil and set a rack on it. Position oven rack 4 inches (10 cm) from the broiler and preheat the broiler.
✤ Rinse fish and pat dry with paper towels. Cut fish lengthwise along the belly and clean, removing guts and bones. Place coriander inside fish.
✤ In a bowl, combine ginger, garlic, and onion and spread mixture inside fish, on both sides. Close fish, insert 5 or 6 toothpicks along each cut side and lace fish closed by hooking kitchen string around the toothpicks. Place on the prepared baking sheet. In a cup, combine honey and sesame oil and brush over fish, then sprinkle with salt.
✤ Broil for 10 minutes per inch (2.5 cm) thickness of fish, probably about 20 minutes total, turning halfway through.
✤ Remove fish from broiler and immediately pour liqueur over top. Sprinkle with cardamom. Pour pan juices into a gravy boat and serve with fish.

Note

Don't cook the fish on the barbecue, as juices will be lost.

Saumon à la gaspésienne

SALMON GASPÉ STYLE

Thick fillets of salmon are immersed in a creamy white sauce in this time-honoured recipe for a luxury comfort food. Part of the pleasure of this dish is fishing into the depths of the sauce for pieces of hard-boiled egg. My daughter Claire, who lived for some years on the Bay of Chaleur, introduced me to this East Coast tradition with a recipe she adapted from one she obtained from Wanda Keys of Fleurant.

SERVES 6

2 pounds (1 kg) thick salmon fillet

Court-bouillon (page 136)

1/3 cup (75 mL) unsalted butter

3 tablespoons (45 mL) all-purpose flour

1/2 cup (125 mL) boiling court-bouillon or water

2 cups (500 mL) whole milk, heated

Salt and whole peppercorns

1 hard-boiled egg, cut in 6 pieces

✤ Place salmon in the court-bouillon and bring to a boil over high heat. Reduce heat to medium and simmer for 10 minutes per 1 inch (2.5 cm) thickness of fish if you have 1 thick fillet, a little less for 2 fillets. Remove fish to a plate, reserving the cooking liquid.

✤ Alternatively, cook salmon wrapped in aluminum foil in an oven preheated to 450°F (230°C) for 10 minutes per 1 inch (2.5 cm) thickness of fish if you have 1 thick fillet, a little less for 2 fillets. Transfer cooked fish to a warmed plate, covering it to keep warm.

✤ In a stovetop-safe casserole dish, melt butter over medium heat. Stir in flour and cook, stirring constantly, for 2 minutes. Add ½ cup (125 mL) of boiling court-bouillon and continue cooking, stirring for 3 to 5 minutes, until mixture is smooth and thick.

✤ Stir in hot milk and continue cooking just until sauce is creamy. Season with salt and peppercorns. Add egg gently so as not to break up the pieces.

✤ Cut fish into 6 portions and place on 6 warmed plates. Serve topped with sauce.

Note

A single thick fillet can be replaced by 2 thinner fillets, but they will need a shorter cooking time. Check for doneness after 8 minutes. The fish will be cooked when it flakes easily with a fork.

Baker Patrick Moubarak shows off French bread at Folles Farines bakery in Le Bic.

Folles Farines (crazy flours) is typical of Quebec's little bakeries flourishing across the province, the bakers using untreated flour and making bread with the long rising time prescribed by Raymond Calvel, the late French bread reformer. It's a cheerful yellow-painted bakery in the village of Le Bic, on the south shore of the lower St. Lawrence River. Seeing through its big windows the loaves on traditional wooden racks, I went in, to be greeted by the aroma of serious baking wafting from the rear. I loaded up with a baguette, both "levain" (sourdough) and "rustique" (unshaped) loaves, a slab of pizza for lunch, and a chocolate croissant. The owners are not unusual; Quebec artisanal, or craft, bakers tend to be a little crazy about what they do. Claude St-Pierre and Valérie Jean opened the bakery in 1996 after changing careers and learning how to bake in order to stay in this beautiful part of eastern Quebec. Another headquarters for superb bread is Boulangerie Owl's Bread in Mansonville, in the Eastern Townships, close to the U.S. border. Driving past, one could easily miss this modest delicatessen and café where French-born chef Denis Mareuge makes the best bread in the region, plus classic pâtés to go with it. His trademark refers to the nearby ski mountain Owl's Head: it's an owl holding the traditional baker's paddle with loaf and includes the towers of the nearby St-Benoît-du-Lac Trappist monastery, makers of exceptional blue and semi-soft cheeses. I once served as a baking contest judge with this chef at the venerable country fair held annually in the village of Brome. Being French, Denis regretted the lack of butter in some loaves. But he really came down on the lack of salt. "People think it's healthy to reduce salt in their cooking," he says. "But bread is heavy without salt. It needs it to rise properly. If you're making bread, don't skimp on the salt."

Pavé de flétan et salsa de tomates fraîches, avocats, et crevettes roses

HALIBUT STEAKS WITH FRESH TOMATO, AVOCADO, AND SHRIMP SALSA

Halibut, fished in deep waters along the north shore of the lower St. Lawrence River and off Anticosti Island in the Gulf of St. Lawrence, is a popular fish in the Gaspé region. Chef-owner Desmond Ogden of Auberge William Wakeham, in the town of Gaspé, finds this fish makes light, firm fillets, which go well with a fresh salsa rather than a heavy sauce. He suggests his salsa recipe could also be seasoned with fresh dill or coriander, plus lemon juice and olive oil. When he has a whole halibut, sometimes weighing up to 30 pounds (13.5 kg), he reserves the cheeks, which have a texture similar to scallops and skate, for a special meal with his wife. He cooks the cheeks in butter, then seasons them with lemon juice and freshly ground pepper.

SERVES 4

Salsa

3 firm ripe tomatoes, seeded and diced

1 firm ripe avocado, diced

Juice of 1 lime

4 tablespoons (60 mL) olive oil

Pinch Espelette pepper or cayenne pepper

2 or 3 garlic scapes, sprigs fresh coriander, or flat-leaf parsley, finely chopped

4 ounces (125 g) cooked Nordic (Matane) shrimp, thawed if frozen, rinsed and patted dry

Pinches salt and freshly ground pepper

Fish

2 tablespoons (30 mL) olive oil

2 tablespoons (30 mL) butter

1 1/4 pounds (625 g) halibut fillets, cut in 4 equal pieces

For salsa:

+ In a resealable plastic bag, mix together tomatoes, avocado, lime juice, oil, Espelette pepper, garlic scapes, shrimp, salt, and pepper. Seal the bag and refrigerate for up to 4 hours.

For fish:

+ In a large, heavy frying pan, heat oil and butter over medium heat until hot. Place fish in the pan; do not crowd (you may need to do this in batches). Cook for about 3 minutes. Carefully turn fish and cook for 1 minute. Turn off heat, leaving fish in the hot pan to finish cooking.
+ Place fish on 4 warmed serving plates, coloured side up. Spoon salsa around fish and top fish with a little oil from salsa.
+ Serve with a green salad or couscous salad.

Notes

Espelette pepper is French cayenne pepper, available in specialty shops.

The salsa can be prepared up to 4 hours in advance. Keep refrigerated until ready to serve.

Fish, odour-free

Use unsalted butter when frying fish, because salted butter burns quickly, warns Montreal chef and fish specialist Jean-Paul Grappe. He recommends that if you want your home completely free of fish smells, fry fish and seafood in equal amounts of peanut oil and unsalted butter.

Ragoût végétarien

DR. JOE'S VEGETARIAN GOULASH

Dishing out the latest nutritional advice in his column in The Gazette, *on CJAD radio, and in his many books, McGill University chemistry professor Joe Schwarcz decided he should make his mother's Hungarian goulash a healthier dish. Instead of the meat she favoured, either Debreziner sausages or chunks of beef, he substituted firm tofu, which he browns in canola oil and sprinkles, crouton-style, on top. His goulash is loaded with summer vegetables and seasonings. Joe advises adding only a modest dollop of sour cream.*

SERVES 8

2 tablespoons (30 mL) sunflower oil

2 medium onions, finely chopped

1 cup (250 mL) water

10 red-skinned potatoes, peeled and cubed

4 Roma or plum tomatoes, peeled, seeded, and chopped

1 cup (250 mL) green beans cut in 1-inch (2.5 cm) slices

3 bell peppers (1 each green, red, and yellow), seeded and coarsely chopped

8 ounces (250 g) mushrooms, thinly sliced

4 or 5 cloves garlic, crushed

2 tablespoons (30 mL) Hungarian paprika

1 teaspoon (5 mL) salt, or to taste

Freshly ground pepper

1 tablespoon (15 mL) sour cream (optional)

Tofu

2 tablespoons (30 mL) sunflower oil

1 medium onion, chopped

1 clove garlic, minced

1 pound (500 g) firm tofu, wiped dry and cubed

1 teaspoon (5 mL) Hungarian paprika

2 bell peppers (1 red, 1 yellow), seeded and chopped

Fresh flat-leaf parsley

✦ In a large, heavy frying pan, heat oil over medium-high heat and sauté onions just until they begin to turn golden, 3 to 4 minutes. Add water and potatoes and boil gently for 10 to 15 minutes. Add tomatoes, green beans, bell peppers, and mushrooms. Reduce heat to low and cook, stirring often, for another 5 minutes or until vegetables and mushrooms are softened. Stir in garlic, paprika, salt, and pepper and cook, stirring constantly, for 5 minutes. Stir in sour cream (if using).

For tofu:

✦ In a large, heavy saucepan, heat oil over medium heat and sauté onion and garlic just until they start to turn golden, about 5 minutes. Add tofu and cook, stirring constantly, until tofu begins to turn crisp and golden.

✦ Add paprika and continue cooking, stirring occasionally, for 5 minutes. Add bell peppers and cook until tender. Taste and add more paprika, if desired.

✦ Ladle goulash into shallow, warmed bowls and sprinkle with the fried tofu. Sprinkle generously with parsley and serve.

Steak de bavette au fromage Gorgonzola

SKIRT STEAK WITH GORGONZOLA SAUCE

Quebec is dotted with neighbourhood restaurants with faithful clientele. One such establishment is Alex H, in Montreal's Notre-Dame-de-Grâce district. Many a Tuesday night Jacques Hendlisz, a gifted, French-born amateur cook, drops in to help the Syrian owner-chef, Alex Haddad, in the kitchen. This lively beef dish is one of his specialties.

SERVES 6

1 1/4 cups (310 mL) dry white wine
1 cup (250 mL) whipping cream
8 ounces (250 g) picante or plain Gorgonzola cheese, or other blue cheese, crumbled
1 tablespoon (15 mL) grated Parmesan cheese
Freshly grated nutmeg
Olive oil or canola oil, for frying
6 skirt or flank steaks (6 ounces/180 g each)

✤ In a small saucepan, heat wine over medium heat until reduced by half. Add cream and reduce mixture by half. Reduce heat to low and add cheese, mixing well. Cook, stirring constantly, until cheese is melted. Add Parmesan and nutmeg and set sauce aside, keeping it warm.

✤ Place the oven rack in the lowest position. Preheat the oven to 325°F (160°C).

✤ Heat 2 large, heavy frying pans over medium heat. Add enough oil to each pan to oil lightly. Cook steaks for 2 minutes on each side, then place the pans in the oven and cook steaks for 5 minutes.

✤ Remove from the oven and let steaks rest, covered, for 5 minutes at room temperature. Slice on an angle.

✤ Transfer steaks to 6 warmed serving plates, spoon pan juices over each steak, then spoon about 2 tablespoons (30 mL) cheese sauce over top.

Salade tiède de joue de veau braisé, champignons sauvages, pommes de terre nouvelles, et vinaigre de zérès

WARM SALAD WITH BRAISED VEAL CHEEKS, WILD MUSHROOMS, AND NEW POTATOES

Veal cheeks are an expensive cut of meat, valued by chefs because they keep their flavour and silky texture during long braising. Sutton chef Christian Beaulieu likes to liven up his recipe with mushrooms and sherry vinegar. Combining small pieces of freshly cooked hot meat with chilled greens is popular in Quebec restaurants. Chicken livers are often served in this fashion.

SERVES 4

8 veal cheeks (about 20 ounces/600 g), trimmed of fat

2 to 3 tablespoons (30 to 45 mL) Dijon mustard

4 tablespoons (60 mL) sunflower oil or other oil of your choice

4 tablespoons (60 mL) cold butter

1/2 cup (125 mL) dry white wine

2 cups (500 mL) fond de veau (page 56)

8 new potatoes, scrubbed and quartered

2 shallots, coarsely chopped

4 ounces (125 g) mushrooms, preferably wild

2 tablespoons (30 mL) sherry vinegar

Mesclun or baby salad greens, to serve

✦ Preheat the oven to 375°F (190°C).

✦ Brush meat with Dijon. In a large, heavy frying pan over medium-high heat, heat 2 tablespoons (30 mL) of the oil and 2 tablespoons (30 mL) of the butter and brown meat quickly on all sides. Transfer meat to a plate.

✦ Deglaze pan by adding wine and scraping up brown bits from the bottom. Reduce heat to low and simmer until mixture is reduced by half. Stir in fond de veau and heat until simmering.

✦ Place meat in a heavy 2-quart (2 L) casserole dish and cover with fond de veau. Cover casserole dish and bake for 1½ to 2 hours, depending on the size of the veal cheeks, until meat is tender to the fork. Remove meat from its liquid and set aside.

- Meanwhile, cook potatoes in boiling salted water just until tender, then drain.
- In a large nonstick frying pan, heat remaining 2 tablespoons (30 mL) oil and cook shallots, potatoes, and mushrooms until lightly browned. (Be careful not to overcook wild mushrooms, if using.)
- Add meat to vegetable mixture and continue cooking just to warm all ingredients. Remove from heat, add vinegar, and stir to incorporate brown bits from the bottom of the pan. Thicken sauce by whisking in remaining 2 tablespoons (30 mL) butter, a tablespoon (15 mL) at a time.
- Serve on a bed of mesclun or baby salad greens.

Note

Fond de veau is thickened veal stock. It is sold in cartons, and fresh or frozen at butcher shops. A powdered base that is mixed with water is also available at specialty stores and some supermarkets.

Hamburger d'agneau de Charlevoix

CHARLEVOIX LAMB BURGERS

Lamb is a specialty in the Charlevoix region, where La Ferme Éboulmontaise, a big lamb farm in Les Éboulemonts, has acquired Quebec's first attestation de spécificité, a designation of a unique regional product modelled on Europe's AOC (appellation d'origine contrôlée). This recipe is from Charlevoix chef Régis Hervé, a native of Tours, in France's Loire Valley, and chef for many years in a lamb restaurant. His lamb burgers are seasoned with mint, olives, and onions.

SERVES 4

1 pound (500 g) ground lamb
2 shallots, finely chopped
1 tablespoon (15 mL) Dijon mustard
10 fresh mint leaves, chopped
1/2 teaspoon (2 mL) salt
Freshly ground pepper
4 sesame kaiser rolls, cut in half horizontally
Soft butter, for spreading
4 tablespoons (60 mL) green olive pistou
4 tablespoons (60 mL) onion confit
Fresh spinach and mint leaves
Sliced tomatoes

+ In a mixing bowl, combine lamb, shallots, Dijon, chopped mint, salt, and pepper. Shape mixture into 4 thick patties. Grill on a hot barbecue or under a hot broiler for 5 minutes per side. Set burgers aside and keep warm.
+ Toast and butter rolls. Spread roll bottoms with olive pistou and roll tops with onion confit. Layer spinach and mint leaves on roll bottoms, then stack on hot grilled burgers, tomato slices, and roll tops.

Note

Specialty food shops sell green olive pistou and onion confit. You can substitute green onion paste or green olive tartare for the green olive pistou. Make your own onion confit by sautéing sliced onions gently in butter with a little sugar until they are of marmalade consistency.

Honouring
Specialties

Lamb produced on a big farm in the Charlevoix region made Quebec food history in 2009 when the government gave it the province's first *attestation de spécificité*, the Quebec version of France's *appellation d'origine contrôlée* (AOC). This system of identification of a food or drink as unique to a region has flourished for years in France and Italy. It was initiated in Quebec only after years of study by the agriculture department. On the list for future accreditation are three products considered unique to their areas. Ice cider, the apple version of ice wine produced in Quebec apple orchards, is one. Cheeses made from the milk of the first Canadian cow, known as the Vache canadienne, are another. And the Chantecler chicken, a superior breed, is the third expected to be named by a committee of agricultural scientists and university professors. SlowFood Canada, part of the international organization trying to protect unique foods, maintains its own list of unique specialty products. Quebec is represented on that list by the Chantecler chicken, the Vache canadienne, the Montreal melon (see page 176), and ice cider (see page 382).

The chicken, a large and hardy bird that produces plenty of eggs and flavourful meat, was crossbred a century ago by a Trappist monk at Oka. The cow arrived in the colony of New France from northern France in 1608, became nearly extinct, and is on a comeback because of the discovery that its rich milk is perfect for cheesemaking.

Jocelyn Labbé and Diane Marcoux taste
Le Paillasson cheese they make and sell
on Île d'Orléans.

Cheese Tradition Restored

One of the most noteworthy cheeses in Quebec is believed to be the first to be made in North America. It's a fresh farm cheese called Le Paillasson, from Île d'Orléans, near Quebec City. The cheese is made using a method that has been traced to 17th-century French farm cheeses. Reintroduced in 2004 and using modern cheese technology, it's sold fresh on the island but is so perishable that the handful of cheese shops in Montreal and Quebec City that offer it sell it frozen. Mild-flavoured, the cheese is delectable when melted on a baguette or pizza, or in a fondue, gratin, or sauce.

Today's makers of this cheese are Jocelyn Labbé and his wife, Diane Marcoux, who dress in 17th-century costume to add colour to the story they relate at their little cheese plant and café in the village of Ste-Famille. Gérard Aubin, a long-time island resident, was the last man still making the ancestral cheese. But then his time-honoured method was judged unsanitary by a Quebec agriculture department inspector. The elderly farmer and others before him had always made their fresh cheese at home, curdling raw milk, adding salt, filling moulds, draining whey from the rounds of cheese, and then setting the cheese to lose part of its moisture on mats made of reeds that grow along the shores of the island.

These mats, key to the flavour of the cheese, would be set near the stove in farm kitchens. The cheese was produced from October to May, when it was cold outside but warm in the kitchen, and the dry air helped give the cheese its desired texture. To mature it, it was stored in a maple box and placed in the cellar. A far cry from today's hygiene standards.

The restoration of the historic cheese began when the inspector recommended the elderly farmer consult Jacques Goulet, a Laval University cheese technology professor. Working with Laval graduate food science student Hélène Thiboutot, Jacques looked for a way to identify the microorganisms from an aged cheese produced by Gérard Aubin. Two yeasts were shown to be the dominant microflora, and they were presumed to come originally from the reeds along a shoreline washed by saltwater tides.

The scientists, experimenting with yeast instead of the usual lactic bacteria used in cheese-making, succeeded in recreating the cheese in an aseptic, stainless-steel plant.

Although approved by both health officials and gastronomes, this cheese will not appear in supermarkets, says Jocelyn, even though it won a prize from the prestigious American Cheese Society in 2011. "We have no desire to become big. This cheese is artisanal, from our heritage."

Then he grinned. "But it's the best cheese I've ever tasted."

Gratin de fenouil et jambon au fromage Allegretto

Fennel, ham, and cheese casserole

Michelle Gélinas likes recipes that can be assembled completely in advance and then cooked at the last minute. This recipe the Montreal food specialist also makes with asparagus instead of fennel, blanching the asparagus briefly before rolling the spears in the ham. This treatment of fennel accents its full flavour and differs from Michelle's usual method of grilling it or adding it to a salad.

Serves 4

2 fennel bulbs, trimmed
8 small slices or 4 large slices cooked ham
Dijon mustard, for spreading
4 tablespoons (60 mL) unsalted butter
4 tablespoons (60 mL) all-purpose flour
1 cup (250 mL) light cream, heated
1 1/2 cups (375 mL) grated Allegretto or cheddar cheese
2 tablespoons (30 mL) chopped fresh thyme leaves
2 tablespoons (30 mL) chopped green onions, green part only

✤ Place the oven rack in the middle position. Preheat the oven to 400°F (200°C).

✤ Slice fennel bulbs in half vertically and place in a large saucepan of cold salted water. Bring water to a boil over high heat, then reduce heat to low, cover, and cook fennel for 20 minutes. Drain, reserving 1 cup (250 mL) cooking water.

✤ Spread ham slices with Dijon and wrap each piece of fennel in ham so it is covered completely. Arrange wrapped fennel in a shallow baking pan just wide enough to fit it in a single layer.

✤ In a small, heavy saucepan, melt butter over medium heat. Stir in flour and cook mixture, stirring constantly, for 2 minutes. Stir in reserved fennel cooking water and cream, bring mixture to a boil over medium heat, then reduce heat to low and simmer gently, stirring often, for 10 minutes.

✤ Pour sauce over fennel, sprinkle with cheese, and bake for 30 minutes or until sauce is bubbling and lightly browned. Serve sprinkled with thyme and green onions.

Méli-mélo de salades vertes

DEEP GREEN SALAD

The darker the green, the more nutritious the salad. This recipe contains four dark green vegetables, dressed with a ginger-garlic vinaigrette. It's lively in flavour, and crisp and crunchy. The recipe is from Israeli-born chef and cooking teacher Gigi Cohen, who runs a tiny vegetarian restaurant in Monkland Village, at the heart of the Notre-Dame-de-Grâce district of west-end Montreal. Gigi's café Juicy Lotus and her cookbook, Nourishing Friends, *reveal her travel discoveries. Vary the greens to suit; alternatives Gigi suggests are cabbage, zucchini, cucumber, mustard greens, arugula, and watercress. She is an organic food advocate; if preferred, replace the organic cane sugar with granulated sugar, and the tamari with regular soy sauce.*

SERVES 6

4 cups (1 L) chopped Swiss chard and kale
2 cups (500 mL) chopped green cabbage
2 cups (500 mL) small broccoli florets
1 green bell pepper, diced

Dressing
3 tablespoons (45 mL) olive oil
1 tablespoon + 1 teaspoon (20 mL) organic cane sugar
1/4 cup (60 mL) minced fresh gingerroot
2 cloves garlic, crushed
1 tablespoon (15 mL) toasted sesame oil
Pinch cayenne pepper
2 tablespoons (30 mL) tamari sauce
2 teaspoons (10 mL) sesame seeds

✦ Cut spines from Swiss chard and kale and discard. Rinse, dry, and cut up Swiss chard, kale, cabbage, broccoli, and pepper. Toss together in a salad bowl and put in the refrigerator to chill.
✦ For dressing, in a bowl or a food processor, combine oil, sugar, ginger, garlic, sesame oil, cayenne, and tamari sauce. Whisk or process just until smooth.
✦ When ready to serve, toss salad with dressing and serve, sprinkled with sesame seeds.

Note
The dressing may be made in advance and left at room temperature for several hours or refrigerated, covered, overnight.

Pommes de terre au citron

CHUNKY LEMON POTATOES

Peggy Regan's cooking reflects her Irish-Scottish background. She likes potatoes in many ways, including this refreshing mashed version. The combination of butter and lemon gives the potatoes a distinctive taste. Peggy, who runs a Montreal tearoom and bakery called Gryphon d'Or, likes to use the best butter available in all her cooking, and she uses it with a generous hand.

SERVES 6

5 large potatoes, peeled and quartered
1/4 cup (60 mL) butter, at room temperature
Grated peel of 1 lemon
Juice of 1/2 lemon
2 tablespoons (30 mL) chopped fresh flat-leaf parsley
Salt and freshly ground pepper

✛ In a medium saucepan, cover potatoes with cold, salted water and boil over medium-high heat, uncovered, just until tender. Drain potatoes, return to the pan, and set on the burner with the heat turned off.

✛ Add butter, tossing until potatoes are coated. Stir in lemon peel, lemon juice, and parsley. Mash very coarsely with a potato masher; do not use an electric mixer or food processor, as it would make the potatoes too smooth. They should be chunky and drier than regular mashed potatoes.

✛ Season to taste with salt and pepper and serve at once.

Note

This recipe works with either peeled potatoes or new potatoes with their skins left on.

Tomates d'été au vinaigre de cidre et à la ciboulette

Summer tomatoes with cider-chive dressing

When tomatoes are at their ripest and best, simple slicing is all they need to make a salad. Experimenting with varying the formula during Quebec's tomato season, caterer Jane Livingston of Knowlton adds a lively dressing flavoured with cider and mustard seeds.

Serves 6

Dressing

1/4 cup (60 mL) apple cider

3 tablespoons (45 mL) finely chopped chives

1/2 teaspoon (2 mL) yellow mustard seeds

2 tablespoons (30 mL) sunflower oil (or half sunflower oil, half pumpkin seed oil)

1 tablespoon (15 mL) white wine vinegar

Salt

5 ripe large red tomatoes, sliced or cut in wedges, at room temperature

✤ Using a mini food processor, purée apple cider, 1 tablespoon (15 mL) of the chives, and mustard seeds. Pour into a bowl and mix in oil, vinegar, and salt. Refrigerate for at least 1 hour.

✤ Arrange tomatoes on a platter and drizzle with dressing. Sprinkle with remaining 2 tablespoons (30 mL) chives and serve.

TOMATOES RENEWED

The varieties of tomatoes our grandparents grew have come back into fashion. Raymond Tratt of Montreal, a heritage-seed saver, has spent years growing an assortment of tomato plants for nurseries and friends. My favourite of his 45 varieties is Dufresne, a Quebec tomato dating back to 1936, when two Dufresne brothers identified and named this big, red, extra-sweet treat. Tratt's choice is a sweet, pink variety he named Douceur de Doucet, bred by St-Hyacinthe agricultural scientist Roger Doucet, Tratt's mentor.

Organic market gardener Ken Taylor is another tomato specialist to favour the Dufresne tomato, with the Brandywine a runner-up. The latter, an American heirloom type, is pink with wine-coloured flesh and a sweet and spicy flavour. Ken grows it at his Windmill Point Farm on Île Perrot, west of Montreal. "One slice can fill a whole sandwich.," he says.

Gwynne Basen is another tomato specialist working to bring these heirlooms to public attention. A writer, filmmaker, and member of Seeds of Diversity Canada, the heritage seed organization, she grows about 50 varieties at Mansonville, in the Eastern Townships. While these tomatoes, some brown-skinned and brown-fleshed, some zebra-striped green and yellow, are conversation pieces, their advantage to the home gardener is that they are hardier than the mass-produced types. Another plus factor is their names, such as Mortgage Lifter, a big red one, and Tula, dark red with brownish flesh.

Tomates rôties aux herbes fraîches

ROASTED TOMATOES WITH FRESH HERBS

Kelly Shanahan, who owns the Sutton shop La Rumeur Affamée, one of the best delicatessens in the Eastern Township-ships, makes this dish when the tomato crop ripens. She likes it with grilled or roasted chicken or sausages, or as a topping for grilled sea bass or cooked rice or quinoa. To make it into a soup, she purées the mixture in a blender or food processor. To make it into a pasta sauce, she removes 1 to 2 cups (250 to 500 mL) of the tomatoes and strains them, reserving the liquid, then chops the tomatoes coarsely and combines them with the reserved juice.

MAKES 4 CUPS (1 L)

1 bag (10 ounces/284 g) pearl onions

1 tablespoon (15 mL) cracked black pepper

1 teaspoon (5 mL) salt

1 teaspoon (5 mL) granulated sugar

1 large head garlic

4 pounds (2 kg) ripe red tomatoes

1 container (6 ounces/180 g) yellow grape tomatoes (1 1/4 cups/310 mL)

1 container (9 ounces/254 g) large cherry tomatoes (1 1/2 cups/375 mL)

1/2 cup (125 mL) olive oil

8 sprigs fresh rosemary

1 tablespoon (15 mL) balsamic vinegar

1 cup (250 mL) loosely packed fresh basil leaves

✤ In a pot of boiling water, blanch onions for 1 minute. Drain onions, cool in cold water for 10 minutes, then peel.

✤ In a cup, mix together pepper, salt, and sugar.

✤ Place garlic root end down on a cutting board. Press with the palm of your hand to loosen the cloves. Separate cloves, and peel.

✤ In a large pot of boiling water, immerse red tomatoes for 15 seconds. Drain, peel, and cut in half horizontally. Using a small spoon, remove seeds and squeeze out juice; discard both.

✤ Preheat the oven to 400°F (200°C).

✤ Place half the prepared tomatoes, cut side up, in a rectangular roasting dish just large enough to hold them side by side. Scatter pearl onions and garlic over tomatoes, sprinkle with half the pepper mixture, and the grape and cherry tomatoes. Cover with remaining red tomatoes and drizzle with oil. Place rosemary on top. Sprinkle with vinegar and remaining pepper mixture.

✤ Bake for 1 hour or until softened, checking after 45 minutes to be sure tomatoes are holding their shape and not collapsing into a sauce.

✤ Remove tomatoes from the oven and let stand for 15 minutes, then sprinkle with basil.

Salade tiède de haricots grillés

WARM BEAN SALAD

This is a perfect potluck dish because it can be made in advance, transported easily to the party, and served warm or at room temperature. It's a favourite with my Gazette *colleague and friend Susan Schwartz. She also likes fresh-cooked beans with an Asian vinaigrette of vegetable or olive oil, rice vinegar, soy sauce, and sesame oil. You can use one colour of beans, but she prefers the contrast of two colours.*

SERVES 4

1 pound (500 g) fresh green and yellow string beans, trimmed
1 red onion, sliced in thin rounds, or 2 shallots, minced
1 tablespoon (15 mL) olive oil
1/4 teaspoon (1 mL) coarse salt
Pinch freshly ground pepper
1 tablespoon (15 mL) balsamic vinegar

+ Preheat the oven to 450°F (230°C). Line a large baking pan with parchment paper.
+ Place beans, onion, oil, salt, and pepper in a resealable plastic bag. Close the bag and turn it several times to mix ingredients well.
+ Spread bean mixture in the prepared baking pan in a single layer and roast, stirring three times, for about 20 minutes, until beans start to soften (but are still a little firm) and develop brown spots, and the onion has begun to caramelize.
+ Remove the pan from the oven. Sprinkle beans with vinegar and mix well. Transfer to a platter and serve warm or at room temperature.

Aubergine et tomates au gratin

Eggplant tomato tart

Mansonville chef Denis Mareuge invented this lunch or supper dish for vegetarian customers at his restaurant, Boulangerie Owl's Bread. He also likes to serve it with Italian cold cuts, grilled lamb, or veal cutlets with lemon. If the tomatoes lack flavour, which can happen when summer sun is scarce, the herbs and cheese will conceal the fact, says the chef.

Serves 4

1 large eggplant, cut in half lengthwise, then crosswise into 1/2-inch (1 cm) slices
Olive oil, for brushing
Salt and freshly ground pepper
1 clove garlic, chopped
2 cups (500 mL) peeled, seeded, and chopped Roma tomatoes
2 tablespoons (30 mL) herbes de Provence (or 1 tablespoon/15 mL each chopped fresh thyme and rosemary)
1/2 cup (125 mL) grated Parmesan cheese

✤ Preheat the broiler.
✤ Brush eggplant slices with oil and set on a baking sheet. Broil close to the heat, without flipping, just until eggplant is golden.
✤ Preheat the oven to 350°F (180°C).
✤ Transfer eggplant to a baking pan just large enough to hold all the slices in a single layer. Sprinkle with salt, pepper, and garlic. Cover evenly with tomatoes. Sprinkle with herbes de Provence and bake for 15 minutes.
✤ Remove from the oven and drain off liquid in the pan with a baster. Sprinkle cheese over tomatoes and broil under a preheated broiler just until the cheese is melted and lightly browned.

Salade aux framboises

RASPBERRY SALAD

Laval chef and caterer Franca Mazza is of Italian background, and dedicated to using fresh food in its season. She likes to keep her recipes simple but distinctive. Her salad combining fruit and vegetables accents both with a slightly sweet-and-sour dressing.

SERVES 4

4 cups (1 L) baby lettuce greens (5 ounces/150 g)

1 red onion, minced

1 cup (250 mL) fresh raspberries (8 ounces/250 g)

4 tablespoons (60 mL) raspberry vinegar

2 tablespoons (30 mL) sunflower oil

1 tablespoon (15 mL) honey or maple syrup

Sea salt or coarse salt and freshly ground pepper

Fresh mint leaves

✦ Place greens in salad bowl and add onion and raspberries, turning gently to mix. In a measuring cup, combine vinegar, oil, and honey. Pour over salad. Gently toss to mix. Season with salt and pepper to taste. Trim with mint leaves and serve.

Maïs sucré au coriandre et à la feta

CREAMED CORN WITH CORIANDER AND FETA

Nothing beats fresh corn on the cob when corn is in season. Americans, with their longer corn season, are good sources of variations on this vegetable, says caterer Jane Livingston of Knowlton. She remembers finding this recipe in a Florida magazine and adapting it. She likes to serve this dish with caramelized chipotle chicken or barbecued ribs or steaks, and a tossed green salad. It could be made with frozen corn kernels, but she warns it won't have the same delicate sweet taste. And, she says, sheep's milk feta cheese gives the best effect because it is lighter in taste.

SERVES 4

3 tablespoons (45 mL) unsalted butter

1 1/2 cups (375 mL) chopped green onions

12 cobs corn, kernels removed, or 1 package (26 ounces/750 g) frozen corn kernels

1/2 teaspoon (2 mL) each salt and freshly ground pepper

2/3 cup (150 mL) whipping cream

2 teaspoons (10 mL) cornstarch

1 large clove garlic

6 ounces (180 g) feta cheese (goat's, cow's, or sheep's milk), crumbled

1 cup (250 mL) fresh coriander sprigs, chopped

✦ In a deep, 12-inch (30 cm) frying pan, melt butter over medium heat and cook green onions until softened, about 5 minutes. Add corn, salt, and pepper. Cook, stirring occasionally, for 5 minutes.

✦ In a small bowl, thoroughly combine cream and cornstarch. Add mixture to corn mixture and simmer, stirring constantly, until slightly thickened, about 5 minutes.

✦ Place 1½ cups (375 mL) of the corn mixture in a blender, add garlic, and blend until smooth. Return mixture to the pan and cook, stirring constantly, until heated through. Transfer to a large serving dish, sprinkle with feta and coriander, and serve.

Marinade de maïs épicé

PICKLED SPICED CORN

When Quebec's corn crop is in full season in mid-summer and the kernels have their fullest flavour, this is the time to preserve some of the pleasure of this sweet and crunchy vegetable to enjoy later in the year. Michelle Gélinas, a Montreal food specialist, was inspired by American-style corn relish and experimented with several recipes before coming up with this one. It contains a lively blend of seasonings and chopped red bell peppers, which give colour.

MAKES 15 JARS (1 CUP/250 ML EACH)

15 1-cup (250 mL) preserving jars

8 cups (2 L) fresh corn kernels, about 16 medium cobs (or frozen corn kernels)

2 cups (500 mL) cider vinegar

1 1/2 cups (375 mL) granulated sugar

2 large onions, finely chopped

4 stalks celery, coarsely chopped

4 cups (1 L) peeled and coarsely chopped red bell peppers

3 tablespoons (45 mL) yellow mustard seeds

1 tablespoon (15 mL) salt

1 tablespoon (15 mL) celery seeds

1 tablespoon (15 mL) ground turmeric

1 teaspoon (5 mL) sambal oelek, or to taste

Freshly ground pepper

1 cup (250 mL) water

✦ To sterilize jars, place them in a large pot, preferably a preserving kettle, and cover with water. Heat to 180°F (82°C). Turn off heat, cover the pot, and let stand until corn is ready to jar. Place the lids in a small saucepan, cover with water, and heat to 180°F (82°C), then remove pan from heat. Wash the metal rings; it is not necessary to sterilize them.

✦ Cook corn kernels in boiling water just until tender (if using frozen corn, thaw it but don't cook it). Drain.

✦ In a large, heavy pot, combine vinegar and sugar. Bring to a boil over medium-high heat, stirring to dissolve sugar. Add corn, onions, celery, and bell peppers. Bring to a boil, stirring often.

✦ Stir in mustard seeds, salt, celery seeds, turmeric, sambal oelek, pepper, and water. Simmer mixture, covered, over low heat for 15 minutes.

✦ Using tongs, remove jars from hot water. Fill each jar with corn mixture, leaving a ½-inch (1 cm) space at the top. Insert a clean knife in mixture to release air bubbles. Clean the rims of the jars with a damp paper towel. Add the heated lids and screw on the metal rings without forcing them. Place the jars on a rack in a large pot of water deep enough to cover them by 1 inch (2.5 cm) and set over medium-high heat. Bring the water to a boil and boil the jars for 15 minutes.

✦ Using tongs, remove jars from water and set on a rack to cool for 24 hours.

✦ If properly sealed, disc part of lids will be concave, indicating a vacuum seal. Jars with lids that do not curve down after boiling should be refrigerated once cool and used within 1 month. Properly sealed, the jars can be stored in a cool, dark place for up to 1 year.

Peppers

Coloured bell peppers—the term "coloured" is used for any colour but the basic green—must remain on their plants an extra two weeks to ripen, which is a reason they are usually priced higher than their green counterparts. Red, yellow, and white bell peppers are the sweetest, so are best appreciated raw in a salad or on a crudité platter. Purple and black peppers, which seem to taste the most like green ones, should definitely be used raw because they turn green when cooked and the extra money you spent on them is lost.

Most of Canada's peppers come from Ontario, where long, hot summers allow more than three times the Quebec production. But Quebec produce suppliers maintain that Quebec peppers have thicker walls and therefore offer more crunch and hold up better in cooking. They're easy to spot when they come to market each autumn because they are usually shaped irregularly, in contrast to the symmetrical peppers produced in greenhouses in Ontario, Mexico, and Holland.

Gérard Mathar

When Montreal chef Derek Dammann opens a box of wild foods fresh off a bus from the Gaspé, he often needs an introduction to the foraged products within. Later that day, his customers at Maison Publique, a pub and restaurant in Montreal's Plateau neighbourhood, will find the bounty of a remote coastal forest on their plates, whether it's as a snack, decoration for a salad, ingredient in a meat sauce, or flavouring for an omelette or quiche.

A fresh box of mushrooms, plus wild plants, flowers, herbs, and fruit, comes once a week, from the time of summer's first chanterelles and lobster mushrooms until the first frost. Tender products are replaced in cold weather by dehydrated mushrooms. The delicacies come from Gaspésie Sauvage Produits Forestiers near Douglastown, the boxes filled and dispatched by transplanted Belgian mushroom forager Gérard Mathar. Gérard never knows, day to day, what he'll find when foraging in his woods.

"There will be weeks when I'll look in the box and think, 'Those look scary,'" Derek says, remembering mushrooms that were bright orange and red, with what he calls "an Alice-in-Wonderland look." They turned out to be the obelisk variety, and delicious after the chef had followed Gérard's directions to blanch them three times in boiling water before cooking. Another time, the fungi had been harvested high in up in trees and were as black as charcoal. They turned out to be chaga mushrooms.

Alongside the mushrooms come wild fruits such as highbush cranberries and sea buckthorn. The latter is picked in winter when the fruit is frozen. Wild vegetables include fresh seaweed and sea lettuce. "Gérard goes out into the ocean chest-deep, reaches underwater, and pulls the sea lettuce, covered in barnacles, off rocks, and that water is cold," Derek says. Fried in hot oil "until crisp like a chip" and then trimmed with toasted sesame seeds, salt, and sugar, the sea lettuce "tastes like white truffles," says the chef.

Everything Gérard sends is guaranteed safe, for this forager is experienced at how to select approximately 80 edible varieties of "champis," as he nicknames champignons. Some poke up near tree trunks, others nestle under fallen leaves or are half-buried in the rich soil in what he calls "a symbiotic relationship with nature."

Spotting spruce trees, Gérard will expect to find porcini mushrooms. Near poplars, he anticipates morels. Close to a birch grove, the mushrooms are more likely to be boletes, a variety so delicate he often dries them. "You can even make ice cream with boletes," he says, describing a favourite mixture of these mushrooms with caramel, dark chocolate, and dried fruit or chestnuts.

He recommends generally cooking mushrooms in grapeseed oil. "It improves the mushroom taste," he says. But some varieties, such as lobster mushrooms, go well with seafood and are

Gérard Mathar forages for wild mushrooms near Douglastown in the Gaspé.

best sautéed in butter. Others, such as chanterelles, are good cooked in hazelnut oil with garlic and served with whitefish or chicken. "Chanterelles are called the chicken of the woods," Gérard says.

He has trained upwards of 100 foragers, who scavenge the woods of Quebec's east coast, south into the Atlantic provinces, in the Gatineau hills north of Ottawa, and as far away as British Columbia. They know to look in the woods because, as Gérard explains, "everywhere you have trees you have mushrooms."

Pouding pour chômeurs modernes

ECONOMY PUDDING

Danny St-Pierre, chef-owner of Auguste and Chez Augustine, in Sherbrooke, likes to liven up old Quebec recipes. He adds a layer of fresh raspberries to pouding chômeur, *the economical dessert named for the unemployed—poor man's pudding. The pudding, a cake batter and sweet sauce baked together, is believed to date back to Britain's steamed or treacle puddings. In the mid-19th century, when English-speaking workers joined French Quebecers in the factories of Montreal, recipes were shared. Years ago, maple sugar, now a luxury ingredient, was used. Later, molasses or brown sugar became the sweetener. Whatever the variation, this old-time dish remains one of the most popular desserts in Quebec.*

SERVES 4

1 cup + 1 tablespoon (265 mL) maple syrup
1 cup + 1 tablespoon (265 mL) whipping cream
1/4 cup (60 mL) butter, softened
1/4 cup (60 mL) granulated sugar
1 egg
1 cup (250 mL) all-purpose flour
1 teaspoon (5 mL) baking powder
Pinch salt
1/4 cup (60 mL) whole milk
1 cup (250 mL) fresh raspberries (6 ounces/180 g) (optional)

✤ Preheat the oven to 400°F (200°C). Butter an 8-inch (20 cm) square pan.
✤ In a medium, heavy saucepan, combine maple syrup and cream and bring to a boil over medium-high heat, being careful mixture does not boil over. Reduce heat to medium and simmer for 3 to 4 minutes, then remove from heat.
✤ In a mixing bowl, blend butter and sugar together with a hand-held electric mixer. Beat in egg and continue beating until mixture is light and fluffy, about 2 minutes.
✤ In another mixing bowl, use a fork to stir flour with baking powder and salt. Add ½ cup (125 mL) of the dry ingredients to the butter mixture, using a wire whisk to blend. Whisk in milk, then whisk in remaining dry ingredients.
✤ Arrange raspberries (if using) evenly on the bottom of the prepared pan. Pour batter into the pan, then pour in maple mixture. Bake for 30 minutes or until golden brown.

The Montreal Melon

An air of mystery surrounds this heritage fruit, once prized at Montreal's best restaurants and considered a delicacy at the Plaza and Waldorf Astoria Hotels in New York. The Montreal melon is now a challenge to the few amateur gardeners who try to produce it in the five months it requires from seed to maturity. Grown and enjoyed in 19th-century Montreal, it's a cousin of the Green Nutmeg melon and has made it onto the Ark of Taste of Canada's SlowFood movement, even though no commercial grower produces it and there are few sources for its seeds.

This melon is a giant, weighing from 8 or 9 pounds (3.5 to 4 kg) to as much as 24 pounds (10 kg). It has a soccer ball or torpedo shape, and a thin, ribbed peel, green flesh, and—as old-timers remember—a fine, sweet taste. It was so delicate that growers of the 1880s, such as the Décarie farming family of the Notre-Dame-de-Grâce district of Montreal, would put these melons on the train for New York strapped into large, woven baskets so they wouldn't bruise on the trip.

The seeds for this melon were once listed in the Burpee seed company's catalogue but were discontinued after World War II. They had disappeared until 1996, when Mark Abley, a reporter at *The Gazette* in Montreal, tracked them down at the U.S. agriculture department's National Seed Storage Lab in Ames, Iowa. Obtaining a small packet of seeds, he persuaded an organic market gardener to grow the melons. The gardener, Ken Taylor of Île Perrot, west of Montreal, produced a random assortment of melons from the seeds. He then selected the melons that resembled historic descriptions, grew some more, and ended up, so he thinks, with the Montreal melon so celebrated a century ago.

Another part of Quebec's melon history is the Oka melon, developed when Trappist monks at the Oka monastery west of Montreal crossed a Montreal melon with a banana melon, and came up with a large variety with orange flesh. It's also prized and rare.

Cantaloup /
$2.00 Melon d'eau jaune
ch.
du Québec

Tarte aux framboises

Glazed raspberry tart

Spending our summers near lavish patches of wild raspberries in southern Ontario, we children were taught early on to combine country walks with serious raspberry picking. Mum liked the fruit plain, with very little sugar and thick cream from a neighbour's cows. But she also made raspberry desserts, jam, and jelly. This family recipe plays up the full taste of the fruit with the help of red currant jelly.

SERVES 6 TO 8

Pastry for single-crust, 9-inch (23 cm) pie (page 336) (or ready-made thawed pie shell)
1 cup (250 mL) or 1 jar (8 ounces/250 g) red currant jelly
2 cups (500 mL) fresh raspberries

✦ Place the oven rack in the lowest position, then place a pizza stone or a cast-iron frying pan set upside down on it. Preheat the oven to 375°F (190°C).

✦ Roll out pastry on a floured surface to fit a 9-inch (23 cm) pie pan. Fit it into the pan and crimp the edges. Do not prick the bottom with a fork. Set the pie pan on pizza stone and bake shell for 10 to 12 minutes, until pastry is crisp and golden brown. Transfer to a rack to cool.

✦ In a small saucepan, melt ⅓ cup (75 mL) of the red currant jelly. Using a pastry brush, brush pastry shell on bottom and sides with melted jelly. Arrange raspberries in shell.

✦ Melt remaining jelly and, using the pastry brush, paint berries with jelly. Let stand just until set, then serve right away.

Gelée de framboises aux bleuets

RASPBERRY JELLY WITH FRESH BLUEBERRIES AND RASPBERRIES

Chef Marcel Bouchard serves this crimson fruit jelly on the breakfast buffet at his inn, Auberge des 21, in La Baie, in the Saguenay region. But it could just as well be served as a dessert with a generous dollop of plain yogurt, or cut in cubes and layered into parfait glasses with yogurt. Late-season raspberries, crossbred by Quebec fruit scientists, have extended the raspberry season to the end of September.

SERVES 4 TO 6

1 package (20 ounces/600 g) frozen raspberries
1 package (1/4 ounce/7 g) gelatin (for a firmer jelly, use 2 packages)
1/4 cup (60 mL) granulated sugar
1 cup (250 mL) fresh blueberries (6 ounces/180 g)
1 cup (250 mL) fresh raspberries (6 ounces/180 g)
Fresh raspberries for serving
Plain yogurt, for serving

+ Thaw frozen raspberries in the refrigerator (not at room temperature). Strain and measure juice, reserving fruit.
+ Sprinkle gelatin over the raspberry juice. Let stand for 5 minutes. Meanwhile, pour the same amount of water as you have juice into a saucepan, add sugar, and bring to a boil. Add juice mixture, stirring to dissolve gelatin.
+ Mix together thawed raspberries and fresh blueberries, add juice mixture, and refrigerate, stirring occasionally so fruit is distributed in juice as mixture gels.
+ Serve with fresh raspberries and a dollop of plain yogurt.

Blueberries, the Easy Way

Here's a simple way to serve blueberries. Take a box of blueberries, rinse and dry the fruit, divide into serving bowls, drizzle generously with maple syrup, and top with thick cream or plain yogurt, plus a little maple sugar or brown sugar. The idea comes from Chef Marcel Bouchard, who owns Auberge des 21 in La Baie, an inn and spa on a fjord of the Saguenay River in northern Quebec.

Baker Jacinthe Ouellet poses with blueberry folk art on her lawn at Dolbeau-Mistassini.

Tarte aux mûres

BLACKBERRY PIE

Blackberries grow wild in Brome County, a rural Eastern Townships region where the fruit ripens quietly on the edges of fields and woods. It takes a sharp eye to find them, for the bushes look quite like raspberry canes and hide their black harvest well. Blackberry pie is a category in the annual baking contest held in conjunction with Brome Fair each Labour Day weekend in the village of Brome. Diane Croghan of nearby Foster has made a reputation for herself and also for her son and daughter as expert pie bakers, often winning prizes for their fruit pies. Diane knows where to go to harvest this precious fruit, as well as how to make it into a succulent summer pie. Her other prize-winning pies are made with blueberries, raspberries, and black raspberries.

SERVES 6 TO 8

Pastry for double-crust, 9-inch (23 cm) pie (page 336)
1 cup (250 mL) granulated sugar
4 tablespoons (60 mL) all-purpose flour
4 cups (1 L) fresh blackberries
1 tablespoon (15 mL) cold butter, cut in pea-size pieces
1 tablespoon (15 mL) fresh lemon juice

✤ Place the oven rack in the lowest position, then place a cast-iron frying pan upside down, or a pizza stone, on it. Preheat the oven to 400°F (200°C). Butter an 8- or 9-inch (20 or 23 cm) pie pan.
✤ Roll out half the pastry on a floured surface and fit it into the pan.
✤ In a mixing bowl, stir sugar and flour together. Place half the blackberries in pie shell and sprinkle with half the flour mixture. Add remaining blackberries and sprinkle with remaining flour mixture.
✤ Dot with butter and sprinkle with lemon juice. Roll out remaining pastry and place over berries. Crimp pastry at the edges to seal, then cut 3 small steam vents in crust.
✤ Place pie on top of the frying pan in the oven. Immediately reduce the oven temperature to 350°F (180°C) and bake pie for 45 minutes to 1 hour, until pastry is crisp and golden brown.
✤ Let cool on a rack. Serve warm or at room temperature.

Tarte à la rhubarbe et à l'orange

RHUBARB ORANGE PIE

Eastern Townships pie baker Diane Croghan invented this pie some years ago when she was running a restaurant in Knowlton. By chance, Omega Medina, at the time a CBC radio reporter, dropped in, enjoyed the pie, and mentioned it on the air. A star was born, and the pie became a regular on the menu.

SERVES 6 TO 8

Pastry for double-crust, 9-inch (23 cm) pie (page 336)

4 cups (1 L) fresh rhubarb cut in 1/2- to 1-inch (1 to 2.5 cm) pieces

3 to 5 orange segments, cut in small pieces

2 teaspoons (10 mL) grated orange peel

1 1/4 cups (310 mL) granulated sugar

1/2 cup (125 mL) all-purpose flour

1 tablespoon (15 mL) cold butter, cut in pea-size pieces

1 tablespoon (15 mL) fresh lemon juice

+ Place the oven rack in the lowest position, then set a cast-iron frying pan upside down, or a pizza stone, on it. Preheat the oven to 400°F (200°C). Butter a 9-inch (23 cm) pie pan.

+ Roll out half the pastry on a floured surface and fit it into the pan. Roll out remaining pastry for the top crust.

+ In a mixing bowl, mix together rhubarb, orange segments, and orange peel.

+ In another bowl, combine sugar and flour. Sprinkle fruit mixture with half the sugar mixture, tossing to coat fruit well.

+ Spoon fruit into pie shell and sprinkle with remaining sugar mixture. Dot with butter and sprinkle with lemon juice. Cover with top crust and crimp pastry at the edges to seal. Cut small steam vents in crust.

+ Place pie on the cast-iron pan. Immediately reduce the oven temperature to 350°F (180°C) and bake pie for 45 to 50 minutes, until pastry is crisp and golden brown.

+ Let cool on a rack. Serve warm or at room temperature.

Note
If using frozen rhubarb, thaw it only enough so you can separate the pieces.

It took about 4,000 plants a year and several years of test-ing to breed the Quebec strawberries that now ripen beyond the origi-nal June-July season right through into October. Food scientists from McGill University and the federal agriculture department joined with enlightened growers, working to create varieties they liked. Only then did they seek patents, and encourage growers to start planting the new strawberries, launch them on the market, and persuade the public to buy them.

Federal fruit breeder Shahrokh Khanizadeh led the effort to develop what's usually dubbed Quebec's "autumn" strawberry. Over the years, he has developed nearly a dozen varieties. Some, such as the Chambly, because it resists bruising; others, including the bigger, mid-July variety called Oka and hardy mid-season and late-season varieties Saint-Pierre, Harmonie, L'Acadie, Clé des Champs, Yamaska, and Orléans, because they ripen throughout August and September. The latest to appear is a July strawberry called Variété d'été. These berries were all developed by traditional crossbreeding methods. The result has been a non-stop supply of sweet and juicy fruit that comes to market through August and Sep-tember from huge strawberry farms, most of them on Île d'Orléans, near Quebec City, and in Ste-Anne-des-Plaines, northeast of Montreal.

Scientists call these strawberries "day-neutral," and they have been such a commercial success that Quebec strawberry production has increased to the point that only California and Florida grow more of this popular fruit.

Paralleling strawberry inventions are new varieties of raspberries, which have been given the same extended season. Shahrokh's favourite, popular with Île d'Orléans growers, is his big, firm, late-season raspberry called the Jeanne d'Orléans, named for Jeanne Delisle, a pioneer of small-fruit cultivation on Île d'Orléans. Top-quality local raspberries are now available from early July through September.

Louis Gauthier, fruit grower and researcher, at L'Authentique Les Fraises de l'Île d'Orléans.

Gâteau aux fraises

STRAWBERRY-SEASON CAKE

The Eastern Townships was the source of this recipe, says Micheline Mongrain-Dontigny of St-Irénée, in Charlevoix. She has spent years researching Quebec's traditional and regional specialties and publishing collections of the recipes. Fresh strawberries are a must for this cake, she says. Although she does freeze the fruit at its peak for later use in strawberry puddings and sauces, she never uses her frozen strawberries for this cake, because, when thawed, the fruit contains too much liquid. Thanks to Quebec fruit scientists, fresh strawberries have been crossbred to be available from June through September.

SERVES 8

Topping
1/2 cup (125 mL) graham cracker crumbs
1/2 cup (125 mL) granulated sugar
1/4 cup (60 mL) shredded unsweetened coconut
1/3 cup (75 mL) cold butter, diced

Cake
1 1/2 cups (375 mL) all-purpose flour
1/4 cup (60 mL) granulated sugar
1 tablespoon (15 mL) baking powder
1/2 teaspoon (2 mL) salt
2 eggs
1/2 cup (125 mL) whole milk
4 tablespoons (60 mL) melted butter
2 cups (500 mL) thickly sliced fresh strawberries

+ Place the oven rack in the centre position. Preheat the oven to 375°F (190°C). Butter an 8- or 9-inch (20 or 23 cm) square cake pan.

For topping:

+ In a mixing bowl, combine graham cracker crumbs, sugar, and coconut.
+ Sprinkle with diced butter and blend in with a pastry blender. Alternatively, pulse in a food processor, then return to bowl.

For cake:

+ In another bowl, use a fork to blend flour with sugar, baking powder, and salt. Break eggs into a measuring cup, add milk and melted butter, and whisk with a fork.
+ Pour egg mixture into dry ingredients and beat well. Pour batter into the prepared cake pan. Cover batter with half the strawberries, then sprinkle with half the topping. Repeat with remaining strawberries and topping.
+ Bake for 30 minutes or just until a cake tester inserted in the centre comes out clean. Serve warm or cooled from the pan.

Gâteau aux bleuets

BLUEBERRY—SOUR CREAM TORTE

When strawberries are at their best, Jane Livingston of Knowlton makes a variation of this recipe by replacing the blueberries with 4 cups (1 L) strawberries, rinsed and hulled, for a strawberry torte.

SERVES 10 TO 12

Crust
3/4 cup (175 mL) butter, softened
1/4 cup (60 mL) granulated sugar
2 egg yolks
2 cups (500 mL) all-purpose flour
1 teaspoon (5 mL) baking powder
1/2 teaspoon (2 mL) salt

Topping
2 egg yolks, slightly beaten
2 cups (500 mL) sour cream
1/2 cup (125 mL) granulated sugar
1 teaspoon (5 mL) vanilla extract

Filling
4 cups (1 L) fresh blueberries
1/2 cup (125 mL) granulated sugar
1/4 cup (60 mL) quick-cooking tapioca (instant or minute)
1/2 teaspoon (2 mL) finely grated lemon peel
1/2 teaspoon (2 mL) ground cinnamon
Pinch ground nutmeg

For crust:
+ Preheat the oven to 400°F (200°C). Line a 9-inch (23 cm) springform pan with parchment paper.
+ In a mixing bowl using a hand-held electric mixer, beat butter until creamy. Gradually beat in sugar, then beat in egg yolks until mixture is fluffy. In another bowl, use a fork to blend flour with baking powder and salt. Gradually beat dry ingredients into butter mixture.
+ Press 2 cups (500 mL) of the crust mixture onto the bottom of the prepared springform pan. Bake for 10 minutes. Remove from oven and reduce the oven temperature to 350°F (180°C). Press remaining crust mixture 1½ inches (4 cm) up the sides of the pan.

For filling:
+ In a medium saucepan, mix together blueberries, sugar, tapioca, lemon peel, cinnamon, and nutmeg. Let stand for 15 minutes. Then cook over medium heat, stirring occasionally, until bubbling. Spoon into crust in the springform pan.

For topping:
+ In a small bowl, blend beaten egg yolks with sour cream, sugar, and vanilla. Spoon over blueberry filling.
+ Bake cake at 350°F (180°C) for 45 minutes or until firm. Cool and refrigerate to chill well before serving. Torte will keep in the refrigerator for up to 2 days.

Montreal has its own fast foods, and each has a legendary past. Proof of their popularity lies in their many imitations around town and beyond. Here are the favourite four, with suggested sources.

Smoked meat sandwich

Schwartz's, also called Charcuterie Hébraïque de Montréal (Montreal Hebrew Delicatessen), at 3895 St-Laurent Boulevard, is a joint in the full sense of the word, a modest, well-worn little diner on the Main, as St-Laurent Boulevard is known. Patrons often line up along the street, waiting for a seat to enjoy tender, spiced brisket of beef that's been cured and smoked the same way since 1928. If you peer over the sandwich counter, you'll see slabs of blackened, spice-coated Alberta beef that's still processed just as Reuben Schwartz, the Romanian Jew who founded the place, decreed. This place insists on individual hand-slicing of the meat and takes orders for four grades: lean, medium, medium-fat, and fat. I recommend the medium-fat. Trained slicers will cut the brisket across the grain of the meat, their eye assessing the percentage of fat. "If you slice the wrong way, your meat will be stringy," says Jason Lebrun, who has been on the job for more than a decade. Yellow mustard is optional with your sandwich, typically ordered with french fries, a dill pickle, and the traditional black cherry soda. Smoked meat sandwiches sell all over Quebec, but most can't compare to Schwartz's because their meat, say insiders, is pumped with a watery cure rather than dry-cured, as Schwartz's is. The spicing is secret; I once gained access to the smoking room, a dark, redolent lair of a place, and learned that the briskets spend 10 to 14 days dry-curing in barrels under a coating of seasonings before being smoked for six to seven hours. Those seasonings? "More than four spices" is as close as the restaurant will reveal.

Poutine

La Banquise, 994 Rachel Street East, is a one-time ice cream shop that now specializes in a celebrated Quebec snack. It's a combination of hot french fries, fresh cheddar cheese curds, and hot barbecue sauce or chicken gravy. This succulent mixture should be served in a dish (china or Styrofoam) deep enough to encourage the cheese to melt into fondue-like strands from the heat of the potatoes and sauce. Shun any place that serves poutine on a flat plate, is my advice. Poutine began at rural fast-food stands in the region southeast of Montreal in the late 1950s. As the story goes, the proprietor served french fries and offered bowls of fresh cheese curds on his counter. The patrons started combining the two, and then asked the proprietor for some of the gravy simmering on the stove for his hot chicken sandwiches. A popular dish was created. It's now served all over Quebec and beyond, and chefs, even in top restaurants, will offer their version of poutine, including a duck foie gras variation.

Steamie

Montreal Pool Room, a century-old institution at 1217 St-Laurent Boulevard, formerly across the street, is a spotlessly clean diner that long ago cancelled its billiard tables. Specializing in hot dogs, either steamed (the celebrated "steamie" wiener with steamed bun) or toasted (called a "toasté," a grilled hot dog with a toasted bun), the place offers the popular coleslaw topping, plus all the usual condiments—yellow mustard, sweet relish, and ketchup. This easy and economical menu is usually completed with a little brown paper bag of french fries, and these are Quebec-style, soft and moist, according to specialists, rather than the crisper so-called international fries. The red-shirted servers, who do all the cooking at the long counter, appear to be veterans. One has been there since Mayor Jean Drapeau, who ruled Montreal for decades until 1986, would send over for steamies from his office at 3 a.m.

Bagels

In the Mile End district of central Montreal are two bagel bakeries that vie for first place in bagel popularity. Each hand-rolls the dough, dips the uncooked bagels in honey-flavoured water, then bakes them in wood-burning ovens. Their histories are linked, their competition courteous, their product hailed as first-rate. Some customers favour the Original Fairmount Bagel Bakery, at 74 Fairmount Avenue West, which dates to 1919, when Isadore Schlafman, a Jew from Kiev, in Ukraine, opened the Montreal Bagel Bakery. He made the bagels in a shack on a lane behind St-Laurent Boulevard and transported them in a wheelbarrow to a vending stand on the street. Other bagel shoppers patronize St-Viateur Bagel, headquartered at 263 St-Viateur Street West, where the tender rings of dough come in three versions: plain, with poppy seeds, or with sesame seeds. In contrast, Fairmount makes 19 varieties, including flaxseed, chocolate chip, blueberry, and a miniature size. St-Viateur's founder was Myer Lewkowicz, born near Cracow, Poland, and a survivor of the Buchenwald concentration camp. He immigrated in 1953 and worked at Schlafman's bakery before setting up his own shop in 1957. Descendants and long-time bagel-making staff are part of each bakery. Both produce the crisp-tender, slightly chewy rings of lightly sweetened yeast dough, baking them in the original Eastern European fashion. St-Viateur's current owner, Joe Morena, who started working at the bakery at age 15 and has been at it for half a century, doesn't mind comparisons with Fairmount, since the two specialize in the same product. "A good day," he once said, "is when they taste the same from either place."

D'ALLADIN
3.00 CH
2/5.00

BUTTERCUP
3.00 CH
2/5.00

Autumn

Robert Beauregard of Rougemont sells a variety
of squash at Jean-Talon Market

FRESH EGGS

RUNAWAY CREEK FARM
ORGANIC PRODUCE TODAY

Each autumn, when squash ripens in Quebec fields and loads down the stalls in farmers' markets, I think of the squash once grown by Canada's First Nations. Squash is one of the Three Sisters, a trio of Quebec's original vegetables introduced to 17th-century French explorers by the Iroquois. The other two—corn and beans—were grown together with squash in a system that's been compared to modern companion planting.

First, the corn was started and then earth mounded up around its shoots. Next, beans were added so they could climb the cornstalks as well as attract and share nitrogen. Finally, squash was planted so the vines would wind around the mounds, keeping the earth moist under their big leaves and also controlling the weeds.

First Nations cooks prepare the Three Sisters together and separately. They like to combine the trio in a salad, and to make succotash with the corn and beans. Cornbread is popular, and soups of either corn or squash are favourites with Mohawks, one of the six-nation Iroquois League, and also, as it turns out, with Quebec chefs (see pages 123, 226, and 311). The best way to enjoy a squash, says Mohawk cultural researcher Alexis Shackleton, is also my favourite way—cut open, drizzled with maple syrup, and baked.

Alexis, who is director of social development on the Kahnawake Mohawk Territory, south of Montreal, calls the Three Sisters "part of our Creation story." First Nations artists like to depict the three vegetables together. Historically, the corn should be white corn, says Mohawk soapstone sculptor Steve McComber, who likes to group the Three Sisters in his sculptures.

The bounty coming from Quebec farms is overwhelming in autumn, and the best place to see it is in the open-air markets and at country fairs. The markets dazzle the eye and overload the shopping bag, the big public markets in Montreal and Quebec City in particular, but also small markets in villages and towns all over Quebec.

The artistry of displaying produce is celebrated at Brome Fair, Quebec's oldest farm fair. It has taken place annually in the tiny village of Brome since 1856. Vegetable farmers in this area of the Eastern Townships spend hours arranging an assortment of their tomatoes, peppers, cabbage, zucchini, onions, and cantaloupe.

Peppers do the best job of colouring market stands. I alternate pepper shopping at Jean-Talon Market between the Birri brothers, Italian-Canadian grower-vendors with property in Laval and Montreal's South Shore, and Claude Desnoyers and Louisa Lachance, who farm at St-Damase, south of Mont-real. Both offer every variety, shape, and colour of pepper. Louisa credits the relatively new popularity of spicy cuisines—Mexican, Middle Eastern, West Indian, and South American—with the new demand for hot peppers.

Canada's biggest duck producer, Brome Lake Ducks, celebrates autumn with an annual duck festival in Knowlton, its headquarters for growing plump Peking ducks. Festival visitors enjoy a "hot duck," the wiener that replaces the hot dog. Restaurants throughout the area vary their duck recipes for pâté, breast, or confit (the leg cooked in duck fat), often using Quebec wines and ciders from the Eastern Townships wine country in the area around Dunham to accent this rich-tasting bird.

Duck is available whole or cut up and sells widely in supermarkets. Chefs vote for fancier ducks—Muscovy and others—which cost much more and are leaner. But home cooks appreciate the Peking duck's fat when cooking the meat—you can put a duck breast skin side down, right on the barbecue or in a hot frying pan, and its own fat will prevent it from drying out. When roasting, you prick the skin, drain off the fat as the bird cooks, and then use that fat to make the best french fries. The fat is so popular that the company sells it in containers.

My favourite Quebec harvests are cranberries and apples. During September and October, the big apple-growing areas around Montreal are thronged with children, transported in their yellow school buses for a day in the country. The young pickers join hired harvesters in orchards where the apples hang so low off the trees, there's no need for ladders. Walking through a McIntosh apple orchard in St-Joseph-du-Lac, northwest of Montreal, one sunny October day, I could hear four languages (English, French, Italian, and Spanish) being spoken up in the trees, the conversationalists descending from time to time to dump their fresh pickings into the big wooden containers used by growers.

A cranberry bog, flooded for harvesting, becomes a lake of red berries. Watching a harvest machine collect the fruit is mesmerizing; the process is pictured on page 376.

First Courses

Leeks on Toast

Creamed Mushrooms on Toast

Tomato Tarts with Maple Syrup

Beet Salad with Orange and Basil Dressing

Warm Endive, Orange, and Scallop salad

My Favourite Zucchini Soup

Carrot Ginger Soup

Cream of Cauliflower Soup

Main Courses

Pasta with Cherry Tomatoes

Sea Bass and Clams on a Bed of Cauliflower and Potatoes

Salmon Glazed with Maple and Bourbon

Salt Cod, Potato, and Onion Casserole

Sweetbreads with Mushroom Cream Sauce

Braised Lamb Shanks with Poblano Peppers and Pinto Beans

Charlevoix-Style Rabbit with Tarragon Sauce

Beef Carbonnade with Rutabaga, Caramelized Onions, and Alfred le Fermier Cheese

Fresh and Healthy Shepherd's Pie

Beans with Partridge or Rock Cornish Hens

Breast of Duckling with Shallots and Balsamic Sauce

Maple Pork with Apples

Chicken with Apples

Side Dishes

Hot Pepper Paste

Creamed Swiss Chard

Roasted Vegetable Quiche

Brussels Sprouts with Bacon

Marcel's Mashed Roots with Cheese Crumb Crust

Spiced Carrot Salad

Desserts

Spiced Maple Syrup

Spiced Custard Pie

Apple Crumble Tart

Plum Upside-Down Cake

Maple Cheesecake

Rice Pudding

Canapés au beurre de poireaux

LEEKS ON TOAST

Lively, oniony, buttery, these hors d'oeuvres are a favourite with the Jutras family, proprietors of Les Cultures de Chez Nous, a huge leek farm in Ste-Brigitte-des-Saults near Drummondville, northeast of Montreal. You can bake the toasts an hour ahead, let them stand, and then reheat just until hot.

MAKES 24

1 1/2 cups (375 mL) thinly sliced leeks
1/3 cup (75 mL) butter, softened
5 teaspoons (25 mL) whole-grain mustard
2 teaspoons (10 mL) chopped fresh thyme leaves
1/2 teaspoon (2 mL) salt
Freshly ground pepper
24 thin baguette or ciabatta slices, toasted

✤ Preheat the oven to 350°F (180°C).
✤ In a mixing bowl, mix together leeks, butter, mustard, thyme, salt, and pepper.
✤ Spread toasted bread with leek mixture and arrange on a baking sheet. Bake until hot and lightly browned, 5 to 10 minutes.

THE FORGOTTEN ONION

Leeks need promotion or we ignore them. This long, white-stemmed member of the onion family is well appreciated by chefs, but less so by home cooks. In the autumn, Quebec farmers' markets offer big bunches of leeks, so many of them tied together that you need to line up your neighbours to share a bundle. One of Quebec's largest leek farms has made its vegetable easier for small families to use by washing, slicing, and packaging the leeks in various sizes of plastic bags. The cut-up leeks keep well in the refrigerator and also freeze well. The farm, called Les Cultures de Chez Nous, is family-run by Louis-Marie Jutras, his wife,

Louis-Marie Jutras and his daughter Valérie check leeks at their farm, Les Cultures de Chez Nous, at Ste-Brigitte-des-Saults.

Michelle Rajotte, and their three children. Visiting their leek fields east of Montreal, on the south shore of the St. Lawrence River, I was reminded of the delicate grey-blue look of a field of broccoli. Countless rows of leeks—six million leeks are planted each May—stood waving their stiff green leaves high in the air, promising rich flavour below the earth.

Michelle is an expert at leek cuisine. She makes a fast leek-and-potato soup by cooking sliced leeks in a little butter, adding sliced baby potatoes and chicken stock, and then simmering the mixture until the vegetables are tender. To serve, she adds cream, seasons the soup with salt and pepper, and then sprinkles a little shredded Gruyère cheese on top. She also makes an easy supper dish by cooking 6-inch (15 cm) lengths of leeks in chicken stock until tender, then rolling each in a slice of cooked ham. She then arranges the leeks in a shallow baking pan, partly covers them with a cream sauce flavoured with Dijon mustard, tops them with grated cheddar or Gruyère cheese, and bakes the dish at 350°F (180°C) for 30 minutes.

Canapés de chanterelles à la crème

CREAMED MUSHROOMS ON TOAST

When Nancy Hinton calls for wild mushrooms in a recipe, she means freshly picked in the wilderness. The chef at À la table des jardins sauvages in St-Roch-de-l'Achigan, northeast of Montreal, she has learned that mushrooms high in water content require high heat, while firm varieties with less water need longer cooking over medium-low heat and may even need added liquid. The mushroom mixture used for these toasts may also be served over hot fettuccine, with a sprinkle of freshly grated Parmesan cheese, or mixed with hot macaroni, sprinkled with grated cheese, and baked. Or use it to stuff oysters, mushrooms, or zucchini, then broil for a few minutes to brown.

SERVES 4

2 tablespoons (30 mL) olive oil

1 package (8 ounces/250 g) fresh chanterelle mushrooms, trimmed and quartered

2 shallots, finely chopped

1 tablespoon (15 mL) unsalted butter

Pinch chili powder

Pinch dried thyme

1 clove garlic, minced

1/4 cup (60 mL) dry white wine

1/2 cup (125 mL) mushroom stock, chicken stock, or vegetable stock

1/2 cup (125 mL) whipping cream

1/2 cup (125 mL) shredded Ménestrel or mild cheddar cheese (about 3 1/2 ounces/100 g)

1 egg, beaten

Salt and freshly ground pepper

Juice of 1/2 lemon or dash cider vinegar

Dash soy sauce

Dash Worcestershire sauce

1 baguette, thinly sliced

1 tomato, diced (1/2 cup/125 mL)

2 tablespoons (30 mL) finely chopped fresh herbs (chives, parsley, dill, or basil)

+ In a wide, heavy saucepan, heat oil over medium-high heat. Add mushrooms and sauté, stirring often, until they start to colour, about 5 minutes. If they are wet or release juices, keep heat at medium-high, otherwise reduce heat to medium.
+ Add shallots, butter, chili powder, and thyme and continue cooking over medium heat until mushrooms are uniformly coloured and cooked through, about 4 to 5 minutes total. Add garlic and cook for 1 minute.
+ Add wine and bring to a gentle boil, uncovered and stirring often, until it has almost evaporated. Add stock and cream and continue to cook, stirring often, until sauce thickens to desired consistency. Turn off heat. Stir in cheese and then egg. Season with salt, pepper, lemon juice, soy sauce, and Worcestershire sauce.
+ Meanwhile, preheat broiler and toast baguette slices.
+ In a cup, combine tomato and herbs. Spread mushroom mixture on baguette slices and broil for 3 to 5 minutes, just until golden. Top with tomato mixture and serve.

Notes

Wipe mushrooms with damp paper towels to clean them. If they look dirty, immerse them briefly in a large container of cold water. The dirt will sink to the bottom of the container. Then scoop them out of the water using a sieve or colander and spread out on paper towels to dry (or pat dry) before cutting and cooking.

This easy mushroom mixture can be made 1 day in advance, then covered and refrigerated. Reheat when ready to use.

MUSHROOM TIPS

Hunt mushrooms only with a trained mycologist because a few of these fungi are poisonous. Cook all wild mushrooms fully before eating, warns Chicoutimi mushroom forager Luc Godin, who harvests more than 20 varieties in the Saguenay region.

Fresh wild mushrooms are not easily available. Luc often relies on the dehydrated product, finding that it makes a satisfactory—and easy—sauce or soup. He puts dehydrated mushrooms (a 28 g/1 ounce package) in a small bowl, pours boiling water over them and lets them stand on the counter for 15 minutes. Then he drains them, and chops them coarsely. He then heats butter or oil in a pan, sautés the rehydrated mushrooms, and blends in cream and chicken stock.

Luc suggests pulverizing dried mushrooms with a grater or coffee grinder and using the powder instead of flour or bread crumbs to coat fish or seafood. Then sear the fish quickly in hot butter to give a crisp, bronze crust.

Wild mushrooms are found in the woods around Douglastown in the Gaspé.

Tarte aux tomates confites au sirop d'érable et Cru du Clocher

TOMATO TARTS WITH MAPLE SYRUP

Brother and sister Marco and Suzy Latreille, self-taught cooks, grew up in Ville-Marie, in the Abitibi-Témiscamingue region of northwestern Quebec. Their mother kept them out of the kitchen when she cooked but passed on her belief in the importance of family dining. Marco uses a week of holidays from his auto sales job to help at cooking demonstrations at the annual regional Quebec-Ontario food fair called Foire Gourmande.

SERVES 6

Pastry
1 1/3 cups (325 mL) all-purpose flour
Pinch salt
1/3 cup (75 mL) cold butter, chopped
1 egg, beaten
1 tablespoon (15 mL) ice water

Filling
8 ounces (250 g) cherry tomatoes
  (1 1/2 cups/375 mL)
Sea salt and freshly ground pepper
3 tablespoons (45 mL) maple syrup
7 ounces (200 g) shredded Cru du Clocher
  or aged cheddar cheese
Dried basil or oregano, for sprinkling
Small arugula leaves

For pastry:

+ Butter 6 aluminum foil tart shells, each 6 inches (15 cm) in diameter.
+ Combine flour and salt in a food processor. Add butter and pulse until butter is the texture of small peas. Add beaten egg and water, continuing to pulse, until pastry forms a ball. Remove from the food processor, wrap in plastic wrap, and refrigerate for 30 minutes.
+ Preheat the oven to 350°F (180°C).
+ Roll out chilled pastry on a floured surface. Cut 6 rounds of pastry, each a little larger than the diameter of the 6 tart shells. Fit pastry into the tart shells. You should have enough pastry to shape or crimp with your fingers or a fork to make a raised border. Place the tart shells on a baking sheet and bake for about 5 minutes, just until the pastry turns golden. Remove baking sheet from oven, leaving the oven on, set on a rack and cool.

For filling:

+ Cut tomatoes in half and press to remove seeds and juice. In a baking pan, arrange tomato halves cut side up. Season with salt and pepper and drizzle with maple syrup. Bake for 15 minutes.
+ Divide grated cheese among the tart shells and top with tomato halves. Return tarts to oven for 5 minutes. Remove from the oven, sprinkle with basil, and trim with arugula.

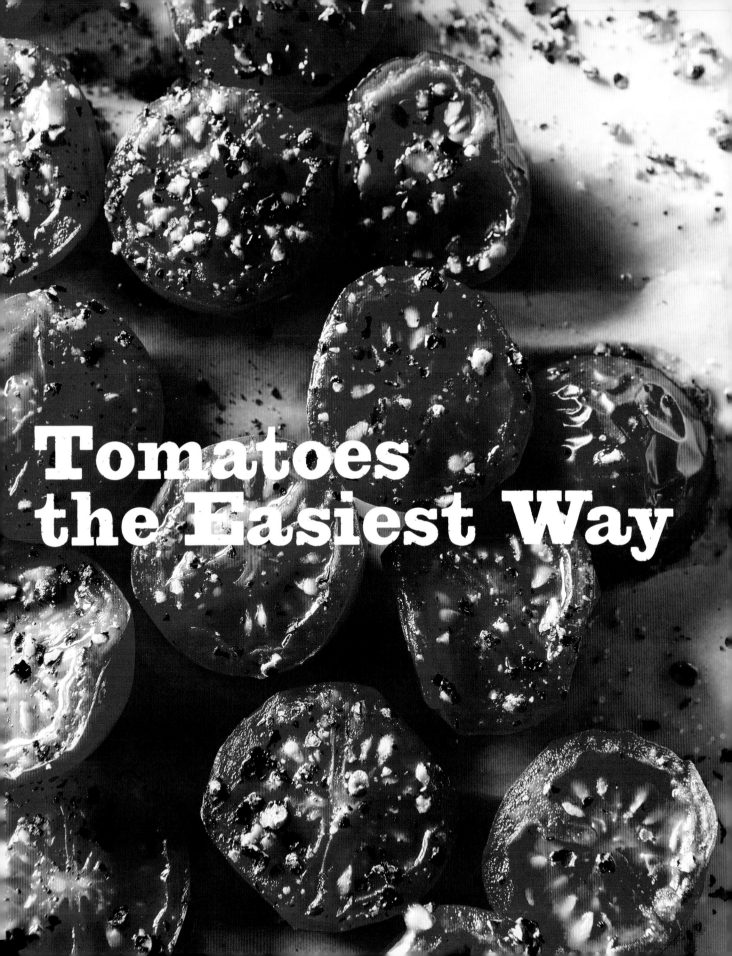

Tomatoes
the Easiest Way

A good, ripe tomato works for you if you allow it to. That's the principle behind two easy tomato sauce recipes, one from a veteran cooking teacher in Montreal's Little Italy community, the other from an heirloom tomato grower in the Eastern Townships south of Montreal.

Elena Faita, partner in Little Italy's kitchen and hardware store Quincaillerie Danté, teaches her cooking classes how to make her authentic Italian tomato sauce. First, remove tomato skins by blanching the tomatoes. This means making a small, criss-cross slash in the bottom of each tomato, then dropping it into a big pot of boiling water for from 30 seconds for small tomatoes up to two minutes for large ones. Quickly transfer the tomatoes to a bowl of ice water to halt the cooking. They will be easy to peel. Dice, removing seeds. Coat the bottom of a heavy pot with olive oil, heat it over medium heat and add two or three whole, peeled cloves of garlic per pound (500 g) of tomatoes. Once the cloves start to sizzle, add tomatoes. (Instead of fresh tomatoes, you may pour in a big can—28 ounces/796 mL—of top quality canned tomatoes.) Simmer over low heat until the garlic is soft. Remove the garlic, mash it, and return it to the pot. Season mixture with salt and six to eight fresh basil leaves. Cook for another five minutes, then cool, bottle, refrigerate, or use right away.

Gwynne Basen likes to use small, meaty tomatoes from her Mansonville garden. Her favourite variety is the Italian Principesse Borghese. Pack peeled tomatoes into a heavy casserole, smashing them together with a potato masher. Stuff in plenty of peeled, whole garlic cloves. Tuck a generous number of fresh basil leaves in among the tomatoes and garlic and pour good olive oil over the top. Bake, covered, in a 350°F (180°C) oven for 45 minutes or until the tomatoes are very soft. If you wish, purée in a food processor or blender.

Salade de betteraves à l'orange et au basilic

BEET SALAD WITH ORANGE AND BASIL DRESSING

Salad doesn't have to be just green, especially when Quebec's beet crop is fresh from the farm and arugula is at its best. Basil is the perfect accent and arugula provides some greenery, says Montreal food specialist Michelle Gélinas of this, her recipe. For flavour, fresh, young beets are best; storage winter beets come second; canned beets, third.

SERVES 4

Vinaigrette
Grated peel and juice of 1 medium orange
Juice of 1 lemon
1 teaspoon (5 mL) honey
Salt and freshly ground pepper
2 tablespoons (30 mL) sunflower oil

Salad
1 pound (500 g) beets (4 or 5 medium)
4 cups (1 L) arugula
3 ounces (90 g) fresh goat cheese, sliced
4 tablespoons (60 mL) chopped fresh
   basil leaves

For vinaigrette:
✤ In a measuring cup, combine orange peel and juice, lemon juice, honey, salt, and pepper. Whisk in oil.

For salad:
✤ Preheat the oven to 400°F (200°C).
✤ Bake unpeeled beets in a baking pan with a little water added and covered with aluminum foil until fork-tender, about 1 hour. Cool in water, then peel and quarter.
✤ In a mixing bowl, toss beets with half the vinaigrette to coat. Divide arugula among 4 plates.
✤ Arrange beets on the arugula, followed by the cheese slices. Pour remaining vinaigrette over salad. Scatter each serving with basil.

BEET GREENS

Trim and sauté these rich-coloured leaves in olive oil with finely chopped garlic or just until wilted, advises my friend Susan Schwartz. Or steam the leaves and, when limp, toss with a vinaigrette made with olive oil, lemon juice, grated fresh gingerroot, salt, and pepper.

Beets offred at Jean-Talon market come in red, white and yellow, and in various shapes, from La Ferme Omer Charbonneau et Fils of St-Lin-Laurentides.

Salade tiède d'endives à l'orange et aux pétoncles

WARM ENDIVE, ORANGE, AND SCALLOP SALAD

Just adding smoked fish or seafood to fresh ingredients can turn a recipe into a specialty, says Belgian-born chef Luc Gielen. He shops at Boucanerie Chelsea Smokehouse in Chelsea, just north of Ottawa, for smoked scallops, salmon, and albacore tuna. His signature salad was demonstrated at a Montreal festival of specialties from the Outaouais region of Quebec. Luc is a chef-teacher at the Gatineau culinary school Centre de formation professionelle Relais de la Lièvre-Seigneurie and also partner in the chocolate shop ChocoMotive in Montebello.

SERVES 4

4 heads endive, leaves separated
1 small head Boston lettuce, trimmed
1 navel orange, segments coarsely chopped, juice reserved
24 toasted almonds or pecans
4 radishes, thinly sliced (optional)
1/2 cup (125 mL) chopped fresh flat-leaf parsley
4 slices bacon
2 tablespoons (30 mL) olive oil
2 shallots, finely chopped
1 tablespoon (15 mL) maple syrup
3 tablespoons (45 mL) sherry vinegar
12 large smoked or fresh scallops

✦ Prepare endive, lettuce, orange, almonds, radishes (if using), and parsley and set aside.
✦ In a heavy frying pan, cook bacon until crisp. Drain on paper towels and then crumble.
✦ Discard bacon fat, then heat oil in the pan over medium heat. Add shallots and cook, stirring often, until lightly coloured. Stir in maple syrup, vinegar, and 2 tablespoons (30 mL) of the reserved orange juice, then set the pan aside.
✦ Smoked scallops do not need cooking. If using fresh scallops, spray the bottom of a heavy frying pan with olive oil and heat over medium heat. Rinse scallops and pat dry with paper towels. Cook scallops for 1 to 2 minutes per side, just until lightly coloured.
✦ Meanwhile, arrange endive and lettuce on 4 serving plates. Scatter with chopped oranges, almonds, radishes, parsley, and bacon. Top with scallops. Warm orange juice dressing in the pan, stirring constantly. Drizzle over salad.

The Endive Challenge

Back in 1975, the sharply flavoured Belgian endive was imported from Belgium and France to Quebec and sold only to French chefs and a few Quebec connoisseurs. Jean-Michel Schryve, a farmer who had emigrated from France, decided to grow it locally. Experimenting with more than 30 varieties of seeds, he eventually settled on a French seed that would mature quickly in Quebec's short growing season. Schryve's endive, while beautiful and crisp, had a milder flavour than the European type, and was slow to catch on. He decided to seek help. Suzanne Paré Leclerc, for decades the dynamic public relations officer for the Quebec agriculture department, can still remember a chilly winter morning in the early 1980s when the burly farmer arrived in her Montreal office holding a box of his endive. "He said, 'I want you to help me market this food,'" she remembers. "I asked him when his crop would be ready. 'It takes 21 days to grow, so we have 21 days.'"

Whipping into action, she had a bus bring the Montreal food journalists to the farm, and even persuaded her boss, Jean Garon, the Parti Québécois minister of agriculture, to attend. Schryve's wife, Francine, made her favourite endive hors d'oeuvres, Suzanne served white wine, and we all stood around in the barn relishing both the food and an unusual food story and listening to Garon talk up specialty-vegetable growing with Schryve. The finale in Suzanne's campaign was a chef's recipe contest she then staged, attracting about a hundred recipes. No matter that European-born chefs beat the Quebecers by winning the top prizes: the public noticed, soon upwards of 10 growers were producing endive in Quebec, and both supermarkets and consumers showed interest in a product that was cheaper than the import and fresh all winter. In the end, the Schryve family came out on top. Philippe, Jean-Michel and Francine's son, saw competition dwindle by 1990. He now supplies the whole province, exports endive to Ontario and the northeastern United States, and has launched an organic version. Taste, and be converted, he says. "People who know it eat a lot. Some buy five pounds a week."

Endive grows in darkened barns near St-Clet.

Ma soupe de courgettes préférée

MY FAVOURITE ZUCCHINI SOUP

Patrick Turcot, executive chef at Fairmont Le Manoir Richelieu in La Malbaie, Charlevoix, got the idea for this recipe when working at the Fairmont Hotel Macdonald in Edmonton. His duck and vegetable supplier was a farm in Leduc, Alberta, called Greens Eggs and Ham. He created the recipe using the farm's duck eggs, which he scrambled. This version calls for poaching eggs and creates a meal in a bowl. Patrick, a native of Quebec City and graduate of Montreal's Institut de tourisme et d'hôtellerie du Québec, praises the quality and variety of fruit and vegetables available to him in the Charlevoix region. He uses duck from La Ferme Basque de Charlevoix in St-Urbain.

SERVES 6

2 duck legs confit (optional)

4 tablespoons (60 mL) butter, or as needed

1 small leek, minced

2 medium onions, chopped

1 clove garlic, mashed (optional)

1/2 cup (125 mL) dry white wine

Salt and freshly ground pepper

2 pounds (1 kg) fresh zucchini, peeled and diced

1 small potato, peeled and diced

2 cups (500 mL) chicken stock

6 small or medium eggs, poached (optional)

+ Remove skin from duck legs (if using), and place skin in a small frying pan over low heat. Cook gently until fat in skin is melted. Discard skin. Measure 3 tablespoons (45 mL) of the duck fat, or use butter if desired, into a saucepan. Set the pan over medium-low heat and sauté leek until softened, about 5 minutes. Cover and keep warm. Meanwhile, remove meat from duck bones, shred meat finely, and add to leeks, mixing well. Again cover to keep warm.

+ Alternatively, sauté the leek in 2 tablespoons (30 mL) of the butter until softened, about 5 minutes. Cover and keep warm.

+ In a large saucepan, melt 2 tablespoons (30 mL) of the butter over medium heat and sauté onions and garlic (if using), stirring often, until tender and lightly caramelized, about 5 minutes. Deglaze pan by adding wine and scraping up brown bits from the bottom.

+ Season onion mixture with salt and pepper. Add zucchini, potato, and stock to the pan. Cover and simmer for 20 to 30 minutes, until potato is tender. In a blender or food processor, purée soup until smooth. Return to the pan and cook until soup is hot.

+ When ready to serve, put a poached egg (if using) into each of 6 warmed shallow bowls. Divide leek-duck mixture between the 6 bowls and finally pour the soup over the top and serve hot.

Velouté de carottes au gingembre

Carrot ginger soup

Carrot soups are popular in Quebec, and carrots grow so well here that there's usually a hefty export business to the United States. This recipe belongs to my friend and Gazette *colleague Susan Schwartz, who originally made it with orange juice as part of the liquid, and rice instead of potatoes. She gradually increased the flavour by adding ginger, and found that potatoes gave the soup more taste than rice.*

SERVES 4 TO 5

1 tablespoon (15 mL) olive oil
1 medium onion, chopped
8 good-sized carrots, sliced in 1/2-inch (1 cm) rounds
1 medium potato, peeled and cubed
1 to 2 tablespoons (15 to 30 mL) grated fresh gingerroot
5 cups (1.25 L) vegetable stock, chicken stock, or water
Salt and freshly ground white pepper

✦ In a large saucepan or stock pot, heat oil over medium heat and sauté onion until translucent, about 5 to 6 minutes. Do not allow onion to brown. Add carrots and potato, stirring briefly. Add ginger and stock, bring to a boil, then reduce heat to medium-low, partly cover, and cook until vegetables are tender, 20 to 25 minutes.

✦ Remove pan from heat and cool soup slightly. Purée in a blender or food processor. If desired, purée half the soup until smooth, and half until blended but not smooth, and then combine.

✦ Return soup to the pan and reheat to serving temperature. Season with salt and white pepper.

Note

The soup can be prepared 1 day in advance, then covered and refrigerated. Reheat before serving. The recipe can be doubled, if desired, and the soup freezes well.

Crème de choufleur

CREAM OF CAULIFLOWER SOUP

Cauliflower comes in four colours in Quebec: the original snowy white ranging to pale cream, plus purple, orange, and green. Chefs Pascal Cormier and Annie Lacombe of Montreal worked together to develop this richly flavoured cool-weather soup when they were both cooking at Restaurant L'Autre Version in Old Montreal. It raises humble cauliflower into the gourmet class. Pascal suggests serving the soup with a topping of smoked fish, either salmon or sturgeon, cut in slivers, and a sprinkling of fresh dill.

SERVES 6

2 tablespoons (30 mL) butter
1 medium onion, chopped
1 clove garlic, crushed
1/2 cup (125 mL) dry white wine
1 small cauliflower, broken into florets
1 cup (250 mL) vegetable stock
1 cup (250 mL) whipping cream
3 sprigs fresh thyme
Pinches salt and freshly ground white pepper
Milk, as needed

✢ In a large, heavy saucepan, melt butter over medium heat and cook onion and garlic, stirring often, until softened. Add wine and simmer until mixture almost dries out.

✢ Reduce heat to low and add cauliflower, stock, cream, thyme, salt, and white pepper. Simmer just until cauliflower is tender. Remove thyme.

✢ Using a potato masher, mash cauliflower until smooth. If soup is too thick, thin with milk to desired consistency. Add more salt and pepper to taste. Serve hot.

Cauliflower

Fresh, crisp, and creamy, cauliflower makes a good salad if you slice the florets top to bottom and dress with a vinaigrette of olive oil, Dijon mustard, and lemon juice. Another way to enjoy this hardy vegetable is to slice a head thickly from top to bottom and grill the slabs as if they were steaks.

Roasting florets intensifies their natural sweetness. Toss first with olive oil, sea salt, and pepper, then spread in a pan in a single layer and roast at 450°F (230°C) for 20 to 30 minutes, stirring occasionally, until crisp and browned. Serve hot or warm, topped with roasted sliced almonds or grated lemon peel, or cooled with chopped radicchio and a vinaigrette.

Cauliflower comes in four colours in Quebec.

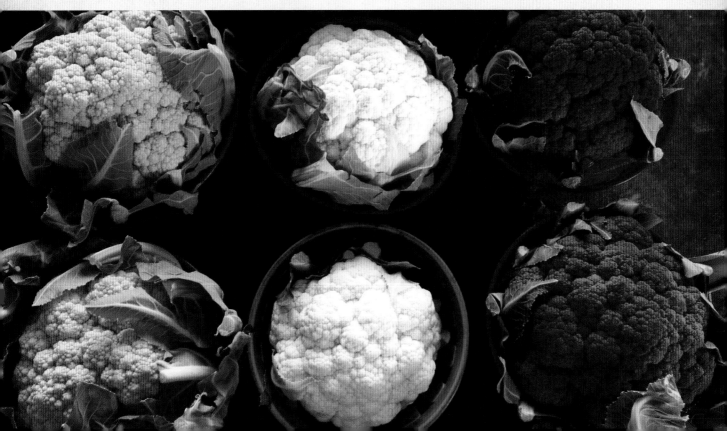

Chef Nancy Hinton shows a harvest of wild mushrooms for À La Table des Jardins Sauvages, St-Roch-de-l'Achigan.

Nancy Hinton

A restaurant seriously off the beaten track and named for its wild gardens is not the usual place for the finest contemporary cuisine. But a cottage on the St-Esprit River near St-Roch-de-l'Achigan, 45 minutes' drive northeast of Montreal, has become a gastronomic haven, its food unique, its cuisine enjoyed by dining critics and customers alike.

At the stove is Nancy Hinton, a diminutive chef whose career includes senior positions in top Quebec restaurants. Supplying her with what she calls "wild edibles" is François Brouillard, a forager who learned to pick and savour weeds and wildflowers from his grandmother.

Bring along fine wine when you reserve for a tasting menu of whatever François has harvested. Nancy serves periodic theme dinners based on mushrooms (see her recipe on page 212), duck, maple, or summer greens, and regular weekend feasts. You will be offered rare delicacies such as oysters baked with sea spinach, a cattail (bulrush) you eat as if it's a cob of corn, organic quail flavoured with wild ginger, venison tourtière with pickled day-lily buds, puffball cooked like eggplant, and chocolate mousse made with chanterelle mushrooms. Her exotic menus may raise the questions, why serve this cuisine, and why here?

It's the result of a food romance. Nancy fell out of love with chemical engineering studies at McGill University and took a professional cooking course. François turned from organic gardening to full-time foraging and met Nancy

at the kitchen door of the celebrated Ste-Adèle restaurant L'Eau à la Bouche, where she was executive sous-chef.

They've been a couple working and living together since 2005, and their stall at Montreal's Jean-Talon Market is a source for his fresh, wild finds and her preserves, be they sous vide, dried, pickled, infused, or frozen.

Growing up in the Quebec City suburb of Ste-Foy, "my nose was always in the kitchen. I spent any extra money eating in fancy restaurants, and I started buying cooking magazines," she recalls. Signing up for a cooking course at Montreal's Pearson School of Culinary Arts, she remembers chef-teacher Rick Oliver giving her a copy of *On Food and Cooking*, by food science writer Harold McGee. That book showed her the link between chemistry and cuisine, and helped set her on a path to becoming a chef. She spent the next 18 years cooking in Quebec restaurants, both bistro and fine dining.

Moving to François's stamping ground in the Lanaudière region, northeast of Montreal, Nancy brought with her knowledge of how to prepare a few wild edibles taught by her former boss, Chef Anne Desjardins, then executive chef of L'Eau à la Bouche, and two other top chefs, Normand Laprise of Montreal and Daniel Vézina of Quebec City, all wild-food fanciers. François added his family's recipes, and Nancy dipped into wild-food books for ideas. "As soon as he guaranteed me that something was edible, I mostly just went with my instincts and cooking experience, trying and testing."

Pâtes aux tomates

PASTA WITH CHERRY TOMATOES

Quebec is blessed with cherry tomatoes year-round, thanks to market gardeners in warm weather and hydroponic growers the rest of the year. Often available yellow, always available red, these morsels of sweet juice are such a basic that cooks use them as an ingredient in recipes. Jane Livingston, a talented Knowlton cook, adds cherry tomatoes to a pasta dish.

SERVES 6

4 cups (1 L) red and yellow cherry tomatoes, quartered

1/3 cup (75 mL) slivered fresh basil leaves

1 clove garlic, crushed and chopped

4 tinned anchovy fillets, diced (optional)

1 tablespoon (15 mL) red wine vinegar

1/2 cup (125 mL) olive oil

Salt and freshly ground pepper

1 pound (500 g) spaghettini or other pasta

1/2 cup (125 mL) freshly grated Parmesan cheese

✛ In a mixing bowl, toss together tomatoes, basil, garlic, anchovies (if using), vinegar, oil, salt, and pepper.

✛ In a large pot of boiling salted water, cook spaghettini until al dente. Transfer to a large, heated serving dish and pour tomato sauce over top, tossing to coat. Sprinkle with cheese and serve at once.

Quebec has been producing beer since the early 17th century, and Quebecers drink it with enthusiasm, an estimated half-million servings a day, 500 million litres a year. Brewing news is made today by the lively microbrewing industry. More than 60 independents and almost 40 artisanal brewers or brew-pub operators make a variety of styles in Quebec, reflecting the beer traditions of Germany, Belgium, and England. Quebec brews regularly win top ratings across Canada. Peter McAuslan, founder of Brasserie McAuslan and a leader in Quebec microbrewing, compares Quebec's brewing scene today to that of Belgium's. "There is a virtual explosion of breweries and styles," says the brewer, now retired. "We are the Cirque du Soleil of beer producers."

Proof of the strength of these craft brews can be found in the behaviour of the major breweries, led by Molson, the oldest operating brewery in North America, and still at its original 1786 location by St. Mary's Current, in east-end Montreal. Aware that microbrews command about 7 per cent of Canada's market share and that that number is climbing, the giants Molson and Labatt keep in the game by producing their own craft-styled products, or by buying up smaller breweries that so far remain independent from their industrial owners.

Before the 1940s, the large brewers still brewed India pale ales, stouts, bocks, and lagers. Gradually they settled on their middle-of-the-road bestselling brands, a trend helped by their becoming part of multinational breweries when Labatt was bought by Anheuser-Busch and Molson joined Coors. Beer critic Philippe Wouters believes the new beers from the microbrewers show that they have dipped back into Quebec and international brewing history to offer modern interpretations of early beers. Beer in New France would have been made of wheat flours, barley, oats, or spruce at the Quebec City brewery founded in 1668 by Intendant Jean Talon. Robust porters and stouts, and pale ales became the norm after the British conquest of 1759, with lagers appearing late in the 1800s. In the period from 1988 to today, variety seems unlimited. Gilles Jourdenais, who sells Quebec microbrews in a tiny beer store attached to his Atwater Market cheese shop, estimates he stocks 400 brands, including beer made with such fruits as black currants, blueberries, peaches, and apricots.

The place to sample new Quebec beers is in brew-pubs and bars, says Wouters, a Belgian-Quebecer who publishes the monthly *Bières et plaisirs* newspaper. A new trend is in restaurants, where some sommeliers will suggest a certain brew with the cuisine instead of the habitual wine.

Filet de bar européen et palourdes

SEA BASS AND CLAMS ON A BED OF CAULIFLOWER AND POTATOES

This Portuguese family dish looks modest but offers a lively combination of flavours and textures. Helena Loureiro, chef-owner of Montreal's popular Portuguese restaurant Portus Calle, remembers her grandmother and mother making it with Mediterranean sea bass in their home in Fatima, Portugal. If you like, substitute carrots, parsnips, celery root, or white beans for the cauliflower, she suggests.

SERVES 4

1 pound (500 g) sea bass fillets, 1 1/2 inches
    (4 cm) thick
Juice of 1 lemon
Salt and freshly ground pepper
2 Yukon Gold or other yellow-fleshed potatoes,
    peeled and cubed (1 1/2 cups/375 mL)

2 cups (500 mL) cauliflower florets
4 tablespoons (60 mL) olive oil
4 tablespoons (60 mL) chopped fresh coriander
1 medium onion, halved and thinly sliced
1/2 cup (125 mL) dry white wine
20 littleneck clams, rinsed

+ Rinse fish and pat dry with paper towels. Combine lemon juice, salt, and pepper in a resealable plastic bag, add fish, turning gently to coat, then marinate in the refrigerator for 1 hour. Just before cooking, drain fish and pat dry.

+ Meanwhile, in a medium saucepan, cook potatoes in boiling salted water over medium heat just until tender. In another medium saucepan, cook cauliflower in boiling salted water over medium heat just until tender, 5 to 10 minutes. (Don't cook vegetables together, as the potatoes will take longer.)

+ Drain both vegetables, return them to their pans and set each pan over very low heat for a few minutes to dry out the vegetables slightly. Transfer cauliflower to the potato pan and mash vegetables together with a potato masher (not a blender or food processor), just until combined.

+ Season with salt and pepper, then toss with 2 tablespoons (30 mL) of the oil and 2 tablespoons (30 mL) of the coriander. Cover and keep warm in a double boiler.

+ In a large, heavy frying pan, heat remaining 2 tablespoons (30 mL) oil over medium heat and cook onion until golden, about 3 minutes. Add wine and stir to deglaze the pan.

+ Place fish on onion and continue cooking for 1 minute. Arrange clams around fish. Cover pan and continue cooking for 8 to 10 minutes, until clams open. Discard any clams that do not open.

+ Have ready 4 deep, wide warmed plates or soup bowls. Spread mashed vegetables on the plates, top with fish, and surround fish with clams. Drizzle cooking juices over the fish and clams and sprinkle with remaining 2 tablespoons (30 mL) coriander.

Pavés de saumon glacés à l'érable et au bourbon

SALMON GLAZED WITH MAPLE AND BOURBON

An inn located in a sugar maple wood is likely to offer maple-flavoured cuisine. At Auberge des Gallant, near Ste-Marthe, west of Montreal, Chef Neil Gallant, son of innkeepers Gérard and Linda, likes to combine maple with liquor and seasonings. Rye whisky can replace the bourbon, and Arctic char, the salmon. Do not use the bourbon mixture as a marinade, Neil warns, as it will overflavour the dish.

SERVES 4

1/2 cup (125 mL) medium or dark maple syrup
1 tablespoon (15 mL) soy sauce
1 tablespoon (15 mL) grated fresh gingerroot
1 teaspoon (5 mL) crushed garlic
Pinch red pepper flakes
2 tablespoons (30 mL) bourbon
Sunflower oil, for searing
4 1-inch-thick (2.5 cm) thick salmon fillets (5 ounces/150 g each)
Freshly ground pepper

✤ Preheat the oven to 400°F (200°C).
✤ In a small saucepan, combine maple syrup, soy sauce, ginger, garlic, red pepper flakes, and bourbon and bring to a boil over medium heat. Simmer for about 1 minute, then remove from heat.
✤ In a large, heavy, oven-safe frying pan with a lid, add just enough oil to coat the bottom of the pan and heat over medium-high heat. Sprinkle fish fillets with pepper and sear, skin side up, for about 1 minute.
✤ Turn fish skin side down and remove pan from heat. Pour maple mixture over fish and bake for 5 minutes. Remove from the oven and baste fish with maple mixture. Cover pan and let stand for 1 minute.
✤ Serve fish on warmed plates, each piece drizzled with sauce.

Morue salée aux pommes de terre et aux oignons

SALT COD, POTATO, AND ONION CASSEROLE

Portuguese Montrealers keep the craze for salt cod alive, despite the near-collapse of the Canadian East Coast cod fishery. That craze can be traced back to the 15th century, when Portuguese fishermen fished along the Gaspé coast and landed to salt their catch. Flora Lopes honours her Portuguese culinary tradition with hearty dishes such as this one, named Bacalhau à Gomes de Sá for the restaurant Gomes de Sa in Porto, in northern Portugal. She uses fish salted and dried on the Bay of Chaleur and sold at fish stores catering to the Portuguese. She might not approve the method, but I discovered that I could reheat this dish in the microwave without losing any of the flavour or texture.

SERVES 6

1 1/2 pounds (750 g) salt cod

4 large potatoes (about 700 g), peeled, cubed

4 tablespoons (60 mL) olive oil

2 large onions, thinly sliced

4 cloves garlic, crushed

1 bay leaf

Salt and freshly ground pepper

4 hard-boiled eggs

Black olives, pitted

Finely chopped fresh flat-leaf parsley

+ In a wide, deep pan, soak the dried cod in cold water in the refrigerator for 24 to 48 hours, changing the water five times. Cover the pan so the refrigerator doesn't smell of fish.

+ In a saucepan of cold salted water, boil potatoes until tender, about 10 minutes. Meanwhile in a large, heavy frying pan, heat oil and cook onions, garlic, and bay leaf, stirring often, until onions are softened, about 10 minutes.

+ Place cod in another large saucepan; it will have softened and be easy to fit into the pan. Cover with cold water. Set over high heat, bring to a boil, and cook until fish is tender, about 20 minutes. Drain and, working quickly so the fish doesn't cool, remove flesh from bones. Discard bones and skin and break fish into bite-size pieces.

+ Preheat the oven to 250°F (120°C) if you're not planning to serve the dish right away. In a deep, 2-quart (2 L) baking dish, arrange layers of potatoes, fish, and onion mixture, finishing with onions. Drizzle each layer with a little olive oil.

+ Slice eggs and arrange over onions. Poke olives in between egg slices. Sprinkle with parsley. Keep warm in the oven until ready to serve.

Driving along the Bay of Chaleur on a sunny afternoon, looking for an old-style fish-processing company, I got lucky. Here, just west of Percé, on grassy slopes overlooking the bay, I could see a fish-preserving process underway that's been going on along this coast for 400 years. It's rarely in operation these days, because the near-demise of the cod fishery in eastern Canada has decimated the cod catch. But on that day, I was able to see Gaspé Cure in the making, just as it has been in these parts since about 1650. The fishermen at Poissonnerie Lelièvre, Lelièvre et Lemoignan (nicknamed "the Three Ls") were at work on some Newfoundland cod, casting an

occasional eye skyward because integral to the process is the Gaspé's steady, dry, northwestern wind.

First, the fish had been cleaned and layered in bins with generous scoops of coarse salt. Then, after marinating in a chilled warehouse for 21 days, the cod had been drained of brine and was in the process of being laid out to dry outdoors on rustic-looking wooden racks called "flakes," made of a network of wood sticks. The remnants of these flakes can be seen all along the southern Gaspé coast. At the Three Ls, some were the originals, others helped along by wooden poles and wire mesh. The fish stays there, covered with small board roofs if it rains, for up to three weeks. Dried this way and refrigerated, the salt cod will keep for a year. "That wind dries the fish so well, we can use less salt . . . and our fish is more tender on the outside and nearly transparent when it's finished drying," says Roch Lelièvre, company manager.

The other source for this product is Nova Scotia, but there more salt is required in the process, Roch says, because Nova Scotia winds are more moist. Besides Quebecers, his customers are mostly in the Mediterranean, accustomed over the centuries to the Gaspé's lightly salted fish. The rest of the month, Roch counts on frozen cod from Alaska for his supplies. City fish shops selling the product cater to people who like their bacalhau (salt cod), most of them with roots in the Mediterranean.

Previous page: Roch Lelièvre dries salt cod on the shore of the Bay of Chaleur at Ste-Thérèse-de-Gaspé.

Right: Fishermen spread salt cod out to dry in the wind and sun of the Gaspé.

Ris de veau aux champignons et à la crème

SWEETBREADS WITH MUSHROOM CREAM SAUCE

This delicately flavoured meat is rare on Quebec menus. Dining my way about the Saguenay region of northern Quebec, I enjoyed this dish at Auberge-Bistro Rose & Basilic in Alma, where Mathieu Gagnon was chef. Gagnon, who is now cooking at the International Café in Chicoutimi, estimates that, once the bouillon is made and the first step in cooking the sweetbreads is complete, it takes only seven minutes to make this dish. It's been called a recipe for people who enjoy cooking, but is not difficult.

SERVES 4

Bouillon (see below)

1 pound (500 g) veal sweetbreads, trimmed of their membrane
Flour, for dredging
1/3 cup (75 mL) clarified butter (see opposite page)
1 pound (500 g) shiitake mushrooms, stems discarded, chopped
1 shallot, minced
2 tablespoons (30 mL) whole-grain mustard
1/2 cup (125 mL) fond de veau (page 56)
3 tablespoons (45 mL) whipping cream
Salt and freshly ground pepper
1/4 cup (60 mL) each chopped fresh flat-leaf parsley, thyme, and chives or
   green parts of green onions

Bouillon:

✦ In a medium saucepan, combine a bouquet garni (2 bay leaves and sprigs of fresh parsley and thyme tied together with string or in a cheesecloth bag), 1 onion cut in quarters, 1 sliced carrot and 1 sliced celery stalk. Cover with cold water, add salt and freshly ground pepper, and bring to a boil over medium heat. Simmer for 30 minutes, then cool, and add juice of 1 lemon. Strain.

+ Pour bouillon into a medium saucepan, add sweetbreads, bring to a boil over medium heat, and simmer for 5 minutes.
+ Drain sweetbreads, dry on paper towels, and transfer to a plate. Cover with paper towels, then place another plate or chopping board on top, followed by a heavy weight. Let stand for 30 minutes to press out the extra moisture.
+ Dry sweetbreads with paper towels and slice into two along the width. Dip in flour, shaking off excess.
+ In a large, heavy frying pan, melt the clarified butter over high heat and sear the sweetbreads on each side just until they are crisp, about 1 to 2 minutes a side. Transfer to a plate, cover, and keep warm.
+ In the same pan over medium heat, cook the mushrooms and shallot just until soft but not browned, 2 to 3 minutes. Add mustard, fond de veau, and cream. Simmer, stirring often, just until thickened to sauce consistency. Season with salt, pepper and fresh herbs. Keep warm.
+ To serve, slice hot sweetbreads into four equal portions, place on heated serving plates, and add the sauce. Serve with mashed potatoes and a green vegetable.

Notes

To make clarified butter, melt butter in a small saucepan over low heat, drain off the clarified, clear liquid, and discard the sediment.

Fond de veau is obtainable commercially or at butcher shops, fresh or frozen. Or, use the powdered product. To make 1/2 cup (125 mL), mix 2 teaspoons (10 mL) powder with 1/2 cup (125 mL) hot water.

Jarrets d'agneau braisés aux piments poblano

BRAISED LAMB SHANKS WITH POBLANO PEPPERS AND PINTO BEANS

Quebec French cuisine "with a Latin accent" is the specialty of Montreal chef David Ferguson, Ontario-raised and a graduate of the Stratford Chefs School. Faithful to French culinary techniques at his midtown bistro, Restaurant Gus, David also adds flavours learned on his cooking sojourns in Mexico and New Mexico.

SERVES 4

2 large onions

3 tablespoons (45 mL) olive oil

4 lamb shanks

1 medium carrot, peeled and sliced

4 cloves garlic, crushed

1 leek, white part only, chopped

5 1/2 cups (1.375 L) cold water

1 tablespoon (15 mL) finely chopped fresh thyme or rosemary

1/2 ancho pepper, rehydrated (see below)

Salt and freshly ground pepper

1 can (19 ounces/540 mL) beans, preferably pinto or red kidney, drained and rinsed

4 Roma tomatoes, peeled and coarsely chopped, or 2 cups (500 mL) canned Italian tomatoes

1 poblano pepper, grilled, peeled, seeded, and cut in strips

✤ Preheat the oven to 300°F (150°C).

✤ Finely chop 1 of the onions. In a 4-quart (4 L) heavy, stovetop-safe casserole dish with a lid, heat 2 tablespoons (30 mL) of the oil over medium-high heat and brown lamb on all sides. Remove to a plate. Reduce heat to medium and, in the same casserole dish, sauté carrot, chopped onion, garlic, and leek just until golden, about 5 minutes.

✤ Add ½ cup (125 mL) of the cold water to the pan and scrape up any brown bits. Return lamb to the casserole dish and add 5 cups (1.25 mL) cold water or enough to cover. Add thyme and ancho pepper. Bring mixture to a boil, then cover, transfer to the oven and roast for 1 hour and 45 minutes, until lamb is tender.

✤ Remove lamb to a plate. Season the cooking liquid with salt and pepper. Discard ancho pepper. Simmer cooking liquid until it is reduced to about 3 cups (750 mL).

✤ Meanwhile, cut remaining onion in half vertically, then slice finely. In a heavy frying pan, heat remaining 1 tablespoon (15 mL) oil over medium-high heat and cook onion until caramelized.

✤ Return lamb to casserole dish. Add beans, tomatoes, caramelized onion, and poblano pepper. Reheat mixture and serve on deep, warmed serving plates.

Note

To rehydrate the ancho pepper, cut it in half and roast in a 350°F (180°C) oven for 5 to 10 minutes. Remove and discard seeds. Place in a small bowl, add boiling water to cover, and soak for 5 to 10 minutes. Drain and pat dry.

Cuisses de lapin des volières Charlevoix

Charlevoix-style rabbit with tarragon sauce

Rabbit, fresh or frozen, has become a regular at Quebec meat counters, and more and more chefs experiment with this tender, lean meat. Treat it as you would chicken and expect less fat in the meat, so don't dry it out with overcooking. This braised rabbit dish comes from Dominique Truchon, veteran Charlevoix chef. He regularly serves rabbit at his restaurant and inn, Chez Truchon, located in a 19th-century mansion in La Malbaie.

Serves 4

10 whole black peppercorns
2 tablespoons (30 mL) butter
2 tablespoons (30 mL) vegetable oil
4 rabbit legs, skin removed
1 carrot, peeled and cut in chunks
3 stalks celery, cut in chunks
1 medium leek, white part cut in chunks, green part reserved
1 1/4 cups (300 mL) dry white wine
6 tablespoons (90 mL) whole-grain mustard
1 bouquet garni (3 bay leaves, sprigs of fresh thyme and flat-leaf parsley, and 1 clove garlic
    enclosed in green part of a leek and tied together with kitchen string)
3 cups (750 mL) chicken stock

Tarragon sauce
1 tablespoon (15 mL) butter
1 shallot, finely chopped
3/4 cup + 1 tablespoon (190 mL) dry white wine
1 cup (250 mL) fond de veau (page 56)
2 tablespoons (30 mL) finely chopped fresh tarragon (or 2 teaspoons/10 mL dried)

For rabbit:

+ Preheat the oven to 400°F (200°C). Place peppercorns in a wire mesh tea infuser or tie in cheesecloth.
+ In a large, heavy saucepan, heat butter and oil over medium heat. Sear rabbit until golden, about 10 minutes per side. Transfer meat to a plate and keep warm.
+ In the same pan, cook carrot, celery, and leek just until lightly browned. Add wine and deglaze pan by scraping brown bits up from the bottom. Simmer liquid for about 5 minutes, then stir in mustard.
+ Place bouquet garni in the bottom of a 3-quart (3 L) oven-safe casserole dish with a lid. Add peppercorns, rabbit legs, stock, and carrot mixture. Bring to a boil over medium heat, then cover and bake for 1 hour or until rabbit is tender to the fork.

For tarragon sauce:

+ While rabbit is in the oven, in a small saucepan, melt butter over medium heat and sauté shallot just until tender and lightly coloured, about 3 minutes. Add wine and simmer until it has reduced almost completely. Stir in fond de veau and tarragon and set aside.

To serve:

+ Remove rabbit from casserole dish and keep warm. Strain mixture in casserole dish. Add tarragon sauce. Heat and serve rabbit with sauce.

Note

Fond de veau is obtainable commercially or at butcher shops, fresh or frozen. Or, use the powdered product.
To make 1/2 cup (125 mL), mix 2 teaspoons (10 mL) powder with 1/2 cup (125 mL) hot water.

Carbonnade de boeuf aux rutabagas, et oignons caramélisés, pain à l'ail, Alfred le fermier

Beef carbonnade with rutabaga, caramelized onions, and Alfred le fermier cheese

This succulent braised and baked stew is Belgian-inspired and a prize-winner developed by Danny St-Pierre, chef-owner of the restaurants Auguste and Chez Augustine in Sherbrooke. He won a silver medal with the dish at the 2011 Montreal contest of Gold Medal Plates, the annual chef fundraiser for Canada's Olympic athletes. The natural sweetness of the vegetables is enriched with beer and cheese.

Serves 6

2 tablespoons (30 mL) salted butter

2 tablespoons (30 mL) vegetable oil

2 pounds (1 kg) beef chuck or blade, trimmed, cut in 1 1/4-inch (3 cm) cubes

4 cups (1 L) finely sliced onions (3 or 4 medium)

1 cup (250 mL) maple syrup

2 cups (500 mL) dark beer

4 cups (1 L) rutabaga cut in 1-inch (2.5 cm) cubes

1 teaspoon (5 mL) salt

Freshly ground pepper

2 1/4 cups (560 mL) dried bread, cut in 1-inch (2.5 cm) cubes

1 clove garlic, mashed in 4 tablespoons (60 mL) vegetable oil

3 cups (750 mL) coarsely grated Alfred le fermier or aged cheddar cheese

1 cup (250 mL) fresh flat-leaf parsley leaves, stems discarded, sprinkled with malt vinegar, for serving

✤ Place the oven rack in centre position. Preheat the oven to 325°F (160°C).

✤ In a heavy, 3-quart (3 L) stovetop-safe casserole dish with a lid, heat butter and oil over medium-high heat, then sear meat on all sides, about a dozen pieces at a time so as not to overcrowd the pan. When browned on all sides, transfer meat to a plate and keep warm.

✤ Cook onions in pan drippings over medium-low heat until golden, then return meat to the pan. Continue cooking, turning the ingredients, until both meat and onions have a rich brown colour. Stir in maple syrup, then beer and rutabaga. Add enough water to cover meat. Cover the casserole dish and put in the oven to bake for 4 hours.

- ✤ Remove carbonnade from the oven. Stir in salt and pepper and let stand on the stovetop.
- ✤ Increase oven temperature to 400°F (200°C). Divide carbonnade among 6 individual baking dishes or ramekins, 1½ to 2 cups (375 to 500 mL) each. In a bowl, mix bread with garlic-oil mixture, salt, and pepper. Scatter bread cubes over top of each dish and sprinkle with cheese.
- ✤ Bake just until the dish is bubbling hot and the cheese is melted. Serve sprinkled with parsley. Serve with Scotch ale or other dark beer.

Note

Alfred le fermier is a firm, washed-rind Quebec cheese. Once topped with the cheese, the carbonnade can be covered and refrigerated for up to 1 day. Bring to room temperature before reheating in the oven.

RUTABAGA

Rutabaga, the big, yellow-fleshed turnip, appeals to both traditional Quebec cooks and adventurous chefs. Admitting that rutabagas "are not the most sexy vegetable," Sophie Perreault of the Quebec Produce Marketing Association notes that 5 pounds (2.5 kg) costs the same as a box of chocolate chip cookies but can feed a family for days in soup or stew.

Bolster a comfort-food supper—pot-au-feu, minestrone, or chef-style ginger-accented soup—with cubes of rutabaga. Sophie suggests mixing rutabaga and potatoes for the mashed topping for a shepherd's pie, and including chicken stock in the meat mixture to harmonize the flavours.

Pâté chinois

Fresh and healthy shepherd's pie

Chef Louis Rhéaume is a multi-talented Montreal chef who is a born teacher, whether on television cooking shows or at the Old Montreal cooking school Académie Culinaire. He likes to reduce the fat in traditional recipes and increase the vegetables. This easy and comforting, yet healthy, dish is a good example.

Serves 6 to 8

1 spaghetti squash
3/4 teaspoon (4 mL) salt, plus extra for sprinkling
Pinches freshly ground pepper
4 tablespoons (60 mL) olive oil, plus extra for coating
1 large onion, finely chopped
1 1/2 pounds (750 g) lean ground beef
1 teaspoon (5 mL) ground cumin, or more to taste
1 large sweet potato, peeled
1/2 teaspoon (2 mL) ground nutmeg, or to taste
4 ounces (125 g) fresh spinach leaves
Chopped fresh thyme, for sprinkling

+ Preheat the oven to 350°F (180°C). Line a baking pan with parchment paper.
+ Cut squash in half, scoop out seeds and filaments, and sprinkle liberally with pinches of salt and pepper. Place both halves cut side down in the prepared baking pan. Roast for 1 to 1½ hours, until tender to the fork but not mushy.
+ Meanwhile, in a large, heavy frying pan, heat 2 tablespoons (30 mL) of the oil over medium heat and sauté onion until softened, about 5 minutes. Add another 2 tablespoons (30 mL) oil to the pan and add beef, breaking it up with a fork. Cook until beef is browned. Season with ¾ teaspoon (4 mL) salt, some grindings of pepper, and cumin. Spread evenly in a 2-quart (2 L) baking pan.
+ Thinly slice sweet potato with a mandoline or very sharp knife. Sprinkle with pinches of salt and pepper and drizzle with enough oil to coat. Set aside.
+ When squash is cooked, hold each half over a bowl and, using a fork, scrape out flesh. (It will form threads.) Season with salt, pepper, and nutmeg. Arrange over meat in pan. Spread spinach leaves on top and sprinkle with thyme. Cover with sweet potato slices, overlapping them if necessary. Bake, uncovered, for 1 hour.

The Shepherd's Pie

Menus in modest restaurants all over Quebec offer shepherd's pie. Its French name is *pâté chinois*, which translates as "Chinese pie." Why such a name for the layered combination of ground beef, corn, and mashed potatoes? For years, according to folklore, the recipe was believed to have come from a town in Maine called China. In fact, this was not the case. However, the pie was found in various places in New England, where between 1850 and 1930 thousands of French-Canadians, who had left Quebec in search of jobs, found work in textile, metal, and lumber mills. Nothing has been discovered to prove the pie's origin, but it had, by the 1930s, become a favourite family recipe in Quebec. Montreal food historian Jean-Pierre Lemasson calls it "our glorious dish."

But still, why "Chinese"? Researching the subject, Lemasson found puzzling details. A shepherd's pie existed in Scotland, where it was made of lamb. But it had no corn, as found in the pie of North America. It is similar to a cottage pie that appeared in *The Boston Cooking-School Cook Book* (the first Fannie Farmer cookbook), published in 1896 in the United States, and containing layers of mashed potatoes and sliced or cubed beef. A 1935 cookbook from Deerfield, New Hampshire, had a Chinese pie, but made with peas, not corn. In Quebec, its meat was usually beef in the cities, a mixture of pork with other meats in the country.

In his 2009 book *Le mystère insondable du pâté chinois*, Lemasson speculates that what he called "the unsolved mystery" of the dish had something to do with the appliance used to mash potatoes, whether that was a ricer or the chef's conical strainer called a chinois. The little town of China had only one Chinese-born resident, and the pie could not be found on New England menus. In a 1941 cookbook published by Montreal nuns of the order Soeurs des Saints Noms de Jésus et de Marie du Québec, the professor found a recipe for *pâté chinois*, but made with rice, rather than mashed potatoes, and with tomato sauce on top. Quebec's bestselling cookbook *La Cuisine raisonnée*, first published in 1919 by nuns of the Congrégation de Notre-Dame, made no mention of the pie until its 1967 edition, when a meat pie, called *pâté chinois*, was included. Although the dish has been a basic in Quebec homes since the 1930s, Lemasson has decided its true origin and Chinese name are lost in time. To the professor, who enjoys it regularly, "*Pâté chinois* is a phantom."

Perdrix rôties aux fèves

BEANS WITH PARTRIDGE OR ROCK CORNISH HENS

For as long as Quebecers have been trapping or raising game birds, they have been cooking them gently, moistened with stock or buried under beans or cabbage or other vegetables so these lean birds don't dry out. Serge Caplette, a chef-teacher at the École hôtelière de Laval, likes to collect the family recipes of different regions of Quebec and refine them, as he has with this dish.

SERVES 6

1 pound (500 g) great northern, cranberry, or pinto beans
1 1/2 teaspoons (7 mL) ground coriander
1 1/2 teaspoons (7 mL) dry mustard
1 teaspoon (5 mL) salt
Freshly ground pepper

1 cup (250 mL) finely chopped onions
1 medium onion, pierced with 2 cloves
1/2 cup (125 mL) molasses
1/2 pound (250 g) salt pork
3 wild partridges or Rock Cornish hens

✤ In a large bowl or pot, soak beans at room temperature in enough cold water to cover them for at least 8 hours. Drain beans through a large strainer, rinse under cold running water, then transfer to a 4-quart (4 L) heavy, stovetop-safe casserole dish with a lid. Cover beans with fresh cold water and bring to a boil over high heat. Reduce heat to low and simmer, covered and stirring occasionally, for 1 hour or until beans are becoming tender but are not mushy. Add more water during cooking if liquid reduces too much. Drain beans, then return them to the casserole dish.

✤ Preheat the oven to 250°F (120°C).

✤ Season beans with coriander, dry mustard, salt, pepper, chopped onions, whole onion, and molasses. Add water just to cover beans and bake, covered, for 3 hours.

✤ Tie legs and wings of birds in place with kitchen string so they are easier to handle when cooked. Bury birds in beans, and continue baking, covered, for 1 hour. Then increase oven temperature to 325°F (160°C) and bake for another 1 to 1½ hours, to add colour to beans, checking the water level occasionally and adding more water if necessary to keep the beans covered.

✤ When ready to serve, remove birds and cut into individual portions, ideally removing bones. Serve about half a bird, plus beans, per serving. Serve with maple syrup on the side, and a green salad.

Note
Farm-raised partridges can be substituted for the wild partridges, though they have much less flavour than the wild birds.

Poitrines de canard aux échalotes et au vinaigre balsamique

BREAST OF DUCKLING WITH SHALLOTS AND BALSAMIC SAUCE

When your restaurant is in the vicinity of Knowlton, home to a big duck farm, you are constantly challenged to create new, appealing ways to serve duck. Knowlton's Restaurant Le St-Martin always has duck on the menu. Over the years, chefs may change but duck continues to be a specialty. Jean-Marc Faucheux, a French-born chef, cooks duck breasts, which are easy to buy throughout the province fresh or frozen, and then perks up the duck flavour with a balsamic vinegar and shallot sauce.

SERVES 4

2 skin-on duck breasts (8 ounces/250 g each), skin scored
4 tablespoons (60 mL) cold butter, cut in 4 equal pieces
2 shallots, finely chopped
7 tablespoons (105 mL) balsamic vinegar
3/4 cup (175 mL) duck, veal, or chicken stock

✤ Preheat the oven to 225°F (110°C).
✤ In a large, heavy frying pan with no added fat, sear duck breasts skin side down over medium-high heat, for 4 minutes. (Their fat will add enough moisture to the pan.) Turn and sear the other side, for another 4 minutes. Transfer breasts to a plate and place in the oven. Wipe out pan with paper towels to remove any fat.
✤ Add 1 tablespoon (15 mL) butter to the pan and sauté shallots over medium heat just until softened and lightly coloured, about 3 minutes. Add vinegar to deglaze pan, scraping up the brown bits from the bottom. Simmer until mixture is almost dry.
✤ Add duck breasts and stock and cook for about 5 minutes, turning halfway through cooking time. Transfer duck to a cutting board and cover with aluminum foil.
✤ Add remaining butter to pan juices 1 piece at a time, whisking vigorously to incorporate and thicken the mixture. Add more salt to taste. Continue to cook just until it has a sauce-like consistency.
✤ Slice duck breasts thinly and spoon sauce over top.

Note

Do not use *magrets de canard*, breasts of ducks force-fed to make foie gras.

In the season for lusty, warming food, France's cassoulet is ideal. Its leading advocate in Quebec is a Carcassonne-born chef who has put the big dish of duck, sausages, and beans on the culinary map in northern Quebec and beyond. Daniel Pachon, chef-owner of Auberge Villa Pachon, in Jonquière, is so dedicated to this classic southern French dish, he has added a kitchen to his inn dedicated to cassoulet cooking and makes it in big quantities year-round to serve and to stock his freezer for orders from home cooks.

Each autumn, he and his wife, Carole Tremblay, load their van with big vats of the dish and head south to various points in Quebec where he stages cassoulet parties. These events attract chefs and food lovers, who enjoy spending convivial hours at table. I attended one such party at an apple orchard in Oka, just west of Montreal. Big casserole dishes of cassoulet lined the centre of the table so that we could help ourselves over and over, all the while sipping wine or sparkling cider as the chefs talked of their favourite cassoulet recipes. Daniel makes the Castelnaudary style of cassoulet, and likes to make his own Toulouse sausages for the dish. Duck confit (legs poached in duck fat, then browned) are essential, and the chef positions them standing up like sentinels in this rich stew of pork knuckles and a pork or ham shank, large white kidney beans (lingots in France), onions, and garlic.

Two other styles of the dish are part of the cassoulet tradition. The Carcassonne recipe contains a leg of mutton and maybe a partridge. The Toulouse version may have a goose along with Toulouse sausages. Daniel's brother, André, a chef working in Japan, started a gastronomic society called the Académie Universelle du Cassoulet and invited his brother to join. You can visit www.academie-du-cassoulet.com for more information.

Porc aux pommes et à l'érable

MAPLE PORK WITH APPLES

For a number of years, pork was the subject of a province-wide cooking contest for chefs. It was run by the Quebec Pork Producers Federation to encourage chefs to put the meat on restaurant menus. Denis Mareuge, chef at Boulangerie Owl's Bread restaurant, in Mansonville, moistens lean Quebec pork by cooking it with both fruit and vegetables, including hot peppers.

SERVES 4 TO 6

2 pounds (1 kg) boneless pork shoulder, trimmed of fat, cut in 2-inch (5 cm) cubes

All-purpose flour, for dredging

3 to 4 tablespoons (45 to 60 mL) peanut or vegetable oil

1/2 teaspoon (2 mL) salt

Freshly ground pepper

2 cooking apples, preferably Cortland, peeled, cored, and cubed

1 medium onion, diced

1 medium carrot, cubed

1 stalk celery, coarsely chopped

1 clove garlic, crushed

1 red bell pepper, cubed

2 small Thai or habanero peppers, finely chopped, or 3/4 teaspoon (4 mL) sambal oelek

6 tablespoons (90 mL) maple syrup

4 tablespoons (60 mL) low-sodium soy sauce

1 to 2 cups (250 to 500 mL) water

3 tablespoons (45 mL) chopped fresh coriander

+ Preheat the oven to 350°F (180°C).

+ Dredge meat in flour, shaking off excess. In a large, heavy frying pan, heat a little oil over medium heat and brown meat on all sides, about 10 cubes at a time, so as not to overcrowd the pan. Transfer browned meat to a 3-quart (3 L) heavy, stovetop-safe casserole dish with a lid. Sprinkle with salt and pepper, stirring to mix.

+ In the same frying pan used to brown the meat, after heating a little more oil if necessary, cook apples, onion, carrot, celery, garlic, bell pepper, and Thai peppers, stirring often, just until softened. Add to the casserole dish.

+ Stir in maple syrup, soy sauce, and enough water to come halfway up the ingredients. Bring to a boil over medium-high heat, then cover and bake for 1½ hours.

+ Remove casserole from the oven. Add more salt and pepper to taste. If meat isn't tender enough, bake for another 15 minutes.

+ Serve, sprinkled with coriander, with basmati rice or Chinese noodles mixed with steamed, slivered vegetables, such as carrots, celery, red onions, and bell peppers.

Note

Wear rubber gloves when handling hot peppers.

If you dine in top Quebec restaurants, you may see a pork chop on the menu at a price as high as filet mignon, venison, and lobster. Pork is usually considered a down-home family meat and not a gastronomic treat, but Quebec's Gaspor pork is changing public opinion in Quebec as well as in Ontario, New York, California, and even Japan. The meat comes from generously sized suckling pigs raised on a special diet. It's like the best veal you have ever eaten but with more flavour, whether you choose such dishes as braised pork chops, flank, or belly, or roasted loin, shoulder, or rack. The source for this treat is the family-run St-Canut Farms, near Mirabel in the Laurentian Mountains, north of Montreal. It's not the species of pig—the commonly raised Yorkshire-Landrace mixed breed—but the treatment the pigs receive that makes it "gastronomic pork"—the basis of the company name Gaspor.

Back in 2003, Alexandre Aubin and Carl Rousseau, both working on the Aubin family farm, decided to experiment with how they fed baby pigs and how large they grew the animals. Tiny piglets, known in French as *cochonnets* or *porcelets*, had been made into roast suckling pig for generations. One day, Ste-Adèle chef Anne Desjardins went on a tour of the farm. Seeing the little pigs, she said, "We don't have this meat any more." That comment, Alexandre remembers, set into motion a three-year experiment to improve the product, which, they recognized, was tender but lacked flavour and had a gelatinous texture. Putting their agricultural science training to work, they invented a diet of powdered milk, sugar, and vanilla, plus iron powder to turn the meat pink, and ran trials to figure out how large to grow the young pigs. The result was animals that made good-sized cuts for their various recipes, said chefs, including Normand Laprise of Montreal's celebrated restaurant Toqué! and Daniel Vézina of Laurie Raphaël in Quebec City and Montreal. The chefs take it from there. As Alexandre puts it, "I give the colours to the artist, and the chef paints the painting."

Émincé de volaille aux pommes

CHICKEN WITH APPLES

Rougemont is in the heart of apple country, southeast of Montreal, so it's natural that Louis Tremblay, chef at Les Quatre Feuilles, a restaurant tucked into an apple orchard and sugar maple grove, adds apples and an Asian tang to this fast and easy chicken dish. You don't always need chicken stock to make a sauce for chicken, he proves with his mixture of apple juice and soy sauce.

SERVES 4

4 boneless, skinless chicken breasts, cut in half lengthwise
All-purpose flour, for dredging
2 tablespoons (30 mL) butter
2 tablespoons (30 mL) sunflower oil
1 medium onion, finely chopped
8 ounces (250 g) mushrooms, thinly sliced
2 firm apples, such as Cortland, Empire, or Spartan, peeled, cored, and quartered
1 tablespoon (15 mL) cornstarch
2 cups (500 mL) apple juice
1 tablespoon (15 mL) soy sauce
1/2 teaspoon (2 mL) salt
Freshly ground pepper

✦ Preheat the oven to 350°F (180°C).

✦ Dredge chicken in flour, shaking off excess. In a heavy, ovenproof frying pan, heat butter and oil over medium heat. Add chicken and brown on all sides. Transfer the pan to the oven and bake chicken for 15 minutes or until juices run clear. Transfer to a plate and keep warm.

✦ In the same frying pan, cook onion, mushrooms, and apples, turning until golden, 5 to 7 minutes. Transfer apple quarters to the plate with chicken and keep warm.

✦ Stir cornstarch with enough apple juice to form a thin paste. Add to the pan of mushrooms and onion, along with remaining apple juice and soy sauce, and bring to a boil, stirring until smooth. Add salt and pepper to taste.

✦ Divide chicken among 4 warmed plates and drizzle with sauce. Arrange apples around chicken. Serve with rice and steamed vegetables.

Apple pickers fill wooden bins in the orchards of St-Joseph-du-Lac.

Shahrokh Khanizadeh

The fruit scientist was checking apple varieties to crossbreed for growers who want fruit that resists disease and stores well. Suddenly he noticed that the flesh of a newly developed apple he had cut apart was staying crisp and white.

An apple that doesn't need a drizzling of lemon juice to stop it from going brown is a find, according to Shahrokh Khanizadeh, a veteran Agriculture and Agri-Food Canada fruit breeder whose new breeds, which include 36 varieties of apples, strawberries, and raspberries, have changed the fresh fruit scene in Quebec.

"A half-hour later, I noticed that it stayed white . . . I couldn't believe it," he says. So he cut into another variety of apple and kept an eye on both in his office at the St-Jean-sur-Richelieu research centre where he worked. Two days later, the first apple still looked freshly cut, whereas the flesh of the second had turned brown and wrinkled.

Colleagues helped name his non-browning apple after the fruit of the Garden of Eden, and the Eden apple has tantalized the food industry ever since news about it leaked out after that day in 2000. Originally developed for makers of apple juice and cider because it didn't fall readily from the tree, it's being grown by prize-winning ice cider–maker François Pouliot at his La Face Cachée de la Pomme ice cider company south of Montreal, in Hemmingford. The advantage is that these apples hang on the tree until midwinter, so the cold concentrates their flavour.

Processors would profit from the Eden because of its non-browning characteristic. They could use it for sliced apples, pie filling, and apple chips, while restaurants see its advantage for making fruit cups that keep their fresh look. So why is Eden slow to reach the market?

Government bureaucracy, answers Shahrokh, describing a jungle of red tape that follows invention. A new variety of fruit needs a patent and certain clearances before growers can obtain the trees. American fruit scientists are working on developing a non-browning apple, says the scientist, who was born in Iran, educated at Tehran and McGill universities, and has worked cooperatively with counterparts in the United States, Europe, and China. He finds the world of fruit development "very, very competitive." This type of food science is not genetic modification but the old-fashioned method of arranged marriages called crossbreeding.

Other apples that he has developed have sold well, including the Diva, another tree-clinging variety used by cider prize-winner Robert Demoy at his Cidrerie du Minot at Hemmingford. Three other of his apple varieties, all scab-resistant, are widely grown in Quebec—Belmac and Primavera, both red, late-season varieties, and SuperMac, a firmer, longer-storing McIntosh derivative.

Right: Fruit scientist Shahrokh Khanizadeh has developed many varieties of apples, strawberries, and raspberries.

Bomba

HOT PEPPER PASTE

When the early autumn sun ripens sweet and hot peppers, Marisa Birri makes this hot pepper condiment she calls "bomba." She has a full range of peppers available to her, as her husband, Lino, grows them in Laval and on Montreal's South Shore and sells them, along with his other crops, at a big stall at Montreal's Jean-Talon Market. She likes to cook the paste in a wok and include the pepper seeds. You can lower the heat by discarding the seeds and upping the quantity of sweet peppers. Use the spread on sandwiches, or for pasta and rice, and to accent grilled meats and fish.

MAKES ABOUT 1¼ CUPS (300 mL)

1 or 2 jalapeño peppers
5 sweet cherry peppers
5 red bell peppers
5 green poblano or Anaheim peppers
1 serrano pepper, or more to taste
4 tablespoons (60 mL) vegetable oil, plus more as needed
5 cloves garlic, chopped
Salt and freshly ground pepper
1 bunch fresh coriander, including stems, chopped

✦ Cut jalapeño peppers in half lengthwise; do not remove seeds. Chop. Trim away stems and interior membranes and discard seeds from all the other peppers, then coarsely chop.

✦ In a large, heavy, stovetop-safe casserole dish, heat oil over medium heat and sauté garlic for 2 minutes. Add the jalapeño, sweet cherry, red bell, and poblano peppers and sauté just until they begin to become tender. Reduce heat to low and add some of the serrano pepper to taste. Continue cooking very gently, uncovered and stirring occasionally, for 45 minutes, until mixture has blended into a thick sauce; if it starts to dry out, add a little more oil. About halfway, taste and add more serrano, if desired. Stir almost constantly at the end of cooking time.

✦ Add coriander and remove the casserole dish from heat. Pour sauce into a food processor (in 2 batches, if necessary) and pulse briefly just until mixture is combined but not completely smooth and still has texture. Store in clean, lidded jars in the refrigerator for up to a month. Do not freeze.

Note

The poblano pepper is large and heart-shaped, mildly hot, brown when dried to make an ancho or mulato, smoked and dried to become a chipotle. The Anaheim pepper is a mild chili pepper. The serrano pepper is another chili pepper, hotter than the jalapeño. Be sure to wear rubber gloves when handling hot peppers.

Michael Rossy prides himself on the different colours of kale at his farm near Arundel.

Healthy Greens

Walking through Michael Rossy's market garden in the Laurentians is an experience. He prides himself on producing what he calls "entertainment vegetables," and my first sight of his patch of kale was certainly entertaining. This dark green leafy plant with a frizzy look to its leaves also comes in black, and I mean black. His favourite varieties of kale are Siberian and Russian Rainbow. Dandelion greens flourish, and Swiss chard brightens up his garden with five colours of stems: red, orange, yellow, fuchsia, and white.

Rossy, whose property near Arundel is called Runaway Creek Farm, is working to put kale on our plates. Start with salad, he suggests. Chop the leaves in bite-size pieces and put in a salad bowl; season with salt and pepper. Then work in a ripe avocado, tossing or pressing with your hands until it is mixed in. Make a dressing of lemon juice and soy sauce and toss with the salad. Final additions: thin slices of onion, and toasted sunflower seeds or sliced almonds or dried cranberries.

Bettes à carde à la crème

CREAMED SWISS CHARD

A vegetable both nutritious and fashionable, chard is a bitter green that originated in Sicily and is used through-out the Middle East. If it's young, make a salad of it as you would with spinach. Mature chard benefits from the creamy treatment given in this recipe from Chef Geneviève Longère. She grows chard in her garden in St-Alexis-de-Montcalm, northeast of Montreal.

SERVES 6

1 1/4 pounds (625 g) Swiss chard
2 cups (500 mL) whipping cream
Salt and freshly ground pepper
Freshly grated nutmeg

✤ Remove stems and spines of Swiss chard and slice into 1-inch (2.5 cm) pieces. Bring a large pot of water to a boil, with 1 tablespoon (15 mL) salt added for every 4 cups (1 L) water. Cook stems and spines just until tender. About 3 minutes before they are done, add leaves and cook for 3 minutes. Drain and cool stems and leaves in cold water, then drain well.

✤ Spread Swiss chard on a baking sheet lined with paper towels or a tea towel and cover with more towels.

✤ In a large, heavy saucepan over medium heat, heat cream to simmering (180°F/82°C) and cook without boiling until it thickens enough to coat the back of a wooden spoon. Remove from heat and set aside. Just before serving, press any remaining liquid out of Swiss chard. Chop leaves and stems coarsely.

✤ Reheat cream, add Swiss chard and warm, stirring often. Season with salt, pepper, and nutmeg. Serve at once.

Note

The Swiss chard can be cooked and drained up to 1 day in advance, then covered and refrigerated until ready to use.

Quiche aux légumes rôtis

ROASTED VEGETABLE QUICHE

Jane Livingston, an Eastern Townships caterer, likes to give familiar vegetables a bit of class by roasting them with herbs, then making them into a vegetarian quiche. You can vary the variety you choose, says Jane, who named her catering business after her home, East Hill Farm, near Knowlton. Yogurt and cheese enrich this combination, as does the all-butter pastry.

SERVES 3 TO 4

Fall vegetables of your choice (carrots, sweet potatoes, onions, zucchini, parsnips),
   about 4 cups (1 L) when sliced (see directions)
3 tablespoons (45 mL) olive oil
1 tablespoon (15 mL) fresh thyme leaves
1 tablespoon (15 mL) fresh rosemary leaves
Salt and freshly ground pepper
4 eggs
1/2 cup (125 mL) plain yogurt or whole milk
3/4 cup (175 mL) shredded aged cheddar cheese
1 deep-dish ready-made frozen pie shell (optional)

✤ Preheat the oven to 375°F (190°C). Oil a baking pan large enough to hold vegetables.
✤ Cut onions, if using, into 8 pieces each. Peel and slice remaining vegetables so they are approximately the same size. In a large bowl, toss vegetables with oil to coat well. Season with thyme, rosemary, and generous pinches of salt and pepper.
✤ Place vegetables in the prepared pan. Cover with aluminum foil and bake for 15 minutes. Remove foil, stir vegetables, reduce the oven temperature to 350°F (180°C), and roast, uncovered and stirring occasionally, for another 20 minutes.
✤ In the same large bowl, beat eggs with yogurt. Season with salt and pepper. Stir in ¼ cup (60 mL) of the cheese. Add vegetables, mix well, and pour into frozen pie shell, spreading mixture out evenly. Sprinkle with remaining cheese and bake for 30 to 40 minutes, until centre doesn't jiggle when the pan is gently shaken.

Note

The pie shell is optional. The vegetables can also be cooked in a baking dish.

Choux de Bruxelles au bacon

BRUSSELS SPROUTS WITH BACON

Choose your favourite pork when making this dish, suggests Peggy Regan, a Montreal baker of Irish-Scottish background. Her recipe calls for the Italian pancetta, but she also suggests "frying pork" if in the Gaspé, scrunchions if in Newfoundland, or thick-cut farm bacon if in Ontario.

SERVES 4

1 pound (500 g) Brussels sprouts, trimmed
1/2 pound (250 g) pancetta (4 thick slices)

+ Preheat the oven to 375°F (190°C).
+ Drop Brussels sprouts into a large pot of boiling salted water and boil for 8 minutes. Drain, rinse under cold running water, and drain again.
+ Place blanched sprouts in a baking dish just large enough to hold them in a single layer. Cover with pancetta slices, draping them over sprouts. Bake until tender, 20 to 25 minutes, depending on the size of the sprouts.
+ Alternatively, use a large, heavy frying pan. Fry pancetta until golden and beginning to crisp up. Toss in the blanched Brussels sprouts, crowding them in with bits of pork resting on top, and transfer the pan to the oven to finish cooking sprouts.
+ Serve with beef, pork, or poultry.

Purée de légumes au gratin

MARCEL'S MASHED ROOTS WITH CHEESE CRUMB CRUST

Veteran chef Marcel Kretz of Val-David, in the Laurentians, designed this recipe when he was commissioned by a major soup company to develop dishes inspired by early Quebec cuisine. This one uses vegetable stock to liven up winter roots. You can vary the vegetables; I add 2 cups (500 mL) cubed parsnips. Marcel, Alsatian-born and one of only a few Canadian chefs to have been honoured with the Order of Canada, spent much of his career leading Canadian and Quebec teams of chefs in international culinary competitions.

SERVES 8

2 cups (500 mL) cubed celery root

2 cups (500 mL) cubed carrots

2 cups (500 mL) cubed parsnips

2 cups (500 mL) cubed peeled rutabaga

1 cup (250 mL) cubed peeled potatoes

2 cups (500 mL) vegetable or chicken stock

Salt and freshly ground pepper

2 tablespoons (30 mL) chopped fresh flat-leaf parsley, green onions, or chives

Cheese crumb crust

2 tablespoons (30 mL) butter

1 1/2 cups (375 mL) finely cubed French bread, crust included

1 1/2 cups (375 mL) coarsely shredded cheddar cheese or crumbled goat or blue cheese

1/2 teaspoon (2 mL) ground nutmeg

Salt and freshly ground pepper

✦ Place celery root, carrots, parsnips, rutabaga, and potatoes in a large saucepan. Add stock. Cover and bring to a boil over medium-high heat. Reduce heat to very low. Simmer gently, stirring occasionally, for about 1 hour. Stock should be absorbed by the vegetables; if not, uncover and continue to simmer, stirring often, until stock is absorbed. Mash vegetables with a hand-held masher. Season with salt and pepper.

✦ For the cheese crumb crust, melt butter in a medium frying pan over medium heat. Add bread cubes and stir until crisp and lightly browned. Cool and stir in cheese and nutmeg.

✦ Spread vegetables in a shallow, buttered casserole or baking dish. Top with cheese crumb mixture.

✦ To serve right away, preheat the broiler, then place the casserole on a rack in the middle of the oven for a few minutes, just until lightly browned. Serve sprinkled with parsley. To serve after dish has been refrigerated, place in a preheated 350°F (180°C) oven until hot, 25 to 35 minutes, then set under the broiler to brown crust.

Note

Once topped with cheese crumb mixture, the casserole can be covered and refrigerated overnight. Bring to room temperature before final cooking.

Salade de carottes épicées

SPICED CARROT SALAD

Carrots, a mainstay vegetable when Quebec weather cools off, become refreshingly new with added spice and fresh herbs. Gigi Cohen, who runs the vegetarian restaurant Café Juicy Lotus in Montreal's Notre-Dame-de-Grâce district, uses a mix of international flavours in her dressing for cooked, cooled carrots. She considers this recipe Moroccan inspired. Use mature carrots; baby or "baby-cut" carrots do not have full flavour when cooked.

SERVES 6

2 pounds (1 kg) carrots, peeled and cut in 1/4-inch (5 mm) slices
1/3 cup (75 mL) olive oil
1/4 cup (60 mL) fresh lime juice or lemon juice
2 tablespoons (30 mL) cider vinegar
1 tablespoon (15 mL) ground cumin
1 tablespoon (15 mL) paprika
1/2 teaspoon (2 mL) sea salt
Pinch cayenne pepper
Pinch cardamom
1 medium ripe tomato, finely chopped
3 cloves garlic, finely chopped
1 cup (250 mL) lightly packed flat-leaf parsley leaves
1 cup (250 mL) lightly packed coriander leaves
1 red bell pepper, finely chopped

✤ Bring carrots to a boil in a medium saucepan of salted water. Reduce heat to low and simmer, covered, just until carrots are tender, about 20 minutes. Drain, transfer to a salad bowl, and let cool to room temperature.

✤ Meanwhile, for dressing, whisk together oil, lime juice, vinegar, cumin, paprika, salt, cayenne, and cardamom in a bowl. Pour dressing over carrots, turning them to coat. Let stand for 30 minutes.

✤ Meanwhile, in a blender or food processor, process tomato, garlic, parsley, coriander, and bell pepper just until roughly mixed; do not purée. Just before serving, toss with the carrots.

Sirop d'érable épicé

SPICED MAPLE SYRUP

Chef Yves Moreau of the Hôtel Forestel in Val-d'Or makes this delectable sauce with Quebec's favourite syrup. It's outstanding on roast pork, ham, and chicken, as well as on desserts such as poached pears or vanilla ice cream. Make a batch and refrigerate it so it's ready for when you suddenly need something special to liven up a simple meal.

MAKES 1⅔ CUPS (400 ML)

1 2/3 cups (400 mL) pure maple syrup
2/3 cup (150 mL) pineapple juice
2/3 cup (150 mL) apple juice
2 star anise
1 cinnamon stick
8 whole cloves
Slices fresh gingerroot, green cardamom pods, or black peppercorns (optional)

✦ In a deep saucepan over medium heat, cook maple syrup, pineapple and apple juices, star anise, cinnamon stick, cloves, and gingerroot (if using) until mixture has thickened and reduced by one-third. Cool at room temperature. Strain through a sieve and discard spices, then bottle.
✦ Stored in the refrigerator, it will last for several months.

Tarte épicée aux oeufs

SPICED CUSTARD TART

When Quebec farms always kept chickens and had a continual supply of fresh eggs, this lightly spiced dessert was not the luxury dish it appears to be today. Chef Serge Caplette, who comes from the region of Sorel-Tracy, where the St. Lawrence and Richelieu Rivers meet, remembers his grandmother making this pie. Now a chef-teacher at École hôtelière de Laval, he specializes in regional dishes and considers this pie a basic in the Richelieu River Valley. Fresh eggs and the combination of nutmeg and orange liven up the flavour.

SERVES 6 TO 8

2 cups (500 mL) milk

4 eggs

3/4 cup (175 mL) granulated sugar

1/2 teaspoon (2 mL) ground nutmeg, plus extra for sprinkling

Pinch salt

Grated peel of 1 medium orange

Pastry for single-crust, 8-inch (20 cm) pie

+ Place the oven rack in the lowest position, then place a pizza stone or a cast-iron frying pan upside down on it. Preheat the oven to 425°F (220°C).

+ In a medium saucepan, heat milk almost to the boiling point.

+ In a mixing bowl, whip eggs and sugar together using a wire whisk. Whisk in nutmeg, salt, and orange peel. Set aside.

+ Butter an 8-inch (20 cm) pie pan. Roll out pastry on a floured surface and fit it into the pan. Crimp the edges; do not prick the bottom with a fork. Cover with aluminum foil and weigh down with dried peas or beans.

+ Set pie shell on the pizza stone for 6 minutes, then remove from the oven and remove foil and peas. Return pie crust to the oven for another 4 minutes, then remove and let cool completely on a rack.

+ Reduce the oven temperature to 400°F (200°C). Pour egg mixture into cooled pie shell, sprinkle with nutmeg, and bake for 15 minutes. Reduce the oven temperature to 350°F (180°C) and bake for another 30 minutes or until a sharp knife inserted in the centre comes out clean. Cool completely before serving.

Tarte aux pommes et son croustillant

APPLE CRUMBLE TART

Chef Serge Caplette wanted to show off a traditional Quebec recipe at a Montreal conference of the International Association of Culinary Professionals. Every Quebec family cook has their own version. This one came from his family and is tried and true.

SERVES 6 TO 8

Pastry for single-crust, 9-inch (23 cm) pie (page 336)

2 tablespoons (30 mL) butter, or more to taste

5 cooking apples, preferably Cortland, Golden Delicious, or Granny Smith, peeled, cored, and cut in 1-inch (2.5 cm) pieces

1 tablespoon (15 mL) granulated sugar

Pinch ground cinnamon

1/2 cup (125 mL) packed brown sugar

2 2/3 cups (650 mL) old-fashioned rolled oats

1/2 cup (125 mL) butter, cut in small pieces and softened

+ Preheat the oven to 400°F (200°C). Roll out pastry on a floured surface to fit a 9-inch (23 cm) pie pan. Fit in pan, crimping the edges.

+ In a large, heavy frying pan, melt butter over medium heat and cook apples, turning to sauté on all sides, just until golden and caramelized. Combine granulated sugar and cinnamon and sprinkle over apples. Transfer to pie shell.

+ In a bowl, mix together brown sugar and oats, then add butter and mix into oat mixture with your fingers. Spread oat topping over apples in pie shell.

+ Bake for 25 minutes or until topping is crisp and lightly browned. Cool on a rack to room temperature before serving.

Headquarters for Plums

When historian Paul-Louis Martin realized that the property he'd acquired in the lower St. Lawrence valley was home to plum trees transplanted from France in the 1620s, he made an ambitious plan. Already restoring the handsome 1840 manor house on his land near St-André-de-Kamouraska, he decided to add to the 100 trees that had been planted by 17th-century settlers and were still growing in an orchard that once numbered some 800 trees. That was in 1973, and the result, thriving today, is called Maison de la Prune (home of the plum) and Martin and his family look after 900 trees in a microclimate formed in the shelter of a hillside near the great river.

Each September, when the plums begin ripening, Martin's wife, Marie de Blois, starts making jam, jelly, and other preserves, which the family sells in an elegant shop on the main floor of their 24-room clapboard house (see her recipe on page 290). The building was erected originally on seigneurial land by Sifroy Guéret dit Dumont as a combination house and store. Dumont was a prosperous merchant, and his family became known for their butter business. His handsome, wood-panelled shop now has shelves crowded with jars of preserves made by the Martin family from Damas plums, ancestor of the damson, both the red and yellow variety, and Lombard plums. You can also buy Martin's books in French; they cover the history of such subjects as the fruit of Quebec, Quebec architecture, and early Quebec gardens.

On Sundays if not too busy, family members—Martin, retired from a career as cultural historian at the Université du Québec à Trois-Rivières, his wife, and their son, Charles, and daughter, Julie—will escort visitors on a tour of the orchard, where apple and cherry trees grow alongside the plums. Historian Martin is proud of his orchard but likes to inform visitors it's a microcosm compared with that of 1900, when 250,000 plum trees flourished on both sides of the St. Lawrence.

Renversé aux prunes de Damas

Plum upside-down cake

The perfect plum for this easy dessert is the Damas, a small red cousin of the damson plum, grown at the restored plum orchard at St-André-de-Kamouraska, in the Lower St. Lawrence. Co-owner Marie de Blois likes to accent her plums with walnuts. If you use large plums, cut in quarters before placing in the cake pan. Whipped cream, plain yogurt, or vanilla ice cream provides a refreshing accent to this dessert.

Serves 8

1/2 cup (125 mL) unsalted butter, softened

1/2 cup (125 mL) firmly packed brown sugar

1/2 cup (125 mL) whole or halved walnuts or other nuts of your choice

2 cups (500 mL) whole plums, cut in half and pitted

1 cup (250 mL) all-purpose flour

1 1/2 teaspoons (7 mL) baking powder

1/2 teaspoon (2 mL) salt

2/3 cup (150 mL) granulated sugar

1/2 teaspoon (2 mL) vanilla extract

1 egg

1/2 cup (125 mL) milk

✤ Place the oven rack in the middle position. Preheat the oven to 350°F (180°C).

✤ Place ¼ cup (60 mL) of the butter in a round 10-inch (25 cm) cake pan. Place the pan in the preheating oven until butter is melted, about 30 seconds. Tilt the pan to spread butter evenly over the bottom. Sprinkle brown sugar and then nuts evenly over melted butter. Place plums on sugar mixture cut side down.

✤ In a small bowl, stir together the flour, baking powder, and salt. In the bowl of an electric mixer, cream the remaining ¼ cup (60 mL) butter with sugar until light and fluffy. Then add vanilla and egg, beating until well blended. Beat in flour mixture alternately with milk to make a smooth batter. Spoon batter over plums and smooth out.

✤ Bake for 40 to 45 minutes, until a cake tester inserted in the centre comes out clean. Remove cake to a rack and let cool for 5 minutes. Run a knife around the edge of pan, then invert cake, fruit side up, onto a serving plate. Serve warm or at room temperature.

Gâteau au fromage à l'érable

MAPLE CHEESECAKE

Maple sugar, growing in popularity, tops this classic cheesecake, which is sweetened with maple syrup. The recipe is from Jane Livingston, a talented cook who has created a business selling the specialties she makes in her East Hill Farm kitchen near Knowlton.

SERVES 10

Crust
1 1/2 cups (375 mL) graham cracker crumbs
1/4 cup (60 mL) maple syrup
1/3 cup (75 mL) melted butter

Filling
2 8-ounce (250 g) packages plain cream cheese
    (2 cups/500 mL), at room temperature
3/4 cup (175 mL) maple syrup
1/3 cup (75 mL) whipping cream
1 teaspoon (5 mL) vanilla extract
4 eggs
3 tablespoons (45 mL) all-purpose flour
Coarse maple sugar or brown sugar, for sprinkling

For crust:
+ Place the oven rack in the middle position. Preheat the oven to 325°F (160°C). Line a 10-inch (25 cm) springform pan with parchment paper.
+ In a mixing bowl, thoroughly combine cracker crumbs, maple syrup, and melted butter.
+ Spread crumb mixture evenly on bottom of prepared springform pan, pressing it down with the bottom of a glass. Bake for 12 minutes or until firm. Cool on a rack.

For filling:
+ In a mixing bowl, beat together cheese and maple syrup until soft and well blended. Beat in cream and vanilla, then beat in eggs, one by one, until well mixed. Sprinkle with flour and blend in. Pour mixture into prepared crust.
+ Bake cheesecake for 20 minutes, then reduce the oven temperature to 300°F (150°C) and bake for another 20 to 25 minutes. The cheesecake surface should jiggle when gently shaken.
+ Turn off the oven, open the oven door, and leave cheesecake in the oven until it has cooled completely or is cool enough to pick up with your bare hands.
+ To serve, unmould onto a serving plate and sprinkle maple sugar over top.

COOKING WITH MAPLE SYRUP

Maple syrup sells in three grades, based on its colour. Light ("clair") is syrup from early in the season, medium comes next, and dark ("ambre") is from the final days of the harvest. A "flavour wheel" designed by the maple industry and federal scientists describes six levels of taste, from light (compared to a marshmallow) to dark (black licorice). Belgian chef Pierre Résimont, who experimented with maple syrup when cooking for the Federation of Quebec Maple Syrup Producers, compared its flavour to vanilla with spices. Sherbrooke chef Danny St-Pierre uses all three grades of maple syrup in his cuisine. The light grade, usually served on breakfast pancakes, he makes into a marinade for fish fillets. Medium grade he uses to flavour sauces and vinaigrettes, and dark in a sweet-and-sour tomato sauce for veal shanks, or to make a creamy dessert. For variations on maple throughout Quebec, meet members of the Maple Gourmet Road, big users of the sweetener listed at creatifsdelerable.ca. These enterprises—restaurants and bakeries, confectioners and caterers, pastry shops and candymakers—guarantee that they will make and sell maple-flavoured treats year-round.

Riz au lait

RICE PUDDING

When the Soares family of Montreal gets together for a meal, they often wind up with Portuguese rice pudding—smooth, creamy, and lightly flavoured with lemon and cinnamon. Fatima Soares Mesquita, manager of Soares et Fils, the Portuguese grocery store in the Plateau neighbourhood of central Montreal, traces her recipe to her grandmother in Caldas da Rainha. It's an easy recipe to make, even for beginners, but you need the right rice. While it's sold at most grocery stores, to get in the mood for a Portuguese classic, you could shop at Soares, founded in 1966 by Fatima's grandfather Julio, after he immigrated from Peniche, on the coast north of Lisbon.

SERVES 4

1 cup (250 mL) arborio or other short-grain rice, rinsed
3 cups (750 mL) cold water
1 strip lemon peel
1 cinnamon stick
1/4 teaspoon (1 mL) salt
1 cup (250 mL) whole milk
1 cup (250 mL) granulated sugar
Ground cinnamon, for sprinkling

✦ In a medium, heavy-bottomed saucepan, combine rice, water, lemon peel, cinnamon stick, and salt. Set over medium-low heat and simmer, uncovered and stirring often, until rice absorbs the water, about 20 to 25 minutes.

✦ Stir in milk and sugar and cook, stirring constantly, for another 5 minutes. Remove lemon peel and cinnamon stick.

✦ Spoon into 4 individual serving dishes or 1 large bowl. Serve warm, or refrigerate for 1 to 2 hours. Sprinkle with ground cinnamon just before serving.

Gilles Jourdenais enjoys selling a big variety of Quebec cheeses at his Montreal cheese shops.

Gilles Jourdenais

A board listing the cheese bargains of the week entices you into Fromagerie Atwater, but there's little indication that, after passing through a little grocery store and descending a staircase, you have arrived at a Montreal headquarters for cheese lovers. The city has other well-stocked cheese shops, but this one, cramped and jammed with products, with no décor or fancy display, is at the heart of Quebec's love affair with cheese.

Many a day, a wiry man in a French beret appears behind the long counter, ready to sell you any of his 850 cheeses. Gilles Jourdenais is the owner and a moving force behind the boom in Quebec cheesemaking and selling. Party givers in the know consult him about the latest and best cheeses to serve. And, when Quebec cheesemakers are considering making a new cheese or wondering about trends in their sales, they call Gilles.

"We're the front line," he says. And tastemakers, he admits. That's because he and his staff talk up their cheese, in particular their 250 Quebec varieties.

Cheese shoppers, in Jourdenais's experience, usually want three varieties: a soft cheese, a semi-soft, and either a hard cheese such as cheddar, or a blue, or maybe a goat cheese. And often something new.

Not long ago, a hefty number of Quebec cheeses were semi-soft. "We must have 75 kinds at a time, and many are bestsellers, such as Le 1608," says Gilles. There was a sameness to these products because Quebec cheesemakers, who all learned from French teachers, found semi-soft cheeses easiest to make and sell. So, when consulted, the merchant started suggesting they make something different. Among the results were Maurice Dufour's Ciel de Charlevoix, a blue that has won prizes, and Laracam, a soft, washed-rind cheese like the French Reblochon, from Fromagerie du Champ à la Meule.

It's a different world since Gilles started selling food 35 years ago, working in his father's little grocery store on the same spot where he now operates his principal shop. That store stocked about two dozen cheeses, only two of them from Quebec—the semi-soft Oka and Ermite, a blue cheese. There are so many Quebec cheeses today, Gilles helped one of his staff, Amélie Tendland, write a guidebook to 100 of them. And he is in constant contact with cheesemakers, refiners, importers, and marketers, keeping up with all matters new in the world of cheese.

His bestselling Quebec varieties? Le 1608, Victor et Berthold, 14 Arpents, Bleu d'Élizabeth, Le Riopelle, and Chèvre Noir.

Winter

When the temporary winter walls go up to shelter vendors at Montreal's big public markets, we face the bitter truth that winter is coming. Another sign is the presence of huge bags of root vegetables, giant bunches of leeks, and bushels of apples. In the old days those bulk quantities were a form of insurance that the cook was prepared to make plenty of warming stews and soups to ward off the Quebec winter. Now that families are smaller and few have those cool, damp spaces in their homes called "root cellars," shoppers for the huge quantities tend to be soup kitchens, food banks, and Cuisine Collective groups that run cooking bees in the inner city. Back when markets were started in Montreal and Quebec City in the mid-1800s, winter shopping would have included sides of beef and live chickens and rabbits, firewood, bales of hay, blocks of ice, and tobacco. There's still the sense that we must batten down the hatches to prepare for grim weather ahead.

Winter menus in restaurants heat up. Old Quebec recipes are revived, even in sophisticated urban establishments. Chefs seem to like offering their spin on their mothers' cooking alongside fancier fare, using a lighter touch of fat than in earlier times. It's not surprising to be offered tourtière, the meatball stew known as ragoût de boulettes, cretons (coarse pork pâté) and baked beans, and, for dessert, pouding chômeur and tarte Tatin.

Braising comes into its own each winter. Home cooks have made cold-weather pot roasts forever, but I notice chefs, particularly those who prefer local foods to imports, serving dishes such as burgundy stews (for example, Bison bourguignon, page 346) and using vegetables from Quebec winter storages to create braised or slow-roasted dishes.

Early Quebecers made pâtés, terrines, galantines, ballotines, and cretons to stretch every scrap of meat. It's been said that the original cuisine was based on scarcity. These mixtures of seasoned meats have gone upscale; sometimes they even contain duck foie gras.

Pork comes into its own in winter. It has always been a favourite Quebec family meat, for the pig was easy to raise and the meat could be salted and stored for months. A pork recipe I have found popular throughout Quebec is a roast that's cooked slowly along with potatoes, plus a sliced onion and dried or salted herbs for flavour. A perfect winter dinner, it's been relished by farmers and fishermen from Quebec's earliest days. My friend Madeleine Kamman, the Paris-born U.S. cooking teacher, traced it for me to Flanders. She could remember her mother, of Flemish background, cooking a rolled shoulder of pork in the Quebec fashion. "The potatoes browned in the natural gravy are unforgettable because of the caramelization," she wrote to me after trying a recipe I'd acquired from the Mauricie region of central Quebec. This recipe turns up all over Quebec, from the Gaspé to the Laurentians.

Today's pork, bred to be lean in the interests of our health, must be cooked gently and with moisture or it dries out. In recent years, some small Quebec producers have begun a return to a fattier meat that's more flavourful and tender. Montreal chef Martin Picard, whose restaurant, Au Pied de Cochon, has been called a palace of pork, is breeding Berkshire pigs for his restaurants. Berkshire pigs are believed to be England's earliest breed, and their meat is juicy, tender, and heavily marbled, with more flavour than mass-produced pork.

First Courses

Gina's Portobello Mushrooms

Halibut or Tuna Tartare with Avocado and Sour Cream

Carpaccio of Quebec Cheeses

Duck Foie Gras

Butternut Squash Soup with Grilled Scallops

Beet Soup

Spiced Pork Spread

My Mother's Pea Soup

Main Courses

Abitibi Trout with Fresh Herbs

Roast Beef with Gravy

Venison Steak with Tea Sauce

Venison Steak with Aurgula Salad and Mushrooms

Tourtière

Tourtière du Saguenay

Pastry

Salted Herbs

Roast pork with Pan-Browned Potatoes

Crispy Chicken Breasts with Honey Glaze

Bison Bourguignon

Cheese Tart

Side Dishes

French Country Bread

Glazed Baby Turnips

Cousin Christine's Yellow Turnip Puff

Beer-Braised Cabbage

Jerusalem Artichokes au Gratin

Mashed Potatoes with Cheese and Truffle Paste

Spiced Squash Cubes

Desserts

Fresh Cranberry Tart

Chocolate Cranberry Cookies

Kathy's Lemon Chocolate Supreme

Tarte Tatin

Maple Bread Pudding

Molasses Cookies

Flourless Chocolate Cake

Apple Charlotte

Champignons grillés

GINA'S PORTOBELLO MUSHROOMS

These big, meaty mushrooms are regarded as better than steak by the family of Gina Balleani, in the Montreal suburb of Kirkland. Italian-born, Gina traces this recipe back to her grandmother in Canosa di Puglia, in southern Italy.

SERVES 4

4 tablespoons (60 mL) olive oil
6 or 7 Portobello mushrooms
Salt and freshly ground pepper
1 tablespoon (15 mL) crushed fresh garlic
3 tablespoons (45 mL) chopped fresh flat-leaf parsley
3 to 4 tablespoons (45 to 60 mL) plain fresh bread crumbs

+ Preheat the oven to 375°F (190°C). Grease a 13 × 9 inch (33 × 23 cm) baking pan with 2 tablespoons (30 mL) of the oil.
+ Remove stems from mushrooms and chop stems finely. Arrange mushroom caps, gills side down, in the pan. Sprinkle chopped stems around caps. Sprinkle mushrooms with salt and pepper, and then with garlic and parsley. Sprinkle with bread crumbs and drizzle with remaining 2 tablespoons (30 mL) oil.
+ Bake, uncovered, for 20 minutes or until crumbs are browned and mushrooms are tender to the fork.

Tartare de flétan ou thon à l'avocat et à la crème

Halibut or tuna tartare with avocado and sour cream

La Maison du Pêcheur is a headquarters for fish and seafood cuisine in the Gaspé town of Percé, the restaurant in full view of the famous rock. Chef-owner Georges Mamelonet enjoys playing with a big variety of fish for his menu.

Serves 4

12 ounces (375 g) sushi-grade halibut or tuna, finely diced
Finely grated peel of 1 lemon
2 tablespoons (30 mL) lemon juice
1 tablespoon (15 mL) chopped fresh flat-leaf parsley
1 tablespoon (15 mL) chopped chives or green onion tops
Salt and freshly ground white pepper
1 ripe avocado
4 tablespoons (60 mL) sour cream, or more to taste
Espelette pepper or cayenne pepper, for sprinkling

✦ Place fish, lemon peel and juice, parsley, chives, salt, and white pepper in a resealable plastic bag. Close the bag and turn it several times to mix ingredients well. Refrigerate for 1 hour.

✦ In a bowl, mash avocado into a purée and combine with sour cream.

✦ Scoop a layer of avocado mixture into each of 4 small serving glasses and sprinkle with pepper. Add a layer of fish and pepper. Continue layering, sprinkling each with pepper and ending with an avocado layer and pepper. Chill in the refrigerator. Serve chilled.

Marion Ferriol of St-Basile-le-Grand catches perch through the ice in Montreal harbour.

Fishing through the Ice

The time-honoured Quebec sport of ice fishing is enjoyed on waterways as varied as the Bay of Chaleur, certain major rivers, and even lakes on golf courses that have been stocked with trout. At streamlined ice-fishing centres, holes are drilled for fishermen, rods installed on sticks, bait provided in the form of buckets of live minnows, and hot soup and hot dogs offered right there on the ice. The major location is at Ste-Anne-de-la-Pérade, east of Trois-Rivières on the St. Lawrence River, where as many as 500 fishing cabins spring up on the ice at the mouth of the Ste-Anne River each winter, and tommy cod (*poisson des chenaux*), up to 8 inches long, can be caught as they make their way to their traditional spawning ground.

All along the Gaspé coast, fishermen cut long, narrow holes in the ice, wait for the tides to start running, and lower nets to trap dozens of tiny smelt no more than 4 inches long. In Montreal harbour, canvas shelters are erected around little stoves to shelter fishermen trying to catch a variety of fish, ranging from the tiny tommy cod to perch and lotte (*barbotte*).

Cooking methods are simplest in the Gaspé, I learned from my daughter, Claire, who lived for several years on the Bay of Chaleur. She would toss smelt onto the ice, where they would freeze in minutes, easy to bag and carry home to store in the freezer or to cook right away.

Thaw the fish in a bowl of cold water, she directs. Clean them, gutting them and removing heads, then dip them in flour, salt, and pepper. Cook for two minutes a side in one of two ways: in a heavy, red-hot frying pan sizzling with oil and butter, or directly on a blazing hot woodstove sprinkled first with salt.

At ice-fishing centres, the favourite technique seems to be to dip the fish in beaten egg, then in flour, salt, and pepper, and fry it quickly in hot oil and butter.

Ice-fishing huts are set up each winter in Montreal harbour.

Carpaccio de fromages du Québec

CARPACCIO OF QUEBEC CHEESES

Chef Marie-Chantal Lepage is dedicated to cooking with foods from the region around her Quebec City restaurant, L'Espace MC Chef. She combines some of her favourite cheeses from the Lower St. Lawrence in this biscuit to enjoy with drinks. One of Quebec's most respected chefs, she has run the kitchens of large restaurants, travelled widely to demonstrate Quebec cuisine outside her city and province, and recently opened her own establishment in Quebec City's Lower Town. Her recipe can be made with other mixtures of cheeses. If you have leftovers, use these snacks to top hot toast.

SERVES 4

2 ounces (60 g) Ciel de Charlevoix cheese
2 ounces (60 g) Brie de Portneuf
2 ounces (60 g) Riopelle de l'Isle
2 ounces (60 g) Chèvre des neiges

✦ Cut each piece of cheese into thirds, discarding the rind from the Brie. Place cheeses in a bowl, mixing them up so varieties are distributed. Let stand at room temperature for several hours.
✦ Cut 2 pieces of parchment or waxed paper, each about 12 inches (30 cm) square. Place a sheet on a cutting board. Place cheeses in the centre of the paper and cover with the second piece of paper. Using a rolling pin, roll out the cheeses to the thickness of a thin cookie.
✦ Place the paper-covered cheeses, still on the cutting board, in the freezer, until cheeses are frozen.
✦ Remove from the freezer. Peel off the top layer of paper and use either a knife or cookie cutter to cut the cheese into small, snack-size shapes. They will take only about 15 minutes to thaw.
✦ Serve cold with olives as hors d'oeuvres with drinks.

Foie gras de canard

DUCK FOIE GRAS

Michelle Gélinas, a Montreal food specialist, considers her recipe for this favourite Quebec appetizer "the classic way" to prepare the delicate livers of specially fattened ducks. Quebec is a major producer of duck foie gras, the industry modelled on that of France, where goose foie gras is a basic food. It's considered part of the French culinary tradition and efforts to ban it as inhumane to the ducks have never been successful in the province.

SERVES 8 TO 10

1 whole uncooked duck foie gras, 1 to 1 1/2 pounds (500 to 750 g)
Salt and freshly ground pepper
1/2 cup (125 mL) cognac, white port, Pineau des Charentes, or Sauternes

+ Place foie gras in a medium bowl. Cover with room-temperature water and let soak, at room temperature, for 2 hours, turning the foie gras in the water from time to time.
+ Remove foie gras from water and dry with paper towels. Place on a cutting board and gently separate the two lobes. Using a sharp knife, cut the larger lobe open along its length. Detach and discard the veins, using the handle of a metal spoon (not a knife, as the meat is very soft). Trim away the sack containing the spleen and discard. Repeat with second lobe.
+ Place the lobes in a terrine or glass baking dish about 9½ × 7½ inches (24 × 19 cm). Sprinkle with salt and pepper and pour the liquor over top. Cover the terrine with plastic wrap and refrigerate for 24 hours.
+ Drain liquid from foie gras and place it on a cutting board. Dry with paper towels and stack one lobe on top of the other. Cut a piece of plastic wrap twice the length of the foie gras. Place the foie gras in the centre of the plastic wrap and wrap it up tightly, twisting the ends of the plastic wrap closed. Repeat this wrap four more times. Then wrap the foie gras package in aluminum foil, twisting the foil ends closed.
+ To steam the foie gras, you will need a stovetop-safe casserole dish or baking dish that has a tightly fitting lid and is large enough to take a marguerite (perforated strainer). Place marguerite in the casserole dish, then add a rack at least the size of the foie gras. Pour 2 cups (500 mL) water into the casserole dish and place over high heat. Bring water to a boil, lay the foie gras package on the rack, and cover with the lid. Immediately start timing the steaming. The foie gras should steam for 15 to 20 minutes, depending on its weight: 1 pound (500 g) for 15 minutes; 1⅓ to 1½ pounds (600 to 750 g) for 20 minutes.
+ When foie gras is cooked, it will be soft. Remove it from the casserole dish, place on the rack on a plate, and refrigerate for 12 hours.
+ Unwrap, then wrap in fresh plastic wrap and refrigerate until ready to serve.
+ Serve cold on toasted brioche or spiced bread as an hors d'oeuvre, plain or with onion marmalade.

Note
The cooked foie gras will keep, refrigerated, for up to 8 days.

COOKING SCALLOPS

Begin by buying scallops that are all one size, says Johanne Vigneau, chef-owner of La Table des Roy in Îles de la Madeleine. Cooking times differ, she explains to a class at her new cooking school. If the scallops are frozen, thaw them in the refrigerator or in cold water. The temperature of the water must be similar to that of the scallops or you'll unintentionally start cooking them. Don't cook them at a low temperature or they'll be rubbery and dispense a cloudy liquid. Here's Johanne's method of searing scallops, demonstrated to a class attended by my friend and *Gazette* colleague Susan Schwartz: Sear scallops quickly in canola oil in a hot frying pan. Transfer the seafood to a hot oven (400 to 450°F/200 to 230°C) for a few minutes, just to complete cooking.

Soupe à la courge musquée et aux pétoncles grillés

Butternut squash soup with grilled scallops

Vegetables grown by the First Nations continue to be part of Quebec cuisine, as Chef Anne Desjardins of Ste-Adèle demonstrates with this soup. She refuses to rely on imported vegetables even when the Laurentian Mountains are covered with snow, often using root vegetables in her cuisine. Quebecers love scallops, but this soup is also good without them, if you prefer to leave them out. Substitute crumbled crisp bacon.

Serves 6

1 butternut squash (2 pounds/1 kg)

1 1-inch (2.5 cm) piece fresh gingerroot, coarsely chopped

2 onions, quartered

4 cups (1 L) chicken stock, plus more as needed

Salt

Lemon juice

2 tablespoons (30 mL) olive oil, plus more for brushing and searing

1/4 teaspoon (1 mL) curry powder

1/4 teaspoon (1 mL) smoked paprika

6 large scallops or 7 ounces (200 g) small scallops (optional)

Chopped chives

✤ Preheat the oven to 425°F (220°C). Line a baking sheet with aluminum foil.

✤ Cut squash in half and discard seeds and threads. Brush inside of squash with olive oil and fill the halves with ginger and onions. Place on the prepared baking sheet and bake for 1 hour or until tender to the fork.

✤ When squash is cool enough to handle, scoop out onion filling and cooked flesh and place in a food processor. Add about half the stock and pulse until mixture is puréed. Pour into a large saucepan. Stir in remaining stock and bring to a boil over medium-high heat. Add salt and a drop or two of lemon juice to taste.

✤ In a cup, combine oil, curry powder, and paprika.

✤ Rinse scallops (if using) and pat dry with paper towels. In a large, heavy frying pan, add enough oil to coat the surface. Heat and sear scallops on one side only, about 2 minutes.

✤ Pour hot soup into 6 deep, warmed bowls. Place a seared scallop in each bowl and top with a little of the spiced oil. Sprinkle with chives and serve.

Note

The soup can be prepared up to 1 day in advance, then covered and refrigerated. When ready to reheat, if the soup is too thick, add enough stock to achieve desired consistency.

Soupe aux betteraves

Beet soup

There are two secrets to Chef Janick Bouchard's beet soup, says the chef-owner of Restaurant Janick, in Beloeil, on the Richelieu River southeast of Montreal. The first is homemade chicken stock, fresh and carefully strained. The second is fresh beets, which give the soup a glowing rosy red colour instead of the deep maroon of borscht, made with older or canned beets. Janick, who trained with top Montreal chefs before opening his own place in 2006, also makes this soup with carrots.

Serves 6

4 ounces (125 g) smoked pork or back bacon, cut in short, thin strips (lardons)
2 tablespoons (30 mL) unsalted butter
1 large onion, coarsely chopped
1 leek, white part only, sliced
4 or 5 medium beets, peeled and cubed
Salt and freshly ground pepper
4 to 5 cups (1 to 1.25 L) chicken stock
1 cup (250 mL) whole milk (optional)
Sour cream, crème fraîche, or plain Greek yogurt
Finely chopped green onions or chives

✦ In a heavy frying pan, fry smoked pork over medium heat until crisp, then drain on paper towels.

✦ In a medium, heavy saucepan over medium-low heat, melt butter and sauté onion and leek, stirring often, until softened but not browned, about 5 minutes. Add beets and cook for another 10 minutes, stirring occasionally. Season with salt and pepper.

✦ Add 4 cups (1 L) of the stock, increase heat to medium, and bring to a boil. Reduce heat to low and simmer, covered, until beets are tender, about 30 minutes.

✦ Purée beet mixture in a food processor, adding more stock to achieve desired consistency. Stir in milk (if using). Heat soup, adding more salt and pepper to taste.

✦ Serve soup in 6 heated bowls, each portion topped with sour cream, crisp pork strips, and green onions.

Cretons

SPICED PORK SPREAD

This spiced pork spread is regularly served at Quebec breakfasts and brunches. Ginette Chapdelaine of Montreal remembers her grandmother making cretons at her home in the Mile End neighbourhood of central Montreal. "For us growing up, this was comfort food," Ginette recalls. Flavouring dishes with this combination of spices dates back to the earliest Quebec settlers, who brought medieval food customs to the New World.

SERVES 6 TO 8

1 pound (500 g) medium-fat ground pork
1/2 pound (250 g) ground veal
2 slices dried bread, shredded into crumbs
1 medium onion, grated
1 teaspoon (5 mL) salt
Pinch freshly ground pepper
1 teaspoon (5 mL) ground cinnamon, or more to taste
1/2 teaspoon (2 mL) ground cloves, or more to taste
1 1/4 cups (310 mL) whole milk

+ Place all ingredients in a large saucepan and cook over medium heat for 1 hour, stirring often at first to break up meat. Let cool, transfer to a mould or several small moulds, and refrigerate, covered, for up to 5 days, or freeze for up to 2 months.
+ Serve with toast or crackers, or as a filling for a sandwich.

Note

Be sure to use medium-fat pork for this recipe. Lean pork will give the cretons a grainy texture so that it does not spread easily.

It has been an uphill fight, a long war with Quebec's severe extremes of weather, as well as the skepticism of wine critics. But the province's winemakers are winning their battle with bitter winters and scorching summers, and even the doubters are enjoying all types of local wine—white, red, and rosé. Montreal wine writer Jean Aubry notes that serious winemaking began in Quebec just over 30 years ago and local wineries, which number more than 100, over 50 of them seriously recognized, have yet to produce what he calls great wines. But they are "on the march," in his view. One of his examples is a 2012 rosé produced by L'Orpailleur, Quebec's largest winery, which he calls "an absolute marvel."

Montreal sommelier André J. Côté is equally enthusiastic about the progress made in what he calls Quebec's "crazy adventure" in trying to produce fine wine when winter temperatures descend to below 40°F (5°C), "killer frost level," for weeks on end. "Winemakers have had a long and difficult journey, but, today, the industry has to be recognized as a force to be reckoned with," in André's view. It's a matter of experience, he believes, and remembers his friend, L'Orpailleur's winemaker Charles-Henri de Coussergues, explaining: "The vines are older, the winemakers are also older and wiser. We are now ready to move on to the second stage."

Considerable recognition for certain vintages has already been achieved. André, who is a past president of the Canadian Association of Professional Sommeliers, notes that Quebec wines have improved greatly in the past decade and have been rating well internationally. "Quebec wines have brought home more than 200 medals over the past 16 years," by his count. And their prices are fair, in his view. One of his favourites is a 2007 red wine from the Domaine des Côtes d'Ardoise, only $16 and his choice with a lusty Italian sausage lasagne dinner. Lately, Jean Aubry has been enjoying Quebec sparkling wines; "the expertise is building up," he says.

Competition with other wines, especially top-selling French, is tough in Quebec, a region of serious wine consumption. With less than 25 per cent of the Canadian population, Quebecers drink 60 per cent of the wine consumed in Canada and the province's estimated annual average of 22 litres per person is higher than U.S. estimates. Quebec winemakers compete by issuing frequent invitations to their premises where tastings, vineyard tours and—sometimes—restaurant meals are offered.

What's ahead for the Quebec wine industry? Jean Aubry would like to see local winemakers move away from their favourite hybrid grapes, in particular the Seyval, which has been called "the motor of the industry." Red hybrid varieties are also popular, these hybrids genetic crossings between European and North American varieties. They are the security blanket of choice in the province, grown for their winter hardiness, resistance to disease, and ability to produce grapes in a shorter growing season. All very well, in Jean's view, but he would like more risks to be taken. His hope is that Quebecers will start producing riesling, chardonnay, gewürztraminer, pinot gris, and pinot noir. Time to move on, he says.

Soupe aux pois de ma mère

My mother's pea soup

Chefs with mothers who enjoyed cooking often give these women credit for launching them on culinary careers. Chef Robin Tremblay of Auberge-Bistro Rose & Basilic, in the northern Quebec town of Alma, remembers his mother, Lucienne Dallaire, as a "cordon bleu" cook and baker who gave him "the love of cooking." Bringing up 10 children in the Saguenay town of Larouche, she grew her own vegetables and herbs and used them in this traditional Quebec winter soup. Be careful when adding salt to the soup, Robin warns, as the salt pork and salted herbs provide plenty of saltiness already.

Serves 8

2 cups (500 mL) dried whole yellow peas, rinsed
1 medium onion, finely chopped
2 carrots, peeled and finely chopped
2 stalks celery, chopped
4 ounces (125 g) salt pork
6 cups (1.5 L) cold water, plus more as needed
1 tablespoon (15 mL) salted herbs (page 337)
Freshly ground pepper
1 tablespoon (15 mL) minced fresh savory, plus more to taste

+ In a large pot, place peas, onion, carrots, celery, salt pork, and water. Bring to a boil over high heat. Reduce heat to low and simmer slowly, uncovered, for 2½ hours, adding more water if soup dries out too much.
+ Add salted herbs and pepper. Continue cooking until peas are very tender. Stir in savory and taste, adding more if necessary. Add more pepper to taste. Serve hot.

Note

If you like, use store-bought salted herbs, available at specialty stores and many supermarkets. If you wish to reduce salt, rinse salted herbs in cold water and drain before using.

Ice-fishing is big business each winter
at Ste-Anne-de-la-Pérade.

Truite de l'Abitibi aux fines herbes

ABITIBI TROUT WITH FRESH HERBS

Ste-Adèle chef Anne Desjardins has been cooking farm-raised trout ever since Quebec fish farmer Roger Perigny pioneered the raising of these fish in the icy cold water of an esker, an ancient glacial riverbed at St-Mathieu-d'Harricana, in the northwestern region of Abitibi-Témiscamingue. Anne likes to use the "unilateral" method, cooking the fish on one side only to give it a sautéed effect without overcooking. She describes her sauce as "a broken emulsion of cream and olive oil, Nordic and Mediterranean, with a touch of acidity from lemon or vinegar."

SERVES 4

1/3 cup (75 mL) olive oil
3 tablespoons (45 mL) whipping cream
1 tablespoon (15 mL) tarragon vinegar or balsamic vinegar, or to taste
Salt
2 skin-on trout fillets (12 ounces/375 g each)
4 tablespoons (60 mL) chopped fresh herbs (parsley, basil, tarragon, and dill)
2 green onions, finely chopped
1 small red bell pepper, finely diced

✤ Preheat the oven to 150°F (65°C). Place 4 serving plates in the oven to warm.

✤ In a small saucepan, combine 1 tablespoon (15 mL) of the oil with cream, vinegar, and salt to taste. Cook over medium heat until hot, then cover and keep warm in the oven.

✤ Pour remaining oil into a large, heavy frying pan and set over medium-high heat. When the oil is hot, add trout, skin side down, and cook, uncovered, just until fillets turn opaque. Do not flip. The edges of the fish should be crisp and the centres slightly underdone.

✤ Cut each fillet in half and arrange on the warmed plates. Pour sauce over fillets and trim each with herbs, green onions, and bell pepper.

Rôti de boeuf au jus

ROAST BEEF WITH GRAVY

Long and slow, then a quick, blazing-hot finale. That's the best way to cook roast beef, according to Montreal chef-professor Jean-Paul Grappe. He credits his French grandparents and parents with this method, which he uses regularly, and finds that the meat is very tender. Chef Grappe estimates that he loses only about 10 per cent of the weight of the meat during cooking. "Even if nothing new has been invented in cuisine in 350 years," says the veteran teacher, "the cooking of roasts has evolved considerably." The late Quebec culinary authority Jehane Benoit used this technique: to calculate roasting time for the beef, she would estimate 30 minutes per pound (500 g) at 250°F (120°C). In my experience, this works best if the roast weighs 4 or more pounds (2+ kg).

SERVES 8

1 standing rib roast, 4 to 4 1/2 pounds (2 to 2.25 kg)
Salt and freshly ground pepper
4 teaspoons (20 mL) spices of your choice (see opposite page)
6 tablespoons (90 mL) vegetable oil
1 medium onion, coarsely chopped
1 medium carrot, coarsely chopped
2 stalks celery, coarsely chopped
4 cloves garlic
2 bay leaves
1 sprig fresh thyme (or 1/2 teaspoon/2 mL dried thyme leaves)
1 2/3 cups (400 mL) beef stock

+ Remove roast from the refrigerator 2 hours before starting to roast. When ready to cook, preheat oven to 250°F (120°C). Sprinkle meat all over with salt, pepper, and spices. Insert a meat thermometer in thickest part of roast, avoiding the bone.

+ Place a rack just a little larger than the meat in a roasting pan and add oil to the pan. Place roast on the rack. (With this method you do not brown the meat before roasting.) Roast for 2 hours, then scatter onion, carrot, celery, garlic, and bay leaves around the meat.

+ Stir thyme into pan juices. Continue roasting for another 2 to 4 hours, depending on the size and thickness of the roast. When the meat thermometer registers 120°F (49°C), the meat will be rare. Remove from the oven or continue roasting until the meat thermometer registers 125°F (52°C) for medium-rare, 130°F (54°C) for medium, or 140°F (60°C) for well done.

+ To brown the roast, increase oven temperature to 500°F (260°C) and continue roasting until richly browned, from 5 to 15 minutes.

+ Remove meat from the oven, cover with aluminum foil, and let stand at room temperature for 20 minutes before carving.

For gravy:

+ Skim fat from pan juices. Place roasting pan over two burners turned to medium-low. Add stock. Bring to a simmer and stir often for 5 minutes, scraping up the brown bits from the pan bottom. Add salt and pepper to taste. For a smooth gravy, strain gravy through a sieve; otherwise include vegetables in the sauce. Slice meat thinly and serve on warmed plates with gravy.

Notes

You can use other cuts of beef too: cross rib, sirloin tip, eye of round, or rolled rump.

For the spice mixture, use a commercial spice mixture or mix seasonings of your choice, such as red pepper flakes, dry mustard, dried thyme and rosemary, about 1 teaspoon (5 mL) of each.

Steak de cerf, sauce au thé

Venison steak with tea sauce

Chef Normand Laprise, co-owner with Christine Lamarche of Montreal's Toqué!, is a specialist in cooking venison. When the large deer farm Cerf de Boileau, near Montebello, was testing animal feed, Normand played a role in deciding which feed produced the best-tasting meat. Venison is lean and distinctively flavoured, so a careful hand must be used to cook and season it. The chef recommends root vegetables with this dish.

Serves 4

3/4 cup (175 mL) boiling water
2 tablespoons (30 mL) whole oolong tea leaves
2 venison steaks (10 ounces/300 g each)
Salt and freshly ground pepper
2 tablespoons (30 mL) olive oil
7 tablespoons (105 mL) unsalted butter

+ Make strong tea with the boiling water and tea leaves.
+ Season the steaks generously with salt and pepper. Heat a cast-iron frying pan over high heat until it is smoking hot, then add oil and 4 tablespoons (60 mL) of the butter. Sear steaks until crusty and golden, about 3 to 4 minutes per side, depending on thickness of steaks. Transfer steaks to a warmed serving plate and let rest for several minutes. Discard pan drippings.
+ Reduce heat to medium-high and add 2 tablespoons (30 mL) of the butter to the pan. Heat until it turns golden. Strain tea into the pan and simmer sauce for about 1 minute. Whisk in remaining 1 tablespoon (15 mL) butter.
+ Slice steaks and serve on 4 warmed serving plates, sauce drizzled generously over top.

Cerf de Boileau, up the Ottawa River near Montebello, was not the first deer farm that I had been to. These enterprises are dotted about Quebec, and I'd also seen plenty of beautiful red deer munching on my flowers at my house in the Eastern Townships. It's quite a show when my dog barks and the deer leap gracefully away into the forest, their white tails bouncing. But a snowy day at the Boileau deer farm left the biggest impression, appropriate since it's Canada's largest, and its venison is a regular on menus of fine restaurants. Enclosed in big, snow-covered pastures, hundreds of the Boileau deer stood perfectly still watching us as photographer Gordon Beck shot picture after picture. We even had close-ups when farm manager Denis Ferrer took us to a field of a few dozen deer. They'd been ostracized by the herd, he explained, because they had been abandoned as babies and raised by humans. Corn, sprinkled on the snow, encouraged the animals to amble close to us. My granddaughter Ann was even able to feed them from her hand, one in particular. "Her name is Candy," said Denis. "She's the leader, the dominatrix."

Deer are fed a special mixture of grains at the
Cerf de Boileau deer farm near Montebello.

Bavette de cerf de Boileau sur une salade roquette aux champignons

VENISON STEAK WITH ARUGULA SALAD AND MUSHROOMS

Serge Jost, an Alsatian-born chef who became expert at cooking venison while living in Montebello near Quebec's giant deer farm, Cerf de Boileau, likes this rich-tasting but lean meat. As executive chef at Fairmont Le Château Montebello, he often braised venison but also grilled it, finding it a pleasant change from beef. Remembering a marinade he used on beef when working in Hong Kong, he invented this dish. His Asian version was based on corn syrup but, with plenty of sugar maple groves on the nearby Ottawa River, he switched to maple syrup. Serve this steak with salad, Serge suggests—and enjoy it winter or summer.

SERVES 4

4 venison skirt steaks (6 ounces/180 g each)

Marinade

1/2 cup (125 mL) soy sauce

1/3 cup (75 mL) maple syrup

1/4 teaspoon (1 mL) freshly ground pepper

Salad

8 ounces (250 g) mushrooms, preferably chanterelle or wild

Olive oil, for sautéing

2 shallots, minced

1 package (10 ounces/280 g) arugula

2 tablespoons (30 mL) finely chopped chives

4 tablespoons (60 mL) dried cranberries

2 tablespoons (30 mL) toasted pine nuts

Dressing

1/3 cup (75 mL) extra-virgin olive oil

2 tablespoons (30 mL) balsamic vinegar

1 teaspoon (5 mL) Dijon mustard

For marinade:

✤ In a resealable plastic bag, combine soy sauce, maple syrup, and pepper. Add venison steaks, turning them in the bag to coat. Seal the bag and refrigerate for 12 hours, turning steaks periodically.

For salad:

✤ Rinse mushrooms and pat dry with paper towels. Heat enough oil in a frying pan to coat bottom and sauté mushrooms over medium heat until they release their liquid and start to turn golden, shaking the pan to loosen mushrooms. Add shallots, turning, until they begin to soften. Remove the pan from heat and set aside. Have ready the arugula, chives, cranberries, and pine nuts.

For dressing:

✤ In a jar with a lid, combine oil, vinegar, and Dijon. Cover and shake to mix well.

For assembly:

✤ Divide arugula among 4 serving plates and drizzle with dressing. Sprinkle with some of the cranberries and pine nuts. Top each plate with lukewarm mushrooms.

✤ Remove meat from marinade, reserving marinade. Heat a large, heavy frying pan over medium-high heat and sear steaks on each side. If they are thin, 2 minutes per side is sufficient. Watch meat closely because the sugar in it will caramelize quickly; reduce heat if necessary to avoid burning. Transfer steaks to a plate, slice thinly on the diagonal, and let stand for a few minutes.

✤ Cook reserved marinade in the frying pan over medium heat until it is reduced to a syrup-like consistency. Arrange steak slices on salad. Trim each serving with chopped chives, the remaining cranberries and pine nuts, and a spoonful of reduced marinade.

Note

The venison needs to marinate for 12 hours, so plan ahead.

Tourtière

Long ago, Quebec's favourite meat pie was traditionally of pork, because every farm raised hogs and the meat was cheap. Now that beef is the most-sold ground meat, tourtières tend to be made of beef, or a mixture of beef and pork. Sometimes veal is used, although it is expensive and adds little to the flavour of the pie. This recipe comes from Montreal's Maison du Rôti, a large east-end meat emporium where about 30,000 tourtières are made and sold annually. The chef, Marcel Pelletier, makes most of the pies of beef and pork but also offers tourtières of duck, game, or lamb. Double the pastry recipe on page 336 to make enough for 2 double-crust 9-inch (23 cm) pies. This pie can be prepared and frozen, then thawed and baked.

MAKES TWO 9-INCH (23 CM) PIES

2 tablespoons (30 mL) butter

1 tablespoon (15 mL) oil

1 large onion, chopped (2 cups/500 mL)

4 cloves garlic, chopped

1 pound (500 g) lean ground pork

1 pound (500 g) lean ground beef

1/2 cup (125 mL) chicken stock

1 teaspoon (5 mL) salt

1/2 teaspoon (2 mL) freshly ground pepper

1/2 teaspoon (2 mL) dried savory

1/4 teaspoon (1 mL) ground cloves

1/4 teaspoon (1 mL) ground cinnamon

3/4 cup (175 mL) old-fashioned rolled oats

Pastry for 2 double-crust 9-inch (23 cm) pies (page 336)

1 egg yolk

2 tablespoons (30 mL) light cream

+ In a large, heavy frying pan, heat butter and oil over medium-low heat and sauté onion and garlic until tender but not brown, about 5 minutes. Add pork and beef, breaking the meat up with a wooden spoon or fork, and cook until no longer pink.

+ Stir in stock, salt, pepper, savory, cloves, and cinnamon. Reduce heat to low and cook, stirring occasionally, for 30 minutes. Cool to room temperature.

+ Preheat the oven to 400°F (200°C).

+ Roll out pastry on a floured surface and line two 9-inch (23 cm) pie pans with pastry. Fill the two pans with the meat mixture. Cover with remaining pastry, crimping edges and cutting slits in the top crust. You can cut decorative pieces of leftover pastry and arrange on top. In a cup, combine egg yolk and cream and brush over top crusts.

+ Bake pies for 30 to 40 minutes, until pastry is crisp and lightly browned. Serve hot.

The pastry-topped meat pie known as tourtière may be Quebec's best-known dish. A centrepiece of Quebec holiday gatherings, particularly at Christmas, it sells year-round from supermarket takeout counters. Region by region, tourtières vary. Most are shallow, ground-meat pies, but in the Saguenay–Lac St-Jean region of northern Quebec, a tourtière is a deep-dish pie made of cubes of meat and vegetables. Savory is the number-one herb, spices are essential, and if a recipe uses cinnamon, cloves, and other spices, it's believed to date back to medieval Europe. The link with the cuisine of the Middle Ages can still be found in Quebec, thanks to the first settlers. They were country people from northwestern France who came to the New World in the 17th century.

Montreal food historian Jean-Pierre Lemasson considers the tourtière "one of the oldest meals of humanity" and the oldest recipe in Quebec cuisine. Originally called "tourte," a French pie with a pastry crust, it became known in Quebec as tourtière because of the name of the cast-iron pan in which the pie was cooked. Descriptions of pastry-topped pies have been located in Mesopotamia as far back as 2000 B.C., he found. The first written recipe for the dish dates from A.D. 300 in ancient Rome, when Marcus Gavius Apicius wrote the first cookbook.

Lemasson calls the Middle Ages "the age of the tourte." Monasteries made it, and he traced it to early Italian and French cuisine, in which it was known by several names, including tourte parmesane, pasticchio, timbale, and casserole. British cooking began playing a part in its Quebec history after the British conquered New France in 1759. British pies such as Parmesan and Battle Pye and Yorkshire Christmas Pie are tourtière predecessors, according to the professor.

Lemasson found tourte recipes in 17th- and 18th-century British and American cookbooks, as well as those of 19th-century Quebec. Quebccers may not realize that the condiments they like with their tourtière—dill pickles, relish, pickled beets, and tomato ketchup—are a British tradition.

The biggest tourtière in Quebec comes from the north, from the shores of Lac St-Jean and the upper Saguenay River. It's made deep and rich with cubes of game meats such as venison, moose, hare, partridge, or pheasant, plus vegetables. If you don't have a hunter in the family, you make it with cubes of beef and pork, and maybe veal, sometimes varied with coarsely ground meats. Pastry, ideally made with lard, encloses the pie, and it's baked for hours, moistened at intervals by stock poured into the pie with a pie funnel, or pie bird, that supports the crust. The pie is so popular in the region that the supermarket Corneau Cantin, with a location in Chicoutimi and another in Jonquière, offers a tourtière filling of the coarsely ground beef and pork at its self-serve counters; if you prefer cubed meats, butchers will cut them to your measure.

Lemasson traces the dish back to British cuisine of the Middle Ages and then to 18th-century cookbooks such as Hannah Glasse's *The Art of Cookery* (1747), and a pie often concocted of leftovers and gravy.

British pies of the 18th century included Cheshire Pork Pie, Mutton Pie, and Goose Pie, all similar in style to the big tourtière. Sea Pie, included in *American Cookery* by Amelia Simmons (1796), was another antecedent, made not of fish but of meat. Fishermen would take it along with them on their boats, hence its name.

It's often confused with a simpler Quebec meat pie called *cipaille*, *cipâte*, or *six-pâte*. The big tourtière made its way north from the Charlevoix area of the Lower St. Lawrence, which was partly settled by the British Army after the British conquest of 1759. When English entrepreneurs opened pulp and paper mills on the river in the mid-19th century, settlers from Charlevoix headed north to work, bringing their cuisine with them. One of the best inns in the region, Auberge des 21 in La Baie, is named for the region's first white settlers, 21 pioneers who came to start a lumber business in 1838.

Tourtière du Saguenay

A big, rich, party dish, this tourtière was traditionally made with game meats but is usually made of beef, pork, and chicken, or, as in this recipe, pork, veal, and either venison or beef. Micheline Mongrain-Dontigny, who lives in St-Irénée, in the Charlevoix region of eastern Quebec, is the author of a series of Quebec regional cookbooks, one on the Saguenay. She makes this slowly baked tourtière with the traditional Quebec seasoning of salted herbs (see page 337).

SERVES 10 TO 12

1 pound (500 g) pork shoulder

1 pound (500 g) veal shoulder

1 pound (500 g) venison shoulder or beef shoulder

6 medium onions, finely chopped

1 cup (250 mL) salted herbs (page 337), rinsed in cold water and drained

1 teaspoon (5 mL) freshly ground pepper

4 large potatoes, peeled and cut in 1/2-inch (1 cm) cubes

Pastry (recipe follows)

2 egg yolks, beaten with a little milk

+ Use a meat grinder to coarsely grind pork, veal, and venison, or cut in ¼-inch (5 mm) cubes. In a large bowl, mix together meat, onions, salted herbs, and pepper. Cover with plastic wrap and refrigerate for 8 hours. Place the potatoes in a large bowl of cold water and soak for 8 hours.

+ Preheat the oven to 350°F (180°C). Butter 2 large, deep tourtière pans, each holding 2 quarts (2 L). Drain potatoes, reserving soaking water. Add to meat mixture, combining well.

+ Roll out half the pastry on a floured surface to fit the 2 tourtière pans and put it into the pans. Fill with meat mixture. Pour potato water into the pans just to the top of filling, adding some cold water if necessary.

+ Roll out remaining pastry and cover pies, crimping the edges. Add decorative pieces cut from leftover pastry, if desired. Brush crusts with egg mixture. Cut a 1-inch (2.5 cm) hole in the centre of each pie so you can pour in more liquid as the pies bake. Make a 1-inch (2.5 cm) tube of aluminum foil and insert it in the hole of each pie.

+ Bake for 1 hour. Reduce the oven temperature to 250°F (120°C) and bake for another 6 hours, adding a little cold water down the tube of each pie at intervals if the pie appears to be drying out.

+ Once baked, the tourtières can be cooled, wrapped well in plastic, and frozen for 6 to 8 months. Thaw in the refrigerator for 24 hours, then reheat in an oven preheated to 250°F (120°C). The tourtières are done when a sharp knife, inserted in the centre, comes out very hot.

Notes

If you like, use store-bought salted herbs, available at specialty stores and many supermarkets.

The meat needs to be chilled and the potatoes soaked for 8 hours, so plan ahead.

Pâte brisée

PASTRY

MAKES ENOUGH FOR 1 DOUBLE-CRUST 9-INCH (23 CM) PIE
OR 2 SINGLE CRUST 9-INCH (23 CM) PIES

(For the Tourtière du Saguenay, you will need to make 3 quantities of this pastry; excess may be frozen.)

2 2/3 cups (650 mL) unbleached all-purpose flour
1 teaspoon (5 mL) salt
1 cup (250 mL) cold lard, cut in 1-inch (2.5 cm) cubes
1 cup (250 mL) ice water, plus more as needed

By hand:
+ In a mixing bowl, combine flour and salt. Sprinkle cubes of lard onto the flour. With a pastry blender or 2 knives, cut lard into the flour until lard chunks are the size of peas. Sprinkle ice water over the surface of flour mixture. Using a fork, incorporate water into flour mixture until it begins to form a ball, adding a little more ice water as needed. Using your hands, form the pastry into a ball. Wrap pastry in plastic wrap and refrigerate for an hour or so until ready to use. Roll out on a floured surface.

In a food processor:
+ Place flour and salt in a food processor, add cubes of lard, and pulse until lard chunks are the size of peas (you may need to pulse mixture 25 or so times). Pour ice water over the surface of flour mixture and pulse to mix in. Once pastry begins to clump together, mix at high speed until a single ball of pastry forms. Wrap pastry in plastic wrap and refrigerate until ready to use. Roll out on a floured surface.

Herbes salées

SALTED HERBS

MAKES ABOUT 6 JARS (1 CUP/250 mL EACH)

1 cup (250 mL) coarsely chopped chives
1 cup (250 mL) finely chopped fresh flat-leaf parsley
1 cup (250 mL) finely chopped leeks, green part only
1 cup (250 mL) finely chopped green onions, green part only
2 cups (500 mL) celery leaves, chopped
2 cups (500 mL) coarse salt

✦ Have ready clean glass jars, lids, and rings. Combine herbs and vegetables in a mixing bowl. Sprinkle salt in jars to cover the bottoms. Add a ¾-inch (2 cm) layer of herb mixture to each jar. Repeat, alternating salt and herb mixture until the jars are filled, ending with salt. Close the jars tightly and refrigerate. Mixture will keep for up to 1 year, refrigerated.

✦ When this seasoning is used in cooking, most recipes require rinsing it first in a sieve under cold running water. Then drain and use.

Note
Rinse and dry all the herbs and vegetables before chopping them.

In Quebec's early days, when meals during the long, cold winters seemed monotonous, family cooks would reach for a jar of salted herbs and vegetables, prepared at harvest time and stored in the root cellar. A spoonful pepped up a ragout, meat pie, pea soup, or root vegetables. Nowadays, the popularity of the seasoning lingers on. Cooks use it in various dishes, including hamburgers, pasta sauces, and salad dressings. Jars of the herb and vegetable mixture sell in food stores all over Quebec, as well as in Ontario and the Atlantic provinces. And they are still "put down" at home, using mixtures of various herbs and vegetables. (You'll find a recipe for salted herbs on page 337.)

The leading commercial brand is Les Herbes Salées du Bas-du-Fleuve (Salted Herbs from the Lower St. Lawrence). The maker is Jean-Yves Roy, a plant science graduate with a farm in Ste-Flavie, on the western edge of the Gaspé. He took his grandmother's recipe and adapted it to commercial production. Instead of cutting up the ingredients with a knife, he uses machines to chop crops from 30 acres (12 hectares) planted with parsley, chervil, savory, chives, spinach, celery, onions, carrots, and parsnips. Each food is seasoned with coarse salt and stored separately in barrels that are kept at about 60°F (15°C), the contents ready to blend, bottle, and send to market.

Jean-Yves offered me tips on using his product. Some recipes call for rinsing the herbs before adding them to a dish, but he likes the salty taste at full strength. His favourite uses for the product are to season barley soup, seafood casserole, macaroni in a beef sauce, mashed potatoes, rice, and a tomato sandwich. He likes a spoonful mixed into fresh ground beef as the only seasoning for hamburgers. "But," he says, "skip the usual salt."

His mother, Gabrielle Roy, who used to make her salted herbs using a knife, told me that with a cold dish such as a salad dressing it doesn't matter when you add the herbs but warned that, with a hot dish, they should be added just at the end of the cooking time. "Pea soup becomes something special when seasoned with this herb mixture," she says.

The product is about to become more convenient, for Jean-Yves has been working with food technologists and engineers to dehydrate it into flake form. "The flavour is good," he says.

Rôti de porc et patates jaunes

ROAST PORK WITH PAN-BROWNED POTATOES

This comfortable dinner dish turns up all over Quebec, flavoured with savory, marjoram, rosemary, or cloves. In the Gaspé, turnip or rutabaga may be included with the potatoes. It's most popular in the Mauricie region, north of Trois-Rivières, where Micheline Mongrain-Dontigny, author of several regional cookbooks, regards it as a perfect winter Sunday dinner dish.

SERVES 6

1 pork loin (3 pounds/1.35 kg)
3 cloves garlic, halved
3-ounce (90 g) piece pork rind
1 medium onion, thickly sliced
Generous pinches salt and freshly ground pepper
2 tablespoons (30 mL) butter, softened
1 tablespoon (15 mL) dry mustard
1/2 teaspoon (2 mL) dried marjoram
1 cup (250 mL) water
6 medium potatoes, peeled

- Preheat the oven to 350°F (180°C).
- Using a sharp knife, make 6 incisions in the top of pork loin and insert garlic halves. Place pork rind in a shallow roasting pan and arrange onion slices on top.
- Sprinkle pork loin with salt and pepper. Blend butter with dry mustard and brush it over lean parts of pork loin. Place loin in the pan on top of the pork rind and onions. Sprinkle with marjoram and pour water into the bottom of the pan. Roast, uncovered, for 1 hour.
- Arrange potatoes around pork. Continue roasting for 1½ hours, or until a meat thermometer registers 160°F (70°C), turning potatoes once and basting meat with pan juices every 15 minutes. If juices dry up, add a little more water.
- Transfer roast and potatoes to a heated serving platter. Skim fat from pan drippings and pour drippings into a warmed gravy boat. Serve with the meat and potatoes.

Poitrine de poulet dans sa peau croustillante, glacé au miel

CRISPY CHICKEN BREASTS WITH HONEY GLAZE

A simple chicken dish becomes something special at the hands of French-born Alain Pignard, for many years the executive chef of the Fairmont The Queen Elizabeth, in Montreal. The meat cooks slowly at a very low temperature and is finished with a honey glaze. Alain uses honey collected from the beehives on the hotel's roof, as well as herbs from its rooftop herb garden, in his cooking.

SERVES 4

9 tablespoons (135 mL) butter

7 tablespoons (105 mL) olive oil

4 bone-in, skin-on chicken breast halves (8 to 10 ounces/250 to 300 g each)

1 medium onion, minced

3 tablespoons + 1 teaspoon (50 mL) honey

2 tablespoons (30 mL) dry white wine

3/4 cup (175 mL) chicken stock

7 tablespoons (105 mL) whipping cream

4 carrots, cut in thick strips on the diagonal

✤ Preheat the oven to 200°F (90°C).

✤ In a large, heavy roasting pan, heat 7 tablespoons (105 mL) of the butter and all of the oil over medium-high heat and brown chicken on both sides for about 5 minutes per side. Discard pan drippings. Insert a meat thermometer in thickest part of a chicken breast. Transfer the pan to the oven and roast chicken, uncovered, for 3 hours or until internal temperature is 165°F (75°C).

✤ Remove the pan from the oven, transfer chicken to a broiler pan, and keep warm. Pour juices rendered by chicken into a measuring cup and put in the freezer until cool enough that the fat can be separated from the juice.

✤ In a small saucepan, heat 1 tablespoon (15 mL) of the chicken fat over low heat. Cook onion in the fat just until it begins to turn golden. Add 2 tablespoons (30 mL) of the honey, along with the wine, and simmer until reduced and almost all the moisture has evaporated.

✤ Add ½ cup (125 mL) of the stock to the pan, increase heat to medium, and boil gently for about 5 minutes. Add cream, then pour mixture into a blender or food processor and purée until smooth. Return to the saucepan and set aside.

Recipe continues . . .

+ In a shallow frying pan, melt the remaining 2 tablespoons (30 mL) butter over medium heat and cook carrots just until warm and glazed with butter. Add remaining ¼ cup (50 mL) stock and a little water, if needed, to cover carrots. Cover the pan with waxed paper and cook over very low heat for about 30 minutes, adding more water if necessary to keep carrots moist.

+ Spread 1 teaspoon (5 mL) of the honey over the skin of each chicken breast. Preheat the broiler and broil chicken, skin side up, for about 5 minutes, just until skin is crisp and chicken is hot. Watch carefully that the skin does not burn.

+ Meanwhile, reheat sauce. Drain carrots and divide among 4 warmed serving plates. Add chicken, drizzle both with sauce, and serve.

Note

This is a convenient dish because the chicken can be cooked hours in advance, then kept in the refrigerator until ready to reheat. Bring to room temperature before glazing with honey. The sauce and carrots too can be made in advance, then reheated.

Honey

H oney is a popular Quebec sweetener that often turns up in dishes other than desserts. Compared to maple, honey came lately, having been brought from Europe to Massachusetts in about 1630, and from there to Quebec only after the American Revolution. Like maple, it's welcomed as a pure, natural ingredient. Some Quebec chefs have started keeping their own beehives to ensure a plentiful supply of honey. A tourist sight not to be missed is a honey museum east of Quebec City, where the history of the bee is explained and all flavours of honey offered for sale.

Bison bourguignon

Josée Toupin, who raises more than 100 buffalo at La Terre des Bisons, her family farm in Rawdon, northeast of Montreal, remembers her mother making boeuf bourguignon as a holiday dish. Looking for ways to enjoy the specialty meat she sells, she adapted the beef version to bison. Bison, to her, has a more refined taste than beef. "It's not strong like venison or caribou, but lean, and good especially with mashed potatoes to mop up the gravy," she says.

SERVES 4

1/2 cup (125 mL) olive oil (approximately)

4 pounds (2 kg) bison shoulder, cut in 1 1/2-inch (4 cm) cubes

3 medium onions, finely chopped

1 clove garlic, crushed

2 tablespoons (30 mL) all-purpose flour

1 bottle (750 mL) red wine, preferably Burgundy

3 cups (750 mL) water

1 teaspoon (5 mL) salt

Freshly ground pepper

1/3 cup (75 mL) tomato paste

1 bouquet garni (2 bay leaves and sprigs of fresh thyme and flat-leaf parsley tied together, or tied in a cheesecloth bag)

1 pound (500 g) mushrooms, sliced

1 cup (250 mL) finely chopped fresh flat-leaf parsley

✦ Heat 2 tablespoons (30 mL) of the oil in a large, heavy-bottomed saucepan or stovetop-safe casserole dish. When hot, add about one-quarter of meat and cook over medium-high heat until richly browned on all sides. Using a slotted spoon, transfer meat to a bowl. Repeat with remaining meat, browning it in batches and adding more oil as needed.

✦ In the same casserole in at least two 2 tablespoons (30 mL) of hot oil, cook onions until they begin to turn golden, about 3 to 5 minutes.

✦ Return meat to the pan and add garlic. Sprinkle with flour and stir for 2 minutes. Stir in wine, water, salt, and pepper, then tomato paste. Add bouquet garni. Simmer over low heat, partially covered and stirring occasionally, for 1½ hours.

✦ In a frying pan, heat 2 tablespoons (30 mL) oil and cook mushrooms over medium heat just until they release their liquid and start to turn brown, 5 to 10 minutes. Add to stew and continue cooking for 30 minutes.

✦ When ready to serve, remove bouquet garni and sprinkle stew with parsley.

Tartiflette au fromage 1608

CHEESE TART

This baked cheese-and-onion tart makes a sustaining lunch or supper dish. It calls for Le 1608 cheese, launched by Laiterie Charlevoix for the 400th anniversary of the founding of Quebec (see page 114). La Malbaie chef Marthe Lemire created this version and serves it at her restaurant, Crêperie Le Passe-Temps.

SERVES 6

4 tablespoons (60 mL) butter
4 medium yellow onions, thickly sliced
2 pounds (1 kg) potatoes (7 or 8 medium), peeled, cooked, and thickly sliced
7 ounces (200 g) Black Forest ham, thinly sliced
8 ounces (250 g) Le 1608 cheese, thinly sliced

+ Preheat the oven to 350°F (180°C). Use a little of the butter to grease a 13 × 9 inch (33 × 23 cm) baking pan.
+ In a large, heavy frying pan, melt remaining butter over medium heat and sauté onions until lightly coloured and softened, about 10 minutes.
+ Add potatoes and cook until heated, about 5 minutes. Spread potato mixture evenly in the prepared baking pan. Arrange slices of ham, then cheese slices, evenly over top.
+ Bake for 30 minutes or until cheese is melted and browned slightly.

Note

You can use Emmenthal or Gruyère cheese instead of Le 1608.

Quebec winters are brutal, electricity relatively cheap, and sunny days frequent, which is why the province has an extensive greenhouse industry. Whatever the temperature outdoors, companies produce huge quantities of lettuce, tomatoes, and even strawberries in see-through plastic buildings. A greenhouse called Lufa Farms, opened in 2011 on top of a Montreal office building, produces 25 kinds of vegetables and herbs. It represents the latest technology in

Richard Dorval harvests tomatoes at Savoura greenhouse in Ste-Marthe-de-Vaudreuil.

indoor agriculture and is due to expand to more buildings in Greater Montreal. The big names in this kind of Quebec food production are HydroSerre Mirabel, which started growing Boston lettuce in 1988, and Savoura, which began growing tomatoes in 1989. "Here, it is summer all year long," Savoura agronomist Richard Dorval says on a chilly February day as he harvests tomatoes from their winding, 30-foot (9 m) long stems. These two companies like to compare their hydroponic greenhouses to football fields, operate numbers of them, and have such huge production that they sell their foods in other parts of Canada as well as in the United States.

The most expensive food to be produced in a Quebec greenhouse is the strawberry, which is grown each spring in two locations: the Legault family farm in Sherrington, southwest of Montreal, where the berry plants are grown in compost, and near Drummondville, on the south shore of the lower St. Lawrence River, in the vast hydroponic greenhouses of Rose Drummond, its principal crop being roses. The price of these strawberries runs from 25 to 50 cents apiece; only top restaurants and a handful of Montreal stores sell them.

The most innovative greenhouse in Quebec is M.L. Aquaponics, a small one in Ste-Agathe-des-Monts, in the Laurentians, where in 2005 fish biologist Marc Laberge started growing two foods at once: lettuce on floating platforms, and rainbow trout in the water below, who provide the fertilizer for the lettuce.

Right: The St-Augustin hydroponic greenhouse of HydroSerre Mirabel produces Boston lettuce in a space larger than a football field.

James MacGuire

The soul of a Quebec neighbourhood is its bakery. You find these places—large establishments in the cities, smaller ones in the towns and villages—all over the province. Crowded onto their shelves, ideally of slatted wood so the bread can breathe, are the classic French breads—skinny baguettes, thicker Parisiens, sourdough loaves ("levain" in French), odd-shaped country loaves called "rustique," croissants, brioches, and whatever else the baker fancies.

One man can be credited with Quebec's bounty of beautiful, satisfying French bread. He's a modest Irish-American named James MacGuire, who trained as a chef in France. When he first started selling his bread at his Montreal restaurant, there were line-ups out the door. After you dined at James's celebrated Le Passe-Partout restaurant-bakery-delicatessen, he would tuck a spare loaf under your arm.

French bread existed in Quebec before his reforms. But most of it only looked the part. Back in the 1970s, most baguettes had a pretty, puffed crust and a soft, white interior. James compares that interior to a mass of cotton balls with no flavour. Made with flour treated to suit assembly-line production, a baguette went stale in five or six hours.

Now, at its best, Quebec French bread is so rich-tasting you don't need butter on it. What's more, your loaf can be a couple of days old and still have its signature creamy interior, chewy texture, and slightly sweet, nutty taste. If you are lucky enough to be present when freshly baked loaves emerge from the oven, you may hear them "sing"—baker's language for the quiet crackle a loaf emits as it cools down.

It actually took three men to launch the use of unbleached flour and revolutionize bread-making in French Canada, beginning in the 1980s: James, the French bread reformer Raymond Calvel (1913–2005), and Jean-Marc Étienne, the Basque-born baker who started the Montreal bakery Boulangerie au Pain Doré. Calvel had weaned French bakers off over-processed flour and overly mechanized methods and taught the original techniques of country bread-making all over the world, including Quebec. Helped by James, who brought Calvel to Quebec several times between 1987 and 1995, and some Calvel converts, including Étienne, the Calvel techniques gradually spread like the aroma of freshly baked bread, first to individual bakers in Montreal and Quebec City, later to bakers throughout Quebec.

Essential to French bread of the quality that would satisfy these three bread gurus was unbleached, untreated flour milled from Canadian hard red spring wheat. This flour contains carotenoid pigments that give it a nutty, wheaty flavour. Made into dough with good-quality yeast, and given a long, cool rising time (called "fermentation" by bakers), the dough forms organic fatty acids that give the bread flavour, texture, and keeping quality.

Part of the Calvel method is hand-shaping each loaf and then slashing it with a razor in slanting cuts along its length so the bread develops in the oven's heat and bakes properly.

A big boost was given to Quebec bread reform by two bakery chains, beginning in the 1980s at Étienne's Pain Doré. He developed a combination of mechanized and manual techniques. The dough was mixed in machines but loaves were shaped and slashed by hand. (Pain Doré was sold to Brioche Dorée in 2008 and some outlets have been renamed.)

Another major reforming role was played by the Première Moisson bakery, led by Liliane Colpron. She opened her first store in 1992 and then launched a chain of outlets with a baker in each one, bringing in bakers from France who used the Calvel method.

James keeps watch on all developments, acting as a consultant to bakeries and teaching in the management and gastronomy department of the Université du Québec à Montréal and at King Arthur Flour in Norwich, Vermont. His current crusade is for better, more natural bread flour. With bread, "what comes out is what you put into it," he says.

James forecasts that small, artisanal bakeries will continue to bake the best bread, although major producers have adapted production to some of Calvel's techniques. "We are now offered very decent machine-made bread," he says, and he's almost sure Calvel would agree.

James MacGuire slashes risen loaves
of French bread before baking

Pain de campagne

FRENCH COUNTRY BREAD

James MacGuire is often credited with making the best bread in Quebec and this recipe highlights his latest method of producing a flavourful, chewy, fragrant loaf. A French-trained chef, he works in grams rather than cups or millilitres. Since most home kitchens do not have kitchen scales, I asked Julie Champagne, a graduate of the professional cooking course at Montreal-based Pearson School of Culinary Arts, to test James's recipe and provide both imperial and metric volume measures. She gave top marks to the bread, and some advice, reflected in this recipe: "In baking, you have to be very accurate. I think to measure in grams is the best." James adds a tip about temperatures: "The dough rises best at normal kitchen temperatures. Having the flour and water at room temperature accomplishes this. For especially cool kitchens, use warmer water to compensate; in hot kitchens, cooler water."

MAKES ONE 10- TO 12-INCH (25 TO 30 CM) ROUND LOAF

3 1/4 cups + 1 tablespoon (825 mL/425 g) unbleached all-purpose flour
1/2 cup + 1/2 tablespoon (130 mL/75 g) whole-wheat flour, preferably stone-ground
2 teaspoons (10 mL/10 g) salt
2 teaspoons (10 mL/2 g) instant or quick-rising yeast (not "traditional")
1 1/2 cups (375 mL/375 g) water

+ In a large mixing bowl, stir together both flours, salt, and yeast. Add water and, using one hand, mix it into the dry ingredients just until there is no more dry flour visible. Cover with plastic wrap and let stand at room temperature for 5 minutes.

+ Using your hands, mix the dough again until it is smoother and comes away from the sides of the bowl when lifted. Cover again with plastic wrap. Set to rise ("ferment") in a warm, draft-free place for 4 hours.

+ Once every hour, give dough a gentle mix, just enough to deflate it. (This means gently mixing the dough a total of four times.) This loaf requires no kneading in the traditional sense.

+ After the 4 hours have elapsed, turn dough out onto a floured surface and shape it into a round loaf. Sprinkle loaf all over with extra flour. Line a colander with a coarse linen towel and put loaf into the colander upside down. Cover with another coarse linen towel. Let loaf rise for 35 to 45 minutes.

+ Meanwhile, place a pizza stone or a clean, unglazed terracotta plant tray about 12 inches (30 cm) in diameter, on the middle oven rack. Place a cast-iron frying pan on the lower rack. Preheat the oven to 450°F (230°C). With the stone in place, the oven will take about 30 minutes to heat; it must be hot for risen dough to start baking. If dough is kept waiting, it will over-rise and then deflate.

+ Check that loaf is ready to bake by poking it with a finger. If the indentation disappears after a second or two, it's ready. If the indentation remains, let loaf rise for another 5 to 10 minutes, then test it again.

- Bring about ½ cup (125 mL) water to a boil. Place a piece of parchment paper over the unbaked loaf and then a baking sheet turned right side up. Flip loaf so it is right side up on the parchment paper on the baking sheet. Using a sharp knife or razor blade, slash the loaf with crisscross slashes, about 1 inch (2.5 cm) apart, all along the loaf.
- Slide loaf onto the pizza stone. Quickly and carefully pour the boiling water into the cast-iron frying pan and shut the oven door. The steam from the water will help form a thinner, crisper crust on the bread.
- Bake for 10 to 12 minutes, until crust is very light brown. Reduce the oven temperature to 400°F (200°C) and bake for another 10 to 12 minutes. Then reduce the oven temperature to 375°F (190°C) and bake for 20 minutes, until dark golden.
- When loaf appears to be done, remove it from the oven and rap it sharply with your knuckles. It should sound hollow. If it doesn't, return it to the oven for a few more minutes, then again test for doneness.
- Once done, remove bread from the oven and cool on a rack.

ROOTS: WINTER WINNERS

The humble potato, carrot, onion, parsnip, and turnip, which were grown, stored, and enjoyed all winter long by the earliest Quebecers, become fashionable with chefs each winter as part of today's trend to eat local foods and forget about vegetables transported long distances from southern growing areas. Montreal chef Nick Hodge calls his winter vegetables "the understated roots . . . [they're] all the durable stuff . . . all the usual suspects. People like these vegetables. They're cleaning their plates." In Nick's restaurant Kitchenette, rutabaga, the larger cousin of the turnip, goes into his minestrone soup or is whipped together with carrots, then accented with fresh celery and frozen baby green peas. Carrots develop sweetness when roasted, and Nick helps along that effect with a little maple syrup.

Montreal chef Stelio Perombelon finds that combinations of roots enhance the simple flavour of each. He'll combine carrots, parsnips, celery root, and barley and serve the vegetables with a roast saddle of rabbit. Stelio's soup of celery root or parsnips with onions is dressed up with a few leaves of deep-fried kale or a few spoonfuls of applesauce and crumbled crisp bacon.

Chef Michel Ross likes carrots best of the roots, particularly their different colours—orange, yellow, and red. He also likes to cook beets, parsnips, and celery root, either alone or in combination.

Casserole de rutabaga

Cousin Christine's yellow turnip puff

Turnips and rutabaga are among Quebec's basic root crops, and have been for centuries. If you have scorned these trusty vegetables in the past, this recipe may change your mind. It's a favourite with Leah Curley, a talented Knowlton cook who traces it to an Ottawa cousin and various relatives, all of whom have been enjoying it for almost half a century. The brown sugar version is good; the maple sugar version, exceptional.

Serves 4 to 6

2 eggs
1 medium turnip or rutabaga, peeled, cubed, cooked, and mashed (about 2 cups/500 mL)
3 tablespoons (45 mL) butter, softened
3 tablespoons (45 mL) all-purpose flour
1 tablespoon (15 mL) brown sugar or granulated maple sugar
1 teaspoon (5 mL) baking powder
Pinches salt and freshly ground pepper
4 slices white or brown bread, buttered and cubed

+ Preheat the oven to 350°F (180°C). Grease a 2-quart (2 L) baking dish.
+ In a bowl and using a hand-held electric mixer, beat eggs. Beat in turnip, butter, flour, brown sugar, baking powder, salt, and pepper. Taste and add more salt and pepper, if desired. Pour mixture into the prepared baking dish and sprinkle surface with bread cubes.
+ Bake for 30 minutes or until puffed and lightly browned.

Note

This dish can be made several hours in advance and baked just before serving. Or freeze the unbaked dish for up to 1 month, thawing in the refrigerator before baking.

Rabioles caramélisées

GLAZED BABY TURNIPS

Chef Serge Jost took on the challenge of livening up Quebec root vegetables during his years as executive chef of the Fairmont Le Château Montebello, on the Ottawa River east of Ottawa. He remembers his mother, who ran a small bistro when he was growing up in the small city of Molsheim, in Alsace, caramelizing rutabaga to serve with roast duck. He adapted her recipe to baby turnips (rabioles), *using maple syrup. He likes to serve these turnips with any poultry, duck in particular, or with pork.*

SERVES 2

10 ounces (300 g) baby turnips, peeled
1 tablespoon (15 mL) melted butter
Salt and freshly ground pepper
3/4 cup + 1 tablespoon (200 mL) maple syrup

✦ If turnips are small, leave whole. If large, cut in halves or quarters. Place in a stovetop-safe casserole dish wide enough that they can fit in a single layer. Stir in butter, salt, pepper, and maple syrup. Add enough cold water to cover turnips.

✦ Bring to a boil over medium-high heat, reduce heat to low, and simmer gently until all the water has evaporated. Turnips should be tender to the fork and syrup should caramelize on the bottom of the casserole dish; if necessary, add a little water to loosen up the glaze, scraping any up from the bottom of the dish with a wooden spoon. Shake the dish to turn turnips in glaze, until turnips are well coated.

Chou braisé à la bière

BEER-BRAISED CABBAGE

Montreal chef Nick Hodge grew up in Texas and remembers his grandmother, who was of German descent, making this sustaining dish. His mother's family were farmers near Rosenberg, not far from Houston, and grew large quantities of vegetables in their garden. Cabbage was a favourite crop. "We would have massive family gatherings to make sauerkraut," Nick recalls. He seasons Quebec ingredients with Texas flavours at his two restaurants, Kitchenette and Icehouse.

SERVES 8

1 large savoy cabbage (3 pounds/1.35 kg)
2 tablespoons (30 mL) butter
1 medium onion, coarsely chopped
1 head garlic, halved
1 or 2 jalapeño peppers, seeded and coarsely chopped (keep seeds for extra heat)
2 stalks celery, coarsely chopped
1 bottle (12 ounces/341 mL) pale beer or ale
2 cups (500 mL) chicken stock
4 ounces (125 g) smoked ham hock or lean slab bacon, cut in short, thin strips (lardons)

+ Cut cabbage into quarters and thickly slice each quarter. In a large pot of boiling water, blanch cabbage for 3 minutes, then drain and rinse under cold water.
+ In a large, heavy, stovetop-safe casserole dish with a lid, melt butter over medium heat. Cook onion, garlic, jalapeño peppers (including seeds, if desired), and celery for 5 minutes or until vegetables are softened.
+ Add beer to deglaze casserole dish, stirring up any brown bits from the bottom, and bring mixture to a boil. Add stock and bring to a boil. Add ham, then place cabbage on top. Reduce heat to low and simmer very slowly, covered, for 20 to 30 minutes, until cabbage is very tender.
+ Remove cabbage, then ham and other vegetables to a plate and strain liquid through a sieve. Return liquid to the casserole dish and boil gently until it is reduced to the consistency of a sauce.
+ Return vegetables (except cabbage) and ham to liquid, cover with cabbage and then with the lid. Reheat briefly. Serve hot.

Note

The dish can be prepared several hours in advance up to the point where the cabbage has cooked until very tender. Cover and refrigerate; reheat before serving.

Gratin de topinambours

JERUSALEM ARTICHOKES AU GRATIN

Michelle Gélinas, Montreal food specialist, likes to keep food traditions alive cooking native foods. The Jerusalem artichoke is a native North American vegetable. Samuel de Champlain, the French explorer who founded Quebec, saw the First Nations eating it, and compared its taste to that of an artichoke, though the two are not related. He took it back to France, where it became popular by the name "topinambour" after some Brazilian natives known as Tupinambá who were visiting the Vatican at the time. It's been compared to a slightly sweet potato, another import from the New World.

SERVES 6

2 pounds (1 kg) Jerusalem artichokes, peeled and sliced 1/4 inch (5 mm) thick
Juice of 1 lemon
1 1/4 cups (310 mL) whipping cream
1/2 cup (125 mL) shredded aged cheddar cheese
1/3 cup (75 mL) bread crumbs or panko crumbs
2 tablespoons (30 mL) chopped fresh thyme
Salt and freshly ground pepper
7 ounces (200 g) salt pork lardons, crisply fried

+ Preheat the oven to 425°F (220°C). Butter a baking pan 2 inches (5 cm) deep.
+ Soak artichoke slices in a large pan of cold water.
+ In another large bowl, combine lemon juice, cream, 4 tablespoons (60 mL) of the cheese, 2 tablespoons (30 mL) of the bread crumbs, thyme, salt, and pepper.
+ Drain artichokes, pat dry with paper towels, and add them and lardons to cream mixture. Stir to coat artichokes.
+ Turn artichokes and sauce into the prepared baking pan, sprinkle with remaining cheese and bread crumbs, and bake for about 30 minutes until golden and bubbly. Artichokes should still be crisp.

Notes

Panko crumbs are a flaked, Japanese style of bread crumbs; they do not absorb grease the way regular bread crumbs do.

Lardons are short, thin strips of meat, often pork. Fried, they are used to flavour various dishes.

Purée de pommes de terre au fromage blanc et à la pâte de truffes

MASHED POTATOES WITH CHEESE AND TRUFFLE PASTE

Ian Perreault, long-time Montreal chef-caterer, credits Paris chef Joël Robuchon for introducing him to the pleasures of this creamy, buttery delicacy. He bakes his potatoes for mashing, rather than boiling them, wrapping each potato in aluminum foil and setting them in a baking pan of coarse salt, which absorbs moisture as the potatoes bake. Now chef at Chez Lionel, a bistro across the St. Lawrence River from Montreal, in Boucherville, Ian continues to give potatoes a lift on his menus.

SERVES 4

1 1/4 pounds (625 g) Yukon Gold or other yellow-fleshed potatoes (about 4 medium)

1/2 cup (125 mL) unsalted butter, softened

Generous pinches salt, preferably Sel de Guérande

4 tablespoons (60 mL) soft white cheese

1 tablespoon (15 mL) truffle paste (optional)

2 teaspoons (10 mL) olive oil, plus extra for drizzling

Finely chopped fresh flat-leaf parsley

✦ Preheat the oven to 350°F (180°C).

✦ Scrub, dry, and wrap each potato in aluminum foil. Bake for 1¼ hours or until tender to the fork.

✦ Immediately remove foil and peel potatoes quickly while still hot. If potatoes have cooled, reheat them before peeling.

✦ Mash with a hand-held masher or put through a potato ricer. (Do not use a food processor.) Immediately beat in butter and season with salt.

✦ Blend in cheese, truffle paste (if using), and oil. Taste and add more salt, if desired. Serve hot, sprinkled with parsley and drizzled with a little more oil.

Note

Use a soft white cheese such as Damablanc, made by Damafro; fresh ricotta; or labneh, a Middle Eastern cheese.

Squash on the Rise

S quash has been growing in the Americas for more than 8,000 years, says Rougemont grower Robert Beauregard, who produces 30 varieties of the vegetable on his farm near Mont Rougemont, southeast of Montreal. Chefs make squash soup, bake it with seasonings, or whip it like potatoes. Beauregard and his wife, Marielle Farley, both agriculture graduates, add recipes to their Beau-Far labels and have seen sales rise steadily. Robert's favourite is the delicata squash, cut in half, the halves filled with Italian sausage meat, and then baked. Marielle likes butternut squash soup made with chicken bouillon and apples, and also stuffed squash, made according to a recipe from the late, celebrated Quebec cookbook author Jehane Benoit. To make Jehane's recipe, Marielle cuts any variety of winter squash in half and steams it until tender, then makes a spinach stuffing with cooked, chopped spinach, nutmeg, butter, grated cheese, and minced garlic. After filling the squash halves with the spinach mixture, she adds fresh bread crumbs and a drizzle of oil, and bakes it for half an hour.

When pumpkins ripen each October, I look for a deep orange variety called the potiron, which looks like an inflated curler's stone, flatter than the regular pumpkin. It's a European favourite that I first encountered one September in Provence, filling the fields with brilliant orange and making superb soup in the restaurants. It originated in South America, whereas the regular pumpkin is a North American native. Potirons have more flavour, are sweeter, are more tender to carve, and have less fibre when cooked than other pumpkins, which can be bland if not well seasoned.

Montreal chef Martin Picard feeds regular pumpkins to the pigs he raises at his maple sugar shack, and makes desserts out of the potiron.

Montreal food writer Louise Gagnon, a columnist for the French edition of *Châtelaine* magazine and author of a book about squash, loves all members of the squash family but is particularly keen on the pumpkin, especially the small ones, which she finds have the best flavour. She wants us to cook pumpkins after Hallowe'en is over. She suggests lining the interior of the pumpkin with aluminum foil to protect it from the candle used to light up the jack-o'-lantern's face. Then you can cut up the flesh and freeze it in cubes or puréed to make into everything from soup to muffins.

Cats, sheep, and even a llama welcome shoppers at Les Jardins du Centre market garden near Les Éboulements.

Cubes de courge au miel, au gingembre, et au panko

Spiced squash cubes

Louise Gagnon likes to promote squash as a naturally sweet food with a Quebec history that dates back to the First Nations. Her cookbook explores the many ways all members of the squash family, pumpkin included, may be enjoyed. She designed this easy recipe to serve with grilled meats or fish. Roasting squash concentrates its flavour, according to Louise, who writes about food in the French edition of Châtelaine *magazine and gives squash cooking classes in Montreal's public markets. A plus factor for Louise, who has a master's degree in nutrition, is that squash, a fruit that's treated as a vegetable, is rich in vitamins and fibre.*

Serves 4

Canola oil or olive oil, for greasing
1 tablespoon (15 mL) honey
2 teaspoons (10 mL) Dijon mustard
2 teaspoons (10 mL) grated fresh gingerroot
1 teaspoon (5 mL) canola oil or olive oil
1/2 teaspoon (2 mL) salt
3 cups (750 mL) (about 20 ounces/600 g) peeled squash cut in 1/2-inch (1 cm) cubes
1/4 cup (60 mL) panko crumbs

✢ Place the oven rack in the centre position. Preheat the oven to 375°F (190°C). Line a cookie sheet or wide baking pan with parchment paper and oil the paper.

✢ In a mixing bowl, stir together honey, Dijon, ginger, oil, and salt. Add squash cubes, stirring to coat with honey mixture. Spread squash in an even layer on the prepared cookie sheet. Sprinkle with panko crumbs, turning to coat all sides.

✢ Bake for 20 minutes. Remove from oven, turn cubes over, then bake for another 10 to 15 minutes or until squash is tender to the fork and crusty. If desired, broil a few inches (8 cm) from the heat for a few minutes to brown.

✢ Check seasoning, adding more salt to taste. Serve hot.

Note
Butternut, buttercup, or blue Hubbard squash are recommended. Pumpkin can also be used.

Marie Bieler relishes the harvest of Atoka Cranberries at Manseau.

Tarte aux canneberges fraîches

FRESH CRANBERRY TART

The Bieler family has pioneered in the production, marketing, and processing of cranberries grown in bogs in St-Louis-de-Blandford, on the south shore of the St. Lawrence River. Marc Bieler, who heads the Atoka and Bieler cranberry companies, has become the largest cranberry producer in Canada. His wife, Marie, promotes the fruit, fresh, frozen, or dried, in cooking and has also developed a wild stretch of their property into an ecological education centre where the cranberries grow unattended. This tart is an example of Marie's cuisine. It's a winner for both flavour and appearance.

SERVES 8 TO 10

Pastry for double-crust, 9-inch (23 cm) pie (page 336)

12 ounces (375 g) fresh cranberries (or frozen, unthawed), halved

1/2 cup (125 mL) raisins

1 cup (250 mL) firmly packed brown sugar or granulated maple sugar

4 tablespoons (60 mL) granulated sugar

4 tablespoons (60 mL) all-purpose flour

Grated peel of 1 lemon

1/4 teaspoon (1 mL) almond extract

2 tablespoons (30 mL) butter, cut into pea-size pieces

1 egg yolk mixed with 1 tablespoon (15 mL) water

+ Place a pizza stone or large cast-iron frying pan (the frying pan upside down, if using), on the centre rack of the oven and preheat the oven to 425°F (220°C). Butter a 9-inch (23 cm) pie pan. Roll out half the pastry on a floured surface and fit it into the pan.

+ In a bowl, mix together cranberries and raisins. Stir together brown sugar, granulated sugar, flour, lemon peel, and almond extract. Toss with cranberries and raisins. Fill pie shell and dot with butter.

+ Roll out remaining pastry to fit the pan, cut it into strips about 1 inch (2.5 cm) wide, and place on top of pie filling, weaving to make a lattice crust. Alternatively, use a regular top crust. Brush pastry with egg mixture.

+ Place tart on pizza stone or frying pan and bake for 10 minutes. Reduce the oven temperature to 375°F (190°C) and continue baking for 35 to 45 minutes, until crust is golden.

+ Serve tart warm or at room temperature, with vanilla or lemon ice cream.

Notes

You can use a frozen pie shell, unthawed, for an open-top tart. The best-quality frozen ready-made pastry is available from pastry shops.

Cut cranberries with kitchen scissors or in a food processor with the chopping blade.

Biscuits au chocolat et aux canneberges

CHOCOLATE CRANBERRY COOKIES

Dried cranberries give a lift to many other foods, from meats to vegetables and fruit to salads and confectionery. Marie Bieler is particularly fond of using them in baked dishes. This recipe makes a firm cookie; if you like cookies soft, soak the oats in 1 cup (250 mL) boiling water until absorbed, then add to the batter with the chocolate chips, cranberries, and orange peel.

MAKES 48 COOKIES

1/2 cup (125 mL) unsalted butter, softened
1 1/2 cups (375 mL) packed brown sugar
2 eggs
1 teaspoon (5 mL) vanilla extract
2 cups (500 mL) all-purpose flour
1 teaspoon (5 mL) baking soda
1 teaspoon (5 mL) baking powder
1 teaspoon (5 mL) salt
2 cups (500 mL) old-fashioned rolled oats
1 cup (250 mL) dark chocolate chips
1 cup (250 mL) dried cranberries
Grated peel of 1 orange

+ Preheat the oven to 350°F (180°C). Line a baking sheet with parchment paper.
+ In a mixing bowl, beat butter until creamy, then gradually beat in brown sugar. Beat in eggs, one by one, then vanilla.
+ Stir flour with baking soda, baking powder, and salt, then stir into butter mixture, mixing well. Mix in the oats, chocolate chips, cranberries, and orange peel.
+ Form heaping teaspoons (7 mL) of cookie batter into balls and place on the prepared baking sheet, spacing them 1 inch (2.5 cm) apart. Do not flatten. Bake for 15 to 18 minutes, until crisp and lightly browned.
+ Using a spatula, transfer cookies to a rack to cool. Store at room temperature in a metal container with a tight-fitting lid for up to 2 weeks.

CRANBERRIES

Cranberry bogs flooded until they are afloat with the red fruit are a spectacular sight. Wild, but managed to increase the harvest, they grow in the sandy soil around St-Louis-de-Blandford, on the south shore of the St. Lawrence River. Big machines are paddled through the mass of berries, whipping them from their plants, then scooping them up.

To extend the season for this nutritious, sharply flavoured fruit, Quebec's huge cranberry company Atoka, also Canada's largest, is now drying some of the crop and working to persuade consumers to regard it, as they do raisins, as a kitchen basic. Besides the all-natural dark red version, the firm is producing two flavours of dried cranberry: orange and cherry.

Cranberries' colour is a plus factor in a neutral-looking dish such as a chicken casserole, an endive salad, or an apple pie. Both flavour and colour suit a dressing for duck. Braised cubes of squash look and taste more interesting with the addition of dried cranberries. Add them to scones or fruit-and-nut bread. For an easy dessert, whip dried cranberries into vanilla ice cream, refreeze, and serve. This dried fruit makes a healthy snack too.

Mousse au citron et au chocolat

KATHY'S LEMON CHOCOLATE SUPREME

This beautiful, creamy mousse confection, from my friend Kathy Keefler, takes about an hour to make and calls for several bowls, but its advantage is that you can prepare it the day before the party and it needs no last-minute attention. It looks its best in a large, deep, glass bowl, so that the layers of pale yellow mousse and rich chocolate can be seen.

SERVES 12

1 cup (250 mL) granulated sugar	Grated peel of 1 lemon
1/3 cup (75 mL) cold water	Juice of 2 lemons
1 package (7 grams) unflavoured gelatin	3 cups (750 mL) whipping cream
4 eggs, separated, at room temperature	3 1-ounce (30 g) squares semi-sweet chocolate
1/2 teaspoon (2 mL) salt	3 teaspoons (15 mL) unsalted butter

✤ In the top of a double boiler, dissolve ½ cup (125 mL) of the sugar in the water. Sprinkle with gelatin and let stand for 5 minutes. Set over simmering water, making sure the bowl does not touch the water, and stir until gelatin has dissolved.

✤ In a small bowl, beat egg yolks slightly and set aside.

✤ Stir salt, lemon peel, and lemon juice into gelatin mixture. Add egg yolks, stirring constantly until mixture thickens slightly and coats the back of a metal spoon. Place in the refrigerator and cool for 10 minutes, removing before mixture sets.

✤ In a large glass or metal bowl and using a hand-held electric mixer, beat egg whites until they stand in soft peaks. Gradually beat in remaining ½ cup (125 mL) of sugar. Continue beating until mixture stands in stiff peaks. In another bowl, whip cream until it stands in soft peaks. Fold egg white into thickened, cooled gelatin mixture. Fold in whipped cream to complete the meringue.

✤ Have ready a bowl holding 8 to 10 cups (2 to 2.5 L). In a small saucepan over very low heat, melt 1 square of the chocolate with 1 teaspoon (5 mL) of the butter.

✤ Spoon about one-third of the meringue into the serving bowl. Drizzle with melted chocolate mixture, streaking the chocolate back and forth over top.

✤ Melt another square of chocolate with 1 teaspoon (5 mL) of the butter. Spoon another one-third of the meringue into the serving bowl and drizzle with chocolate in an attractive pattern over top.

✤ Add the last of the meringue to the bowl and decorate with the final square of chocolate melted with remaining 1 teaspoon (5 mL) butter. Cover with plastic wrap and refrigerate for several hours until firm.

Note

The mousse can be prepared up to 24 hours in advance. Refrigerate, covered, until ready to serve.

Left: A cranberry harvesting machine beats berries from plants in bogs at Manseau.

Tarte Tatin

Montreal gastronomic teacher Rollande Desbois taught me how to make the best version of this upside-down apple pie that I have ever tasted; it was part of a course in classic French cooking she gave at Montreal's Institut de tourisme et d'hôtellerie du Québec. Use firm apples, Rollande directs, or the filling will soften and the circles of apple wedges won't be as distinctive.

SERVES 8

Pastry
1 cup (250 mL) all-purpose flour
Pinch salt
2 tablespoons (30 mL) granulated sugar
1/3 cup (75 mL) unsalted butter, chilled and cubed
3 tablespoons (45 mL) ice water

Apples
2 pounds (1 kg) cooking apples, such as Cortland, Spartan, Empire, Golden Delicious, or Granny Smith
1/3 cup (75 mL) unsalted butter
1/3 cup (75 mL) granulated sugar

For pastry:
+ Stir flour with salt and sugar in a mixing bowl. Add butter, and cut it in using a pastry blender or 2 knives until mixture is the consistency of oatmeal.
+ Add water, mixing it in quickly with a fork or metal spatula, until the pastry forms a ball. Wrap in waxed paper and refrigerate for at least 30 minutes or overnight.

For apples:
+ Peel and core apples, cut in half, and cut each half into 3 wedges. In a heavy 9- to 10-inch (23 to 25 cm) frying pan with an ovenproof handle, melt butter over medium heat. Stir in sugar, then reduce heat to medium-low and cook butter mixture slowly, watching carefully and shaking the pan from time to time, until it turns a caramel colour. Be careful not to let it burn.
+ Arrange apple wedges closely together in circles on top of the caramel and continue cooking until the apples begin to soften and turn golden. Remove pan from heat and let cool.

Assembly:
+ Preheat the oven to 375°F (190°C). Roll out pastry on a floured surface to a circle about 2 inches (5 cm) wider than the diameter of the frying pan. Prick pastry all over with a fork. Spread pastry over apples in pan, tucking in the edges and then crimping them. Bake for 40 minutes or until pastry is firm and lightly browned. Remove the pan from the oven and let stand for 5 minutes.
+ Wearing oven mitts, place a serving plate larger than the pan upside down over the pan. Grip the plate and pan firmly on the sides and turn over quickly. The tart should fall out onto the plate. If some apples stick to the pan or are knocked out of their rows, restore them to their place with a fork.
+ Serve tart warm. Do not refrigerate.

Pouding au pain à l'érable

MAPLE BREAD PUDDING

Bakers regularly recommend amber or dark maple syrup for recipes because the intense flavour remains distinctive during cooking. Lesley Chesterman, a pastry chef who is also the fine dining critic at The Gazette *in Montreal, has experimented with various ways of obtaining the most maple flavour from maple products. In contrast to most cooks, she prefers to cook with the light grade, believing it has the most taste. She also uses maple butter and maple sugar to make her favourite comfort food: bread pudding. Eat it slightly warm, she recommends—perhaps with a dollop of whipped cream.*

SERVES 8

1 tablespoon (15 mL) butter

16 slices good-quality white bread

3 tablespoons (45 mL) maple butter

2 cups (500 mL) milk

2 cups (500 mL) whipping cream

4 tablespoons (60 mL) granulated maple sugar

4 egg yolks

2 tablespoons (30 mL) pearl maple sugar (larger grained) or granulated maple sugar

+ Preheat the oven to 325°F (160°C). Butter a 2-quart (2 L) porcelain or enamelled cast-iron gratin dish.

+ Lightly butter half the bread slices with maple butter. Top each with a slice of unbuttered bread. Slice off crusts, cut sandwiches in half on the diagonal, and line them up snugly in the dish, arranging triangle points in rows, points up.

+ In a medium saucepan, combine milk, cream, and 2 tablespoons (30 mL) of the maple sugar and bring to a boil, whisking constantly. In a large bowl, whisk egg yolks until creamy, then whisk in remaining 2 tablespoons (30 mL) maple sugar. Gradually pour hot milk mixture into the egg mixture, whisking constantly. Strain mixture through a sieve. Pour half the mixture all over bread, letting bread absorb it. Slowly pour in remaining liquid.

+ Sprinkle pearl maple sugar over the top. Bake for 40 minutes. When done, the pudding will puff up and tremble slightly in the centre when you gently shake the dish, but the filling should not be liquid. Let cool and serve warm or at room temperature.

Note

You can use a loaf of challah or brioche, end crusts removed, instead of white bread. Brown sugar may be substituted for maple sugar.

Galettes à la mélasse

MOLASSES COOKIES

Molasses has been a basic ingredient in the traditional Quebec kitchen since the earliest times and turns up in both baking and lustier dishes such as baked beans. Its popularity dates back to long-ago trade exchanges between Quebec (salt cod) and the West Indies (molasses). Molasses pie (tarte à la ferlouche) and molasses cookies are traditional favourites. This big, soft snack resembles a flat little cake. Micheline Mongrain-Dontigny, who lives in St-Irénée, in the Charlevoix region, remembers her mother making a white-sugar version and later obtained this recipe from her mother-in-law. She included it in her 1988 cookbook focusing on the Saguenay–Lac St-Jean area of northern Quebec. Treat the batter gently, as if you were making a cake, she advises. When mixed, it should be moister than tea biscuit batter and thicker than a cake batter.

MAKES ABOUT 24 COOKIES

1 cup (250 mL) lard, at room temperature
1 cup (250 mL) brown sugar
1 egg
1 cup (250 mL) molasses
2 teaspoons (10 mL) baking soda
4 cups (1 L) all-purpose flour
1 tablespoon (15 mL) ground ginger
1 cup (250 mL) milk

✦ Place the oven rack in the middle position. Preheat the oven to 350°F (180°C). Grease a baking sheet.

✦ In a large mixing bowl, beat lard until softened, then beat in brown sugar and then egg. Measure molasses into a cup and stir in baking soda, then stir molasses into lard mixture.

✦ In a second bowl, combine flour and ginger and add to lard mixture, one-third at a time, alternately with milk until all ingredients are blended together.

✦ Sprinkle work surface generously with flour. Divide batter into thirds and place one-third on the floured surface. Sprinkle it with more flour, then use your fingertips to flatten it gently to ¼ inch (5 mm) thickness. Cut cookies with a cookie cutter or glass tumbler in rounds about 2½ inches (6 cm) in diameter. Use a spatula to lift each cookie and transfer it from one hand to the other to remove excess flour. Set on the prepared baking sheet, placing 6 to 8 cookies on the sheet.

✦ Bake for 15 minutes or until slightly crisp. Remove cookies while still hot, to cool on a rack. Repeat until all batter has been used.

ICE CIDER

Sometimes good ideas start with a theory. French winemaker Christian Barthomeuf, founder in 1980 of the first vineyard in what's now the thriving Eastern Townships wine region of Dunham, had begun observing the boom in ice wine elsewhere in Canada. He fantasized about an apple version and, in 1989, tried using apples that had frozen on his trees, crushing them, fermenting their nectar, and making his first apple ice wine. Liking the crisp, dry flavour of the drink he called ice cider (*cidre de glace*), he collaborated with François Pouliot, a video and movie producer who owned an apple orchard at Hemmingford. The result, named Neige (Snow), was launched on the market in 1998 from François's orchard La Face Cachée de la Pomme (the hidden face of the apple). The label describes how the apples that do not fall from the trees in the autumn are "dehydrated by the sun and literally cooked by the cold and the wind," their sugars concentrated naturally. From the start, the wine was welcomed by sommeliers as wonderful for serving with dessert and also with slightly sweet foods such as foie gras and cheese. Domaine Pinnacle of nearby Frelighsburg started production in the early 2000s, and lately Christian, the inventor, has opened an apple winery called Clos Saraganat near Domaine Pinnacle. Upwards of 50 producers now make ice cider, which has been winning prizes at home and abroad for years and is a candidate for the Quebec government's unique products list, called "protected geographical indication" (IGP). Tall 12-ounce

(375 mL) bottles contain from 9 to 12 per cent alcohol and sell in Société des alcools du Québec stores, at the cidermakers (cidreduquebec.com), and at Montreal's Marché des Saveurs du Québec shop in Jean-Talon Market. Chefs like to use these delicately flavoured wines to deglaze their pans when making a sauce for veal, chicken, or fish. Ice cider can replace cognac, brandy, or any slightly sweet liqueur in cooking.

Gâteau au chocolat et aux noix sans farine

FLOURLESS CHOCOLATE CAKE

Not only do Quebecers love chocolate but they've developed a taste for the finest dark chocolate, used in this rich and delectable cake. The recipe is a favourite at Olive + Gourmando, a café and bakery in Old Montreal co-owned by pastry chef Dyan Solomon. She adapted a classic French flourless cake, switching from walnuts to pecans and adding the rum. Dyan, who has a master's degree in English literature from McGill University, learned her craft at Vermont's New England Culinary Institute and worked for a time as head pastry chef at the celebrated Montreal restaurant Toqué! "The quality of the chocolate and rum are an essential part of the success of this cake," she says.

SERVES 12

2 cups (500 mL) whole pecans
8 ounces (250 g) unsalted butter, cut in several pieces, at room temperature
   (1 1/4 cups/310 mL)
8 ounces (250 g) dark chocolate, 70% cocoa solids, coarsely chopped
1 cup (250 mL) cocoa powder, sifted
1 teaspoon (5 mL) salt
6 eggs, at room temperature
1 1/2 cups (375 mL) granulated sugar
1/2 cup (125 mL) good-quality aged dark rum
Ganache icing (recipe follows)

✤ Place the oven rack in the centre position. Preheat the oven to 325°F (160°C).

✤ Spread pecans on a baking sheet and toast in oven for about 15 minutes, stirring halfway through. Remove from the oven and let cool. Divide pecans into two equal batches and pulse each batch separately in a food processor just until lightly granular but not powdered. (Processing all the pecans in one batch is likely to turn them into powder, losing the texture.) Set aside ½ cup (125 mL) of the processed nuts to decorate the cake.

✤ Increase oven temperature to 350°F (180°C). Butter the bottom and sides of a 9-inch (23 cm) springform pan. Line pan, both bottom and sides, with parchment paper and butter the paper, both bottom and sides.

✤ Combine butter and chocolate in the top of a double boiler set over simmering water. Stir gently until melted, then set aside.

✤ In a mixing bowl, stir processed pecans with cocoa powder and salt.

✤ Using an electric mixer, beat eggs and sugar just until combined; do not overbeat. Continuing to beat gently, slowly add rum and then melted butter-chocolate mixture. Beat in cocoa mixture.

✤ Pour batter into the prepared pan and gently smooth it out. Bake until cake starts to come away from the sides of the pan, about 1 hour. Place the pan on a rack to cool, then unmould cake and refrigerate until cold.

Ganache icing

4 ounces (125 g) dark chocolate, 70% cocoa solids, coarsely chopped
1 cup (250 mL) whipping cream
5 tablespoons (75 mL) unsalted butter, cut in cubes, at room temperature

+ Place chocolate in a metal bowl. In a small saucepan, bring cream to a boil and pour it over the chocolate. Immediately stir with a wooden spoon until smooth.
+ Add the butter, a cube at a time, whisking constantly to blend; do not whip.
+ Let icing stand until it is lukewarm and pourable.

To finish cake:
+ Unmould cake onto a serving plate or trivet. Pour a large puddle of ganache onto the centre of the cake. Using a rubber spatula, gently and evenly nudge the icing all over the top and over the edges so it rolls down the sides of the cade.
+ Sprinkle with reserved ½ cup (125 mL) prepared pecans, perhaps as a border around the edges.

Note
Valrhona brand or another top-grade chocolate and cocoa powder are recommended for both cake and icing.

Apple Charlotte

This homey apple dessert was a favourite of my mother's. As children, we fought over the crisp, sugar-coated bread that surrounds the apples. Versions can be found in many cookbooks, but none that I have found call for a brown-sugar coating on the bread. Most, including Julia Child's, are designed as a bread mould that completely encloses the apple filling. *Toronto food writer Elizabeth Baird, who has studied early Ontario cooking, traces the Canadian history of the dessert back to the 1861* Canadian Housewife's Manual of Cookery. *I like to use Quebec's best cooking apple, the Cortland, to make this charlotte, but any variety works.*

SERVES 6

4 medium apples, peeled and cored
1 tablespoon (15 mL) fresh lemon juice
1 teaspoon (5 mL) granulated sugar
1 teaspoon (5 mL) butter
Pinch ground cinnamon
1/2 cup (125 mL) firmly packed brown sugar
4 or more slices white bread, crusts removed
2 tablespoons (30 mL) butter, at room temperature

✤ Slice apples thinly and place in a medium saucepan. Measure lemon juice into measuring cup and fill with water to make ¼ cup (60 mL) liquid. Stir into apples along with granulated sugar, butter, and cinnamon. Place over medium-low heat and cook, stirring often, just until apples are tender, about 15 minutes. Let cool.

✤ Butter a 6-cup (1.5 L) baking dish. A classic soufflé dish is ideal; a baking dish with sides at least 3 inches (7.5 cm) high is recommended. Sprinkle the bottom of the dish with a little brown sugar. Butter the bread on both sides. Then, dividing brown sugar evenly, pat onto each side of buttered bread slices. Cut 2 of the slices in half. Press a full slice onto the bottom of the baking dish; if necessary, add more bread slices to cover bottom of dish. Line the sides with the 4 half slices, pressing them firmly into place.

✤ When ready to bake, preheat the oven to 375°F (190°C).

✤ Pour apple mixture into bread-lined baking dish. Cover apples with remaining slice of buttered, sugared bread and gently press down. (If you like, you can butter and sugar an extra slice of bread, then cut it in strips, to cover any exposed apples.)

✤ Bake, uncovered, for 30 to 35 minutes or until bread is browned and crisp. Serve hot or at room temperature, with whipped cream or ice cream.

Notes

Some apples, particularly in winter, may be dry and lacking in flavour. Add a little more water if apples are dry and increase the lemon juice, sugar, butter, and cinnamon if flavour is lacking. McIntosh, a juicy variety, may be used but the water should be reduced to 2 tablespoons (30 mL).

The apples can be cooked in the saucepan several hours in advance, then covered and left at room temperature until ready to use. The baking dish can be lined with the bread several hours in advance, then covered and kept at room temperature until you're ready to bake the charlotte. (Keep the final slice of bread covered too, so it doesn't dry out.)

Acknowledge-ments

Writing about Quebec cuisine is challenging, even for a food reporter who has lived in the province most of her life, but particularly for an anglophone. "La patrimoine gastronomique"—the food tradition of Canada's oldest culinary region—is a complex story, needing many an explanation, source of information, and original recipe, and I have received all of this from generous Quebecers.

I will start by thanking three women who opened my eyes to Quebec's food culture. These Quebec food celebrities have passed on but I will never forget them. Soeur Berthe Sansregret, the stocky little Congrégation de Notre Dame nun who ran a successful Montreal cooking school, had me, a bride, as a devoted student decades ago. Later on when I had turned food journalist, Soeur Berthe liked to take credit for any success I was having. I remember her classes well, each stove with a crucifix on the wall behind. Later on, I studied at the cooking school run by Soeur Monique Chevrier, also a CND nun. Soeur Monique shared stories about how she had once taught farm girls how to cook on wood stoves, as well as the history of the original cuisine: tourtière, cipaille, cretons, pea soup, etc.—all recipes from Quebec's best-selling basic cookbook *La Cuisine Raisonnée*, first published by her order in 1919. During those years, I was counselled by Jehane Benoit, a pioneer in interpreting Quebec cuisine beyond the borders of the province. Jehane pushed all of us Quebec food reporters to write down the dishes of cooks who never used a recipe and record this oral history before it disappeared.

On the gastronomy front, chefs in city or country restaurants have taken precious minutes to share information and provide requested recipes, a task they normally shun. Government officials throughout the province, fellow cookbook authors, and food journalists have been endlessly helpful.

My treasured colleague and friend Michelle Gélinas of Montreal, who tested the recipes in this book, has been a goldmine of culinary information and good will. Faced with the dozens of recipes I was amassing from chefs and home cooks from all over the province, she would read, mark, and inwardly digest before pronouncing her version of pro and con: "This looks interesting," or "That would never work at home."

For detailed information on the various regions of Quebec and assorted subjects, my thanks go to the following. Montreal and area: Chefs Normand Laprise, David McMillan, James MacGuire, Jean-Paul Grappe, David Ferguson, Stelio Perombelon, Serge Caplette, Mario Julien, and Nick Hodge; food scholar Jean-Pierre Lemasson; butcher Victor Lopes; cheese merchant Gilles Jourdenais; journalists Mario Hinse, Lesley Chesterman, Rollande Desbois and Hélène-Andrée Bizier. Quebec City and area: Chef Jean Soulard; food scientist Jacques Goulet. Charlevoix: Chefs Eric Bertrand and Dominique Truchon; cookbook author Micheline Mongrain-Dontigny. Gaspé and the Lower St. Lawrence: Chefs Desmond Ogden and Georges Mamelonet; Reford Gardens director Alexander Reford; food sleuth Helen Meredith. Eastern Townships: Chefs Denis Mareuge and Danny St-Pierre. Laurentians-Outaouais: Chefs Anne Desjardins, Marcel Kretz, and Serge Jost.

Lanaudière-Mauricie: Chef Geneviève Longère. Saguenay: Chefs Marcel Bouchard and Daniel Pachon. Abitibi: Chef Yves Moreau.

A pair of dynamic Quebec public relations specialists never failed me in my many times of need and I thank them now. Suzanne Paré Leclerc, longtime official with the Quebec Ministry of Agriculture, now retired, was famous for her bus tours to the Quebec countryside. We food writers climbed aboard her bus, never knowing where we were headed, but confident Suzanne would give us a story as well as an immersion course in Quebec agriculture. Mimi Vallée, Montreal's top food "relationniste" of today, is our cheerful informant about wine and cheese festivals, maple celebrations, gastronomic meals with visiting chefs, and whatever else is cooking.

I give thanks here to produce marketing specialists who fill me in, week after week, on what's good, bad, fresh or coming soon to our fruit and vegetable counters. For news and tips about the Quebec growing scene, I am indebted to the Quebec Market Gardeners Association, led by André Plante, and his assistant Chantal Cadieux. Tourist office staff far and wide always have a favourite or undiscovered chef or home cook or food source they're eager to talk about; all I had to do was ask.

Fellow journalists who have written many cookbooks gave sage advice: Monda Rosenberg, Elizabeth Baird and Anne Lindsay of Toronto, and Marian Burros of Washington, D.C. Alison Fryer, who ran Toronto's Cookbook Store, regularly encouraged me by saying it was time for another book.

I was lucky to work with two top photographers, Ryan Szulc of Toronto, who took my recipe close-ups, and longtime Montreal *Gazette* colleague Gordon Beck, now of Brockville, Ontario, who travelled the province photographing Quebec food and its producers.

At *The Gazette*, my project was endorsed by publisher Alan Allnutt, who approved including some material that previously appeared in *The Gazette*. I was immeasurably aided by fellow reporter and friend Susan Schwartz, who read the text and made constructive suggestions as well as providing recipes. Colleagues Susan Semenak, Denise Duguay and Pat Wright were helpful supporters.

At HarperCollins Canada, Kirsten Hanson, cookbook editor, trimmed and revised my writing and made useful suggestions. Alan Jones created the design, Ruth Pincoe crafted the index, and Judy Phillips, Shaun Oakey, Avivah Wargon, Simon Honeyman, and Kelly Hope finessed the text. My agent, Denise Schon of Toronto, seized on my book idea with enthusiasm and sold it with flair and good business sense.

My family supported the project all along, beginning with daughter Claire, who tested many of the recipes, daughter Jane, who boosted my spirits and helped with taste-testing, and son Charles, who advised on legal matters along with my niece Janet Ferrier. My sister, Jo LaPierre, was a cheerful fellow traveller over the three years of retracing earlier food trips throughout Quebec. I thank them all.

Sources

English:

Culinary Landmarks: A Bibliography of Canadian Cookbooks, 1825–1949, by Elizabeth Driver. Toronto: University of Toronto Press, 2008.

What's to Eat? Entrées in Canadian Food History, ed. by Nathalie Cooke. Montreal: McGill-Queen's University Press, 2009.

A Taste of History: The Origins of Quebec's Gastronomy, by Marc Lafrance and Yvon Desloges. Ottawa: Environment Canada; Montreal: Les Éditions de la Chenelière, 1989. (Also in French.)

A Taste of Quebec, 2nd edition, by Julian Armstrong. Toronto: Macmillan Canada, 2001.

Toqué! Creators of a New Quebec Gastronomy, by Normand Laprise. Montreal: Les Éditions du Passage, 2012. (Also in French.)

Anne Desjardins Cooks at L'Eau à la Bouche, by Anne Desjardins. Vancouver: Douglas & McIntyre, 2003. (Also in French.)

Locavore: From Farmers' Fields to Rooftop Gardens: How Canadians Are Changing the Way We Eat, by Sarah Elton. Toronto: HarperCollins Canada, 2010.

Cooking with Québec Maple Syrup, by Anne Fortin. Montreal: Éditions Cardinal, 2010. (Also in French.)

Au Pied de Cochon: The Album, by Martin Picard. Montreal: Douglas & McIntyre, 2008. (Also in French.)

Au Pied de Cochon Sugar Shack, by Martin Picard. Montreal: Douglas & McIntyre, 2012. (Also in French.)

The Art of Living According to Joe Beef: A Cookbook of Sorts, by David McMillan, Frédéric Morin and Meredith Erickson. New York: Ten Speed Press, 2011. (Also in French.)

A Taste of Maple: History and Recipes, by Micheline Mongrain-Dontigny. St. Irénée, Quebec: Les Éditions La Bonne Recette, 2003. (Also in French.)

Traditional Quebec Cooking: A Treasure of Heirloom Recipes, by Micheline Mongrain-Dontigny. La Tuque, Quebec: Les Éditions La Bonne Recette, 1995. (Also in French.)

Best Quebec Recipes of Bygone Days, by Suzette Couillard and Roseline Normand. L'Islet, Quebec: Éditions Suzette Couillard, 1986.

French:

La cuisine traditionnelle du Québec: Découvrez la cuisine de nos régions, 3rd edition, by Institut de tourisme et d'hôtellerie du Québec, edited by Jean-Paul Grappe. Montreal: Les Éditions de l'Homme, 2006.

À table en Nouvelle-France, by Yvon Desloges. Quebec City: Les éditions du Septentrion, 2009.

Le menu quotidien en Nouvelle-France, by Hélène-Andrée Bizier. Montreal: Art Global, 2004.

Fromages: 100 produits du Québec à découvrir, by Amélie Tendland. Montreal: Éditions Caractère, 2010.

Cuisine amérindienne: Un nouveau regard, by Françoise Kayler and André Michel. Montreal: Les Éditions de l'Homme, 1996.

La cuisine raisonnée, new abridged edition, by Congrégation de Notre-Dame. Anjou, Quebec: Fides, 2008.

L'incroyable odyssée de la tourtière, by Jean-Pierre Lemasson. Montreal: Amérik Media, 2011.

Le mystère insondable du pâté chinois, by Jean-Pierre Lemasson. Montreal: Amérik Media, 2009.

Les produits du marché au Québec, by Michèle Serre. Montreal: Éditions du Trécarré, 2005.

Maudite poutine! L'histoire approximative d'un plat populaire, by Charles-Alexandre Théorêt. Montreal: Héliotrope, 2007.

Le grand Soulard de la cuisine, by Jean Soulard. Montreal: Les Éditions La Presse, 2011.

Sous le charme des courges et des citrouilles, by Louise Gagnon. Montreal: Les Éditions de l'Homme, 2011.

Les fruits du Québec: Histoire et traditions des douceurs de la table, by Paul-Louis Martin. Quebec City: Les éditions du Septentrion, 2002.

Index